China's Left-Behind Children

Rutgers Series in Childhood Studies

The Rutgers Series in Childhood Studies is dedicated to increasing our understanding of children and childhoods throughout the world, reflecting a perspective that highlights cultural dimensions of the human experience. The books in this series are intended for students, scholars, practitioners, and those who formulate policies that affect children's everyday lives and futures.

Series Board

Stuart Aitken, geography, San Diego State University
Jill Duerr Berrick, social welfare, University of California, Berkeley
Susan Danby, education, Queensland University of Technology
Julian Gill-Peterson, transgender and queer studies, University of Pittsburgh
Afua Twum-Danso Imoh, sociology, University of Sheffield
Stacey Lee, educational policy studies, University of Wisconsin-Madison
Sunaina Maira, Asian American studies, University of California, Davis
David M. Rosen, anthropology and sociology, Fairleigh Dickinson University
Rachael Stryker, human development and women's studies, Cal State East Bay
Tom Weisner, anthropology, University of California, Los Angeles

For a list of all the titles in the series, please see the last page of the book.

China's Left-Behind Children

Caretaking, Parenting, and Struggles

XIAOJIN CHEN

RUTGERS UNIVERSITY PRESS

NEW BRUNSWICK, CAMDEN, AND NEWARK, NEW JERSEY

LONDON AND OXFORD

Rutgers University Press is a department of Rutgers, The State University of New Jersey, one of the leading public research universities in the nation. By publishing worldwide, it furthers the University's mission of dedication to excellence in teaching, scholarship, research, and clinical care.

Library of Congress Cataloging-in-Publication Data

Names: Chen, Xiaojin, author.
Title: China's left-behind children : caretaking, parenting, and struggles / Xiaojin Chen.
Description: New Brunswick : Rutgers University Press, [2024] | Series: Rutgers series in childhood studies | Includes bibliographical references and index.
Identifiers: LCCN 2023036647 | ISBN 9781978837140 (paperback) | ISBN 9781978837157 (hardcover) | ISBN 9781978837164 (epub) | ISBN 9781978837171 (pdf)
Subjects: LCSH: Children—China—Social conditions. | Children of single parents—China. | Rural-urban migration—China.
Classification: LCC HQ792.C5 C4154 2024 | DDC 362.70951—dc23/eng/20230919
LC record available at https://lccn.loc.gov/2023036647

A British Cataloging-in-Publication record for this book is available from the British Library.

Copyright © 2024 by Xiaojin Chen

All rights reserved

No part of this book may be reproduced or utilized in any form or by any means, electronic or mechanical, or by any information storage and retrieval system, without written permission from the publisher. Please contact Rutgers University Press, 106 Somerset Street, New Brunswick, NJ 08901. The only exception to this prohibition is "fair use" as defined by U.S. copyright law.

References to internet websites (URLs) were accurate at the time of writing. Neither the author nor Rutgers University Press is responsible for URLs that may have expired or changed since the manuscript was prepared.

∞ The paper used in this publication meets the requirements of the American National Standard for Information Sciences—Permanence of Paper for Printed Library Materials, ANSI Z39.48-1992.

rutgersuniversitypress.org

For my father, Tianbao Chen

CONTENTS

List of Illustrations   ix

1	Introduction	1
2	Who Leaves and Who Stays? Factors Associated with Parental Migration and Caretaking Arrangements	23
3	Caretaking at Home: Grandparenting and One-Parent Caretaking	47
4	Parenting from Afar: Long-Distance Parenting and Short Visits	70
5	"Have You Finished Your Homework?": Parental Migration, Caretaking Practices, and Children's Schooling	96
6	Are Left-Behind Children More Deviance- and Delinquency-Prone?	120
7	Children's Psychological Well-Being: Caretaking Practices, Long-Distance Parenting, and Ambiguous Loss	142
8	Conclusion	166

Acknowledgments   189
References   191
Index   203

ILLUSTRATIONS

Figures

1.1. The overarching theoretical model	14
2.1. Prevalent types of childcare arrangement	26
4.1. Time of migrant parents working "outside" (%)	86
4.2. Time of migrant parents visiting children and family members (%)	88
4.3. The length of stay during parental visits	92
5.1. Children's academic performance	100
5.2. Children's level of school bonding	105
6.1. Caretaking arrangements, gender, and deviant peer affiliation	123
8.1. Status of left behind, gender, and children's participation in household chores	179

Tables

1.1. Sample individual and household characteristics	17
2.1. Multinomial logistic regression models predicting alternative caretaking arrangements versus nonmigration	31
3.1. Multivariate regression model predicting caretaker monitoring/supervision and caretaker–child bonding	53
3.2. Multivariate regression model predicting caretaker–child conflict and harsh discipline	64
4.1. Ordinal regression model predicting children's visits to migrant parents	83
4.2. Ordinal regression model predicting frequency of parental visits	89
4.3. Ordinal regression model predicting the duration of parental visits to children and family	93
5.1. Multivariate regression models predicting children's academic performance	102
5.2. Multivariate regression models predicting children's school bonding	106
5.3. Distant parenting and children's school involvement	116

6.1. Multivariate regression models predicting children's association with deviant peers	124
6.2. Ordinal regression models predicting children's participation in deviant activities	127
6.3. Logistic regression model predicting children's participation in minor delinquency	130
6.4. Multivariate regression model predicting long-distance parenting and problematic behaviors	139
7.1. Sex, caretaking arrangements, and children's negative emotions	145
7.2. Multivariate regression models predicting the associations between caretaking practices, school bonding, and children's psychological well-being	149
7.3. Multivariate regression models predicting long-distance parenting and negative emotions	153
7.4. Frequency of indicators of ambiguous loss	161
7.5. Exploratory factor analysis of ambiguous loss	162
7.6. Multivariate regression models predicting associations between ambiguous loss and psychological well-being	163

China's Left-Behind Children

1

Introduction

It's a big problem, a big problem. Grandparents in rural areas treat their children as a treasure and do not let them do anything. You [children] just sit there and eat, put on weight, [grandparents] are then happy. They cannot eat any bitterness. They are even less able to eat bitterness than city kids. Do you know that? Children in urban areas are taught by their parents. Parents are better at teaching their children. City kids, parents will teach them, let them do chores from childhood, right? Washing dishes, washing socks, washing clothes, right? In the future, city kids will become better and better. I will say, these rural children, the post-2000 generation, when they grow up, what is the use of them? They are useless.

–grandpa Lian

During the last three decades, modern China has witnessed an unprecedented increase in urbanization alongside the movement of labor from agricultural to manufacturing and service sectors—a phenomenon placing rural-to-urban migration and its ramifications at the forefront of sociological inquiry. In 1982, only 6.57 million rural migrants worked in Chinese cities (Zhao, 2000). By 1994, the size of this population had increased to 37 million (Du, 2000), and it has climbed exponentially since, reaching the unprecedented levels of 130 million in 2005 (World Bank, 2009) and 172 million in 2021. The population of rural-to-urban migrants now comprises more than one-third of the entire Chinese workforce (National Bureau of Statistics of China, 2022). Impressed by its sheer size and speed of growth, sociologists Meng and Manning (2010) dubbed China's rural-to-urban migration as the largest migration in human history, surpassing mass migrations such as the California Gold Rush (1848–1850), the partition of India in 1947, and the Great Migration of African Americans in the United States during the early twentieth century.

China's rapidly increasing "left-behind children" (LBC) population is widely understood as an unintended consequence of this massive migration. Although the definition of LBC varies across studies and government reports, this term typically describes children who live with one parent, grandparents, or other extended family members in rural China after one or both parents have migrated to more developed areas for better job opportunities. Numerous social, cultural, community, family, and individual factors are associated with the emergence and dramatic growth of this subpopulation. Among them, structural barriers such as China's Household Registration System (*hukou*) and its urban-rural dual structure—a system that restricts access to state-funded education, health, and pension systems for migrants and their children—stand out. These structural constraints have driven the substantial growth of the LBC population, from 22.9 million in 2000 to an astonishing 69.7 million in 2018 (UNICEF, 2019). Notably, this demographic subgroup now accounts for one-third of the rural child population and more than 20 percent of China's entire child population (UNICEF, 2019). In predominantly migrant-sending provinces (e.g., Jiangxi, Anhui, Chongqing, Sichuan, Jiangsu, and Hunan provinces), more than half of rural children are left behind by one or both parents (ACWF, 2013). The rapid rise of this population has sparked widespread concerns and anxieties in private and public spheres; in fact, multiple news outlets, including newspapers outside main China (e.g., CNN and HAARETZ), assert that modern China is now raising "a generation of left-behind children" (Ma, 2014; Shani, 2021).

The left-behind children subpopulation has become a hotly contested topic among China's concerned citizens, researchers, and government officials, spurring continuing and heated debate about its size, origin, and potential short- and long-term impacts. Nevertheless, the emergence of LBC and its ensuing individual, social, and cultural implications do not solely exist in China. The rapid growth of LBC has been observed in many developing countries, effectively becoming a global phenomenon. From the Philippines and Vietnam in Southeast Asia to Ethiopia in Africa to Ecuador in South America, hundreds of millions of children are left behind by parents who migrate within or across state borders. Although no official estimates are available globally, prior research has revealed high proportions of children left behind in many developing countries. For example, 27 percent of children in the Philippines—approximately 9 million children—have at least one parent living abroad. Similarly, at least 10 percent of children in Kyrgyzstan, 36 percent in Ecuador, and more than 40 percent in rural South Africa are left behind by one or both migrant parents (Fellmeth et al., 2018).

English-language studies regarding left-behind children have focused almost exclusively on transnational migration. Due to inequalities in global economic development, young adults from the global south and developing countries often overcome numerous financial, cultural, and political barriers to migrate to northern and developed countries to better provide for their families. In 2020, 281 million people lived outside their country of origin, representing roughly 3.6 percent of the world's population (United Nations Department of Economic and Social Affairs, Population Division, 2022). Many of these migrants are chronically separated from their loved family members, are exposed to blatant discrimination and abuse, and even suffer unspeakable brutality and inhumanity at the hands of smugglers, traffickers, and in some cases government officials. As a result, children are often left behind in their countries of origin, regardless of whether the migration is legal or undocumented. For example, in the context of labor migration, many working visas do not allow children to move with their parents, and the alternative—visiting visas—are often costly and difficult to obtain. Even when children have legal visas, parents are hesitant to bring their children with them due to limited resources for childcare or other essential services. Undocumented migrants face even more difficult circumstances. Barred from crossing borders legally, these migrants face severe challenges in not only bringing their children to host countries but also providing them access to quality education and other necessary services.

The majority of transnational and internal migration is motivated by similar economic push and pull factors, including poverty and unemployment in migrant-sending countries/regions and the expectation of better job opportunities and higher income in destination areas. As such, remittances—funds sent by migrant workers to their countries/regions of origin—play a critical role in the decision-making process. In 2017, the total volume of remittances by transnational migration workers surpassed US$466 billion. This amount is likely to be substantially higher for internal migrants—although no official global data are available—given their significantly larger population. Nevertheless, domestic migration and transnational migration differ in a myriad of ways, with many uniquely influencing children's short- and long-term development. For example, when compared with those who have internally migrated, families of transnational migration generally fare better financially—a reflection of income inequality between developing (origin) and developed (host) countries. Meanwhile, children of internal migrants typically experience more frequent face-to-face interaction with their migrant parents. Left-behind children in China, for example, regularly visit their internally migrated parents during summer breaks or other holidays, creating more opportunities for parent–child face-to-face interaction and the development of intimacy.

Given that the majority of English-language studies focus on children left behind by transnational migrants, it is perhaps unsurprising that relatively few researchers have systematically investigated internal migration and its potential impact on children's well-being. As such, many research questions—at both the theoretical and empirical levels—need to be further investigated. For example, are findings from transnational migration conveniently applied to internal migration? How do the similarities and differences between internal and transnational migration influence children's development and well-being? Specifically, to what degree do cultural and institutional constraints and opportunities influence children of internal migration? With global migration as the larger context, I now turn to China's internal migration and its potential impact on the well-being of children left behind in rural China.

I FIRST MET GRANDPA LIAN (introductory quote) in 2015 in a small village in Peace County (pseudonym), Jiangxi province, where he lived with his wife and two grandchildren—ten-year-old Xin and nine-year-old Bing. The parents of the two grandchildren, like most young people in the village, were "outside" *dagong* (working as migrants) at that time. In fact, Xin and Bin each had only lived with their parents for a single year—the year after their migrant mothers briefly returned to give birth to and care for them in their infancy. Since then, Xin and Bing had been living with and raised by their grandparents. Grandpa Lian's two adult sons initially migrated in 2000 to Ningbo, Zhejiang province—a city that is more than seven hundred kilometers away. In 2015, his younger son then moved to Shenzhen in southern China, while his elder son remained in Ningbo. Because of their tight working schedule and the high cost of long-distance travel, the two couples rarely visited their parents and children, only traveling home once a year within the first few years of their migration. This type of caretaking arrangement—grandparents providing essential caregiving for children left behind while adult children work "outside" to meet household financial needs—has become highly prevalent in Peace County. Meanwhile, this caretaking arrangement elicits many concerns and anxieties among local villagers and the larger society. Grandpa Lian, in his aforementioned quote, expressed concerns that children left behind are not cared for by their parents and are not properly disciplined and that grandparenting—grandparents serving as surrogate parents for a prolonged period—may engender negative behavioral outcomes, including children's inability to "eat bitterness," poor educational performance, and a lack of upward mobility relative to urban children.

My follow-up interview with grandpa and grandma Lian a few years later appeared to validate their initial concerns. Xin, the older grandson, became quite rebellious during middle school, constantly missing classes, hanging out with older and delinquent friends, and frequently running away from home. After completing junior high school, neither grandchild qualified for enrollment in academic-track high schools, and both were sent to a private technical school in Nanchang city, the capital of Jiangxi province, by their parents. Unfortunately, Xin dropped out after only one month. After eventually returning for a few additional semesters, he ultimately failed to graduate. The children's failure to attend academic-track high schools and colleges brought grandpa Lian much shame and internal pain. Two years after his grandchildren graduated from middle school, he was diagnosed with cancer, became seriously ill, and ultimately passed away. Even as grandpa Lian was barely conscious before his death, he continued asking his two grandsons whether they had been admitted to the county's First High School—the most prestigious high school in Peace County. The year after grandpa Lian's death, Xin followed in his parents' footsteps and became a rural-to-urban migrant himself, at the age of seventeen, without even graduating from the technical school.

Skip-generation households such as grandpa Lian's family—with grandparents serving as primary caretakers and parents working "outside" to make the ends meet—have become highly prevalent in Peace County and other parts of rural China. This type of family structure emerged during the beginning of the 1990s when rural China began to experience rapid rural-to-urban migration alongside other dramatic social, economic, and demographic changes. Before that time, villagers of all ages in Peace County were inextricably tied to small pieces of farmland allocated to each household—planting rice seedlings and vegetables in the spring, harvesting crops in the summer and fall, and plowing the land in the winter. A mere twenty years later, Peace County's young and middle-aged residents had all but disappeared, the majority having migrated to more economically developed areas and megacities, returning only for special events (e.g., Spring Festivals). Most remaining villagers fall into two age groups: those aged fifty and above (most of them grandparents) and those younger than sixteen (nearly all in school). A small number of villagers outside these two groups can sometimes be found, remaining at home due to child or eldercare obligations, physical or mental health problems, or their possession of skills considered more profitable in rural areas (e.g., carpentry or interior house decoration). Nevertheless, so few residents exist within this group that a villager once commented that in the case of a funeral, it is difficult to find eight men to carry the coffin to the graveyard, threatening a tradition that has lasted for thousands of years in Peace County.

My conversation with villagers, schoolteachers, and local cadres—generally casual and informal—often naturally gravitated toward how *dagong* influences children's academic performance and psychological well-being as well as interpersonal relationships between migrant parents, at-home caretakers, and children left behind. I have heard numerous stories about migrant parents becoming strangers to children or children hysterically chasing parents upon their departure after a recent home visit. Like grandpa Lian, many are concerned about the potential adverse effects of this chronic absence of parents, worrying that a lack of parental discipline and poor school performance will set their children on a life trajectory plagued with problematic behaviors, mental health struggles, and a lack of overall economic success. These concerns and anxieties are studied, expanded, and exaggerated by the media and the academic community, who coined a new term—"left-behind-child syndrome"—to describe a variety of behavioral (e.g., delinquency and crime) and mental problems (e.g., depression and social withdrawal) presumedly exhibited among LBC (Fellmeth et al., 2018; Ge et al., 2019).

This newly coined term has since gained much attention in the public discourse and the academic community. Overall, sociologists and public health experts have accumulated substantial evidence supporting the existence of "left-behind-child syndrome," suggesting that children left behind are more likely to develop behavioral problems such as poor school performance (Bai et al., 2020; Dong et al., 2021; S. Hu, 2019), victimization (X. Chen et al., 2022a, 2022b), conduct problems, and delinquency (X. Chen, 2021; X. Chen et al., 2017), as well as physical and mental health issues such as malnutrition, depression, anxiety, and suicidal ideation (Fellmeth et al., 2018; Ge et al., 2019). Interestingly, researchers have also produced many conflictual findings, revealing that parental migration and the experiences of being left behind have nonsignificant negative but minor or positive effects on children's physical, psychological, and emotional development. These findings—while puzzling—are also somewhat intuitive. On the one hand, the chronic absence of parents is a major life stressor, negatively influencing a child's normative physical and mental development. On the other hand, parental migration is fundamentally different from other types of parental absence (e.g., parental divorce and separation)—often, migration results in improved household financial status, housing access, nutrition, education, and medical care and other essential benefits for children and family members.

Many factors—including variation in the local cultures and levels of economic development of migrant-sending communities, sample characteristics, sampling methods, and theoretical frameworks adopted by researchers—contribute to these inconsistent or conflictual findings. To fully understand the effects of parental migration on children's objective and subjective well-being, many questions need to be thoroughly explored and answered. For example, what is growing up like for young boys and girls like Xin and Bing—primarily raised by grandparents, one at-home parent, or other extended family members? How does parental migration reconfigure family structure and influence caretaking arrangements? How do migrant parents attempt to perform traditional parenting from afar? Can grandparents and other extended family members, now serving as surrogate parents, adapt and effectively adjust to their new caregiving roles? Finally, to what extent do the reconfigured family structure, altered caretaking arrangements, and caretaking practices collectively shape children's academic, emotional, and social development?

Using in-depth interview and survey data, this book addresses these intriguing questions, providing an up-close examination of family life as experienced by a cohort of left-behind children in rural China. Specifically, the book aims to understand whether and how structural and cultural factors shape decision-making regarding rural-to-urban migration and caretaking arrangements and to what extent these decisions—directly and indirectly—influence a child's general well-being, including school performance, delinquency, resilience, and mental health. In particular, I investigate how structural/cultural factors (e.g., the *hukou* system) shape family structures in rural China and to what degree these reconfigured family structures influence the dynamic relationships among family members, with a focus on caretaking practices such as at-home parent caretaking, grandparenting, and long-distance parenting. Finally, I explore how these familial relationships, embedded in and greatly shaped by structural and cultural contexts, influence children's behavioral and psychological outcomes.

The remainder of this chapter is organized into three sections. First, guided by the bioecological model developed by psychologist Urie Bronfenbrenner (2005a), I built an overarching theoretical model, which identifies the interrelationships among predisposing individual, familial, cultural, and structural factors; parental migration decision-making; caretaking arrangements; and children's behavioral and psychological outcomes. This overarching theoretical model provides a blueprint for the analyses of the qualitative and quantitative data. In the second section, I describe the methodology of this study, detailing the sampling methods and procedures of the quantitative and qualitative data collection. Finally, the conclusion of this chapter presents the organization of the book, providing a summary of each chapter.

The Overarching Theoretical Model

Research on child development often utilizes psychologist Urie Bronfenbrenner's ecological systems theory (1979) to investigate how a child's individual characteristics (e.g., age, gender, and personality), a child's immediate life circumstances (e.g., family, school, and peers), and the social and cultural environments in which they are embedded shape their physical, mental, and emotional development. This theory has been widely applied by researchers and has received much empirical support; nevertheless, it has also been criticized for its neglect of the effects of children's biological and personality characteristics (e.g., temper) as well as the interactive relationships between these biological/personality characteristics and multiple environmental contexts. Addressing these critiques, Bronfenbrenner later modified and expanded the original theoretical construct (Bronfenbrenner, 1979, 2005b), proposing a bioecological model that focuses on the dynamic and bidirectional relationships between a person and his or her immediate and remote environmental contexts. An application of Bronfenbrenner's (2005b) theoretical model to the large body of literature on left-behind children in China facilitates an in-depth understanding of the progressively evolving, dynamic, and reciprocal relationships among the individual and environment at multiple levels and—importantly—how these relationships collectively influence and are influenced by children's psychological and behavioral outcomes.

Bronfenbrenner's Bioecological Model

Bronfenbrenner's ecological systems theory focuses on the influence of social, cultural, and immediate environments on children's life development (Bronfenbrenner, 1979). Built on and extending his classic ecological systems theory (Bronfenbrenner, 1979; Darling, 2007; Ettekal & Mahoney, 2017), Bronfenbrenner's bioecological model proposes that children's development is the outcome of four inextricably linked components: process, person, context, and time. Each of these four components exerts an independent effect, interacts with the other components, and produces joint and/or interactional effects on children's short- and long-term development.

PROCESS. The first core concept in this bioecological model is processes, or proximal processes, which encompass "particular forms of interaction between organism and environment" that operate over time. These particular forms of interaction, according to Bronfenbrenner and colleagues, are the primary mechanisms responsible for human development (Bronfenbrenner & Morris, 2007, p. 795). Highlighting their bidirectional and mutually reinforcing nature, Bronfenbrenner states that the direction and magnitude of these processes are presumed to "vary substantially as a function of the characteristics of the developing *person*, of the immediate and more remote environmental *contexts*, and the *time* periods" (p. 795, emphasis original). In other words, the bioecological model investigates key social processes collectively shaped by forces of personal characteristics, the external physical and social environment, and the historical time in which social values, norms, and other structural factors are embedded.

PERSON. The second principal component is that of the developing person. An individual's physical, emotional, and cognitive characteristics are not only determinants of their biopsychological development but are also outcomes to be investigated. Person-level characteristics include aspects such as forces, resources, and demands (Bronfenbrenner, 2005b). Person forces are active behavioral dispositions "that can set proximal processes in motion and sustain their operation, or—conversely—actively interfere with, retard, or even prevent their occurrence" (Bronfenbrenner & Morris, 2007, p. 810). A person's high self-control, for example, is a kind of disposition that can steer a child away from risky, shortsighted, and impulsive behaviors. The second aspect includes a person's resources, which are biopsychological assets required for the effective functioning of proximal processes but which do not, in themselves, involve selective responses to certain social contexts, conditions, and activities. Typical person resources include conditions that limit or disrupt an individual's functional integrity—such as genetic defects, physical handicaps, or damage to brain functions—as well as developmental assets such as ability, knowledge, experiences, and skills. The third person aspect, demand, includes personal traits that "invite or discourage reactions from the social environment that can disrupt or foster processes of psychological growth" (Bronfenbrenner & Morris, 2007, p. 812). Physical (e.g., physical attractiveness) and personality traits (e.g., hot temper), for example, may promote differential person–environment interactions. Notably, the familiar demographic factors of age, gender, and race can be considered as both personal resources *and* demand characteristics, defining a person's position and role in a society while also shaping how this person is perceived and treated by others in both immediate and remote environmental contexts. In Chinese society, a person's *hukou* status is one critical embodiment of person resources and demand characteristics. An agricultural/rural *hukou*, for example, indicates an inferior socioeconomic status and a lack of access to limited resources (e.g., access to education and medical needs).

CONTEXT. The third principal component, context, is derived from Bronfenbrenner's original ecological systems theory (Bronfenbrenner, 1979), which proposes four interrelated types of environmental systems: the (1) micro-, (2) meso-, (3) exo-, and (4) macrosystems. These four systems are interrelated in such a way that the lower/micro levels are both embedded within and a product or function of the higher/macro-level systems. Specifically, the *microsystem* is the lowest level of the four, encompassing settings such as family, school, church, and peers, within which individuals directly interact on a daily and face-to-face basis. The second level is the *mesosystem*, which involves dynamic and reciprocal relationships among multiple microsystems, such as dynamic interplays between family and school, family and church, and school and sports clubs. The third level is the *exosystem*, in which the developing person is involved but not directly embedded. The influence of the exosystem is thus mostly indirect, "trickling down" to influence the development of the focal person through other individuals involved. Neighborhood and community context, family networks, and parents' workplaces are the three exosystems greatly affecting a child's development. Finally, the fourth level of the ecological system is the *macrosystem*, consisting of the overarching pattern of micro-, meso-, and exosystem characteristics of a given culture or subculture. Importantly, these macrosystems structure and shape a person's access to valuable opportunities and varying life course options, setting up distinctive life trajectories for those within different macrosystems. Typical examples of macrosystems include social and health systems, policies, laws, cultural values, and beliefs, which serve as filters and lenses through which people live and interpret past and future experiences.

TIME. The final key component of Bronfenbrenner's bioecological model is *time*, which can be understood at the micro, meso, and macro levels. Micro-time is defined as the time during specific episodes of proximal processes, such as when certain events occur. Meso-time refers to the temporal dimension of the mesosystem or how the interactions between microsystems occur and change over time, such as changes in a child's school or family environment. The macro-time generally refers to two related but distinct dimensions: timing in lives and historical time and place. The timing in lives thesis proposes that the developmental impact of life events and transitions is contingent on when they occur in a person's life. Pregnancy during adolescence, for example, has a more detrimental impact on a person's life trajectory relative to pregnancy during the age of middle thirties. The second dimension of time—the principle of historical time and place—stipulates that a person's life trajectories are shaped by historical times and events. A given cohort, for example, may be exposed to specific social changes and historical events, thereby experiencing distinctive life trajectories and transitions. China's "Up to the Mountains and Down to the Countryside Movement" during the 1950s and 1960s, for example, uprooted an entire cohort of urban youth and dramatically altered their education, marriage, and employment trajectories (Singer, 2020).

The Overarching Theoretical Model

Guided by Bronfenbrenner's bioecological model (Bronfenbrenner, 1979, 2005b), I developed an overarching theoretical model, specifying the dynamic, interactive, and reciprocal processes linking children's developmental outcomes (e.g., education, delinquency, and psychological well-being) to micro-, meso-, exo-, and macrosystems. Specifically, I investigate how the higher and more powerful exo- and macrosystems shape decisions regarding parental migration and caretaking arrangements and to what extent these decisions, in turn, influence parenting and caretaking at home, long-distance parenting, and ultimately children's short- and long-term development.

Numerous studies have emphasized the profound influence of macrostructural factors on China's massive rural-to-urban migration. The enormous urban–rural divide and pervasive economic inequality—largely shaped by the central government's policies and regulations—are the most cited influences driving rural labor toward more economically developed areas and megacities (Chan & Ren, 2018; J. Shen, 2013). According to recent data from the National Bureau of Statistics of China (2022), urbanites earned on average 43,834 yuan, which was about 2.56 times higher than what the rural residents averaged (17,131 yuan). The income gap between more developed coastal regions or megacities (e.g., Guangzhou, Beijing, Shenzhen, and Shanghai) and rural areas in central and southwestern provinces—the predominantly migrant-sending communities—is even more pronounced. In fact, given such a wide rural–urban income gap, researchers (Kong & Meng, 2010) suggest that the study should not focus on *why* many rural residents migrate to more economically developed coastal areas or megacities but *why not*?

The most cited macrostructural factor associated with China's rural-to-urban migration is likely China's *hukou* system. Officially enacted in the "People's Republic of China *Hukou* Registration Regulation" in 1958, the *hukou* system has had a deep and long-lasting influence on Chinese people's access to institutionalized rights and privileges and their daily lives. The early version, built on population registration systems and the "mutual responsibility" system developed in early China's history, included two of the most critical features of the modern *hukou* system. First, it officially cemented the division of the town and country and restrictions on rural–urban migration, with each Chinese citizen being classified as either an agricultural or nonagricultural *hukou* and further categorized by location of origin. Second, the 1958 *Hukou* Registration Regulation institutionally linked the *hukou* status to the state provision of rights and privileges, heavily favoring urban residents. For example, citizens of nonagricultural (or urban) *hukou* received benefits ranging from education to health care to retirement pensions, whereas those of agricultural (or rural) *hukou* were often left to fend for themselves.

There have been incremental changes in the *hukou* system since the age of "Reform and Opening" in the 1980s. For example, one of the original functions of *hukou*—the control of rural-to-urban migration—has been substantially diminished due to the increasing pressure of urbanization and a demanding labor market. Nevertheless, the link between *hukou* and access to social welfare programs such as retirement, public school education, and health care remains largely intact. To date, it remains difficult, if not impossible, for rural-to-urban migrants to permanently settle down in host cities because of the lack of access to these privileges. For example, migrant children are generally excluded from the state-funded public school system, forcing them to attend more expensive private schools or lower-quality migrant schools in host cities. China's rural-to-urban migrants fully understand these institutional constraints, seldom considering permanently settling down in host cities as a viable option. This view, in turn, influences important decisions such as forms of migration (e.g., individual versus family migration), caretaking arrangements, consumption patterns, and investment strategies. For example, leaving children and other family members behind is rarely condemned as abandonment, as rural-to-urban migration is often considered "temporary," regardless of how long the migration lasts. Migrant parents expect—and are often expected by family members or the larger society—to ultimately return and reunite with their family members.

In addition to institutional constraints, social and cultural norms—particularly the patriarchal system that has defined the familial social structure of rural China for thousands of years—greatly influence decisions made regarding parental migration and caretaking arrangements, both immediate factors associated with children's physical and mental well-being. One example of such influence is that left-behind children in rural China are generally cared for by paternal grandparents, whereas in other cultures such as the Philippines, Indonesia, or Mexico, these caregiving duties are often performed by maternal grandparents (Graham & Jordan, 2011). The traditional gender value system is another critical macrostructural factor profoundly influencing migration, shaping a family's decisions (e.g., who goes, for how long, and when to return) and post-migration adaptation strategies (e.g., caretaking arrangements and parenting practices). The changes brought about due to migration also have the potential to transform or greatly modify the attitudes and behaviors of both migrants and family members. Finally, the development of advanced technology, particularly the widespread use of modern information and communication technologies (ICT), radically alters the forms, frequency, and content of interpersonal interaction among Chinese migrant families. The popular multipurpose social media and messaging app WeChat—which registered 811 million monthly active users in China in 2022—for example, presents a plethora of novel opportunities for translocal family members to communicate with one another remotely.

At the exosystem level, I have identified two exosystems potentially influencing left-behind children's developmental outcomes—the rural village and the migrant parents' workplaces. The rural village in which children are embedded is important since community social norms such as the attitude toward and culture of out-migration may deeply influence how children perceive the migration and chronic absence of their parents, as well as the ways children impute meaning to events and circumstances associated with migration and relevant experiences. For example, in a community where migration is highly prevalent, children may consider parental migration as routine, desensitizing and normalizing migration and its personal and family-related implications. The second potential exosystem is the workplace of migrants. Both LBC and at-home caretakers are highly concerned about migrant parents' overextended working hours, their tremendous work pressure, and the tolls these take on migrant parents' physical and mental health. These concerns, in turn, become sources of stress for children, grandparents, and other family members at home (Jingzhong & Lu, 2011).

At the micro level, two institutions—family and school—are most frequently referenced. Previous studies of LBC and caretakers have focused on the immediate family—consisting of the focal child, siblings, and at-home caretakers (e.g., a left-behind parent, grandparents, or other extended family members). While the immediate family plays a critical role in a child's development, migrated family members, including migrant parent(s) and siblings, are part of a family microsystem for children left behind. Although these children generally do not engage in daily interactions with geographically separated family members, many had already established strong bonds with parents or migrant siblings before their migration or remain in frequent communication (e.g., weekly) with their migrated parents or siblings after migration. These separated family members thus occupy critical physical and mental space in LBC's daily lives. This body of research is also consistent with propositions offered by the widely applied family process theory (Broderick, 1993), which argues that family is a system and children's development is an outcome of dynamic interactions within this system. The second crucial microsystem in which LBC are embedded is the school setting (Murphy, 2014), consisting primarily of teachers and student peers. Children in rural China typically spend about ten to eleven hours a day and at least five days a week in school, devoting much of their time, effort, and emotions to grades, peer relationships, student–teacher relationships, and other school-related activities.

At the mesosystem level, the dynamic family–school relationship has the most prominent influence on children's behavioral, psychological, and emotional development. Academic success is highly valued by Chinese parents and the larger society and is one of the most important criteria—if not the only one—by which to evaluate a child's potential success. This practice is further reinforced by the rapid spread of education fever—characterized by parents' unrealistically high expectations of children's academic performance and intensive investment in children's schooling—from the urban middle class to rural peasants. As such, activities, events, and attitudes related to the school sphere are reciprocally influenced by activities and relationships within the family sphere. Children's academic performance, for example, shapes parents' decisions relative to material and emotional investment in children's schooling, which in turn, impacts children's school performance. A study by Chen and colleagues (Y. Chen et al., 2021) found that children's academic performance was positively associated with parents' life satisfaction, with a one-unit rise in the class ranking of the child associated with a 3.4 percent increase in parents' life satisfaction score. These dynamic relationships are further complicated in translocal families, as the two microsystems—the immediate family and the geographically separated family—entail distinctive resources and demands, thereby adding new and differing developmental processes. Grandparent caretakers in dual-migrant parent households, due to their lack of education, often face challenges in effectively communicating with schoolteachers and helping children with schoolwork. Migrant parents, on the other hand, have great difficulties overcoming their physical and temporal distance to physically attend school activities (e.g., parent–teacher meetings) or to communicate with schoolteachers promptly.

The dynamics between the immediate family in which a child is embedded and the geographically distant family is another intriguing mesosystem in need of further research. Left-behind children's short- and long-term development is often a function of these dynamics, shaped by resource exchange (e.g., remittance–care exchange), the frequency of communication and visits, and interpersonal relationships between members of the two microsystems. These translocal family members may be united and collectively strive for a common goal, thereby creating a harmonious and loving environment for the child. Sociologist Rachel Murphy (2020), for example, proposes the lens of "striving" be used to study the lives of left-behind children in rural China. Murphy frames children's study efforts—similar to the labor of migrant parents or domestic care work by at-home parents or grandparents—as a form of work that contributes to a common family goal of accomplishing intergenerational mobility. Conversely, these translocal families may be filled with contested arguments, conflicts, and negative emotions, with migrant parents and at-home caretakers constantly fighting to exert control over limited financial resources, childrearing, and affection or respect from children.

Figure 1.1 depicts the underlying social processes linking varying environmental contexts and children's general well-being. In essence, this guiding theoretical model hypothesizes that children's physical, mental, and emotional well-being are, directly and indirectly, influenced by multiple social systems at the macro, exo, micro, and meso levels. First, systems of upper levels (e.g., the macrosystem) influence children's well-being, directly and indirectly, through social processes operated within and among systems at lower levels (e.g., exo, micro, and meso levels). For example, the rural–urban income gap and the *hukou* system exert substantial and direct effects on parents' decisions on migration and child caretaking arrangements, which, in turn, directly influence children's short- and long-term development. Likewise, exosystems such as migrant-sending communities and migrant parents' workplaces influence children's general well-being both directly and indirectly through social processes at micro- and mesosystem levels. Finally, the micro- and mesosystems themselves exert immediate and direct effects on children's general well-being.

The influence of structural (e.g., the *hukou* system and rural–urban inequality) factors has been extensively discussed and debated in the literature; however, the key proximal factors—caretaking arrangements and practices by at-home

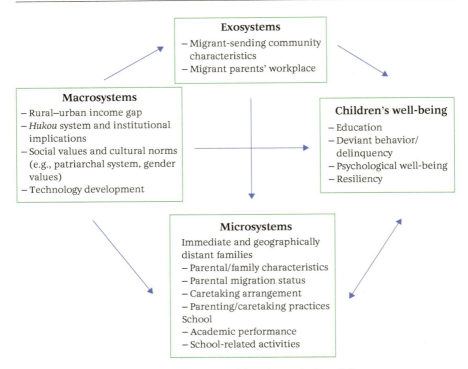

FIGURE 1.1 The overarching theoretical model.

caregivers—are surprisingly understudied. Addressing this limitation, my theoretical model highlights the critical role of alternative caregiving arrangements, identifying structural, cultural, and situational factors leading to such arrangements and exploring how these arrangements influence caretaking practices (e.g., caretaker–child bonding and long-distance parenting), ultimately shaping children's behavioral and psychological outcomes.

Another salient aspect of the theoretical model is its emphasis on reciprocal relationships within and across the person, micro, and meso levels. The left-behind-children literature, for example, studies a myriad of physical, psychological, and behavioral outcomes, including children's physical health, mental health, educational performance, and deviant or delinquent behaviors. However, this body of literature rarely examines such characteristics as precursors and outcomes simultaneously, neglecting the possibility of reciprocal relationships. For instance, the association between a student's academic performance and parenting or caretaking practices is dynamic and mutually reinforcing. A student's academic performance, on the one hand, is greatly influenced by previous and current parenting/caretaking practices and child–caretaker relationships; on the other hand, children's academic performance has an instant and lasting effect on parents' and caretakers' behaviors, significantly shaping future caretaking and parenting practices and child–parent/caretaker relationships. A variety of other behavioral outcomes and social processes, such as children's participation in deviant/delinquent activities, have similar reciprocal effects on children's academic performance and other behavioral outcomes. Leveraging the rich and context sensitive qualitative data (i.e., in-depth interviews and field observation), I examine these possibilities.

Sampling Methods and Procedures of Data Collection

This project adopts a mixed methods research approach, collecting and analyzing data using both quantitative and qualitative methods. As briefly outlined previously, the purpose of this project is to understand the impact of parental migration on family structure and interpersonal relationships among members of translocal families and to explore the extent to which these changes influence children's behavioral and psychological development. I used survey methods to collect quantitative data from a probability sample of middle school students in Peace County, Jiangxi province, and gathered qualitative data through multiyear field observations and interviews with left-behind children, matched at-home caretakers (with most of them being grandparents), and matched and unmatched migrant parents. These two disparate data sources, when combined, greatly complement one another and provide a complete and nuanced picture of the lives of children left behind. Specifically, the qualitative data offer detailed and contextualized insights into lived experiences of LBC at the research site, while the survey results produce generalizable and externally valid findings regarding the attendant effects of parental migration.

I selected Peace County, located in the northwest of Jiangxi province, as my research site primarily because of its prevalence of out-migration and the large number of children left behind. Jiangxi province is one of the least economically developed provinces in China and has been a major migrant-sending province since the 1980s. Most migrants from Peace County seek job opportunities in southern provinces such as Fujian and Guangdong or the eastern coast like Jiangsu, Shanghai, and Zhejiang. The 2010 census data revealed that half of the rural children in Jiangxi province were left behind by one or both parents (ACWF, 2013). As a typical rural county with a high prevalence of LBC, Peace County is an ideal place for researchers to understand how these children's lives are impacted by migration and chronic parental absence.

Survey: Sampling Design and Sample Characteristics

The primary method for quantitative data collection in this project includes survey data collected from approximately 1,200 middle school students in Peace County in May 2017. The survey includes a wide range of questions, including questions and statements regarding parental migration; caretaking arrangements; children's bonding with schools, caretakers, and migrant parents; and children's behavioral and psychological development.

The survey used a multistage cluster sampling design. First, I obtained a list of rural middle schools from the Department of Education in Peace County. A total of nineteen schools—all located in small towns—were considered rural schools and used as the primary sampling frame. Second, I contacted each school's principal and obtained a list of all classes. Note that there are generally three grades—grades 7 to 9—in Chinese public middle schools, and students of the same classes take exactly the same courses with other classmates. These nineteen schools had a total of 148 classes from seventh to ninth grades and 6,556 students enrolled. Each grade had roughly one-third of the classes, with fifty-four seventh-grade classes (36.5%), forty-eight eighth-grade classes (32.4%), and forty-six ninth-grade classes (31.1%). Based on the list of classes and the class student size, I created a list of seventh- and eighth-grade classes and used the proportionate stratified sampling method to randomly select twenty-six classes of seventh and eighth graders. All ninth-grade classes were excluded from the sampling frame because principals of selected schools were concerned that the data collection would disrupt the study of ninth graders, who were intensively preparing for the critical high school entrance examination held within one month. In the final sample, twenty-six seventh- and eighth-grade classes, with a total of 1,239 students enrolled, were randomly selected from this list. These classes were embedded in ten middle schools, with class sizes ranging from thirty-six to fifty-six students.

After obtaining permission from the local Department of Education and selected school principals, I proceeded to distribute letters of parental consent to the students of selected classes. I distributed the questionnaires to these selected classes on a regular school day, with teachers and school administrators not on the site during the survey period. Researchers and assistants explained to the students the purpose of the research project at the beginning of the survey, assuring them that participation was voluntary, that data were confidential and safely stored, and that students could withdraw from the survey at any time. A total of 1,210 or 97.66 percent of students selected provided valid answers for most of the questions in the survey.

Table 1.1 provides detailed information for this sample, including children's demographic information and household characteristics. Among the participating respondents, 49 percent of children were left behind, living with one at-home parent, grandparents, or other extended family members, with some even living alone. Forty-two percent of students surveyed were eighth graders, and the remaining (58%) were seventh graders. Fifty-four percent of the students were boys, and 46 percent were girls. The ages of these students ranged from ten to eighteen, with an average of 13.74 years. About 14 percent of the sample reported that they lived in school dorms during school days, primarily because of the long distances between their villages and the schools, a lack of modern transportation, or tight class schedules.

Regarding parental characteristics, parental education ranged from illiterate or no education (1) to having graduated from specialized or technical school (8),

TABLE 1.1
Sample individual and household characteristics

	Minimum	Maximum	Mean	Standard deviation
Left-behind status	0	1	0.49	0.50
Grade	7	8	7.42	0.49
Male	0	1	0.54	0.50
Age	10	18	13.74	0.84
Boarding school	0	1	0.14	0.34
Parental education	1	8	4.15	1.35
Household property	0	3	1.19	0.75
Perceived economic status	1	5	2.79	0.66
Marital status of biological parents	0	1	0.90	0.30
Number of siblings	0	3	0.62	0.88

Note: N = 1,210.

with an average of 4.15 (not graduated from middle school). Further analyses indicate that for fathers of these children, close to half (45.3%) had less than a middle school education, one-third (31.3%) graduated from middle school but did not attend high school, and 13.5% had more than a middle school education. In addition, about one-tenth of the students (9.9%) reported that they did not know the education levels of their fathers. The education levels of the mothers had a similar distribution. Close to half (47.4%) had less than a middle school education, about a quarter (26.8%) graduated from middle school but did not attend high school, about one-tenth (9.3%) had more than a middle school education, and 16.4% of the students reported that they did not know about the education level of their mother. For parents whose children did not know their education levels, I suspected that most of them had little education and could not provide any tutoring for children—tutoring being one important way for children to gather information about their parents' education levels.

In terms of family economic status, I asked children whether their family had one of three household properties: a two- or more than a two-story house, a car, or a truck. The typical household had at least one of the three major items. Specifically, 16.4 percent reported that their families did not have any of the three, about half (51.3%) had one, more than a quarter (28.7%) had two, and a small percentage (3.6%) had all three. In addition, I included a perceived measure of family economic status, asking children to rank their family's economic status in their local villages.

The average family economic status was at the middle level, with responses ranging from the lowest (1) to the highest (5). Only a small fraction of the children ranked their family economic status at the lowest (1.9%) or the highest (0.6%) levels, and more than half ranked their family economic status at the middle level (59.7%). For the remaining children, more than a quarter (28%) ranked their family at the lower middle, and 9.7 percent ranked their family at the upper middle. Regarding other family characteristics, about 10 percent of the students reported that their biological parents were divorced or separated, a surprisingly high number given the historically low rate of divorce in rural China (Platte, 1988). Finally, more than half of the students were the only child in the family (59.8%), one-quarter had one sibling (22.8%), and 17.4 percent had two or more siblings.

Qualitative Data Collection: In-Depth Interviews and Field Observations

I supplemented my quantitative data with field research, collecting data through field observations and in-depth interviews with left-behind children, matched caretakers (i.e., grandparents and at-home parents), and matched and unmatched migrant parents during the summers of 2017 and 2018. First, I interviewed a total of thirty middle school students, strategically selected from two middle schools based on types of caretaking arrangement (i.e., grandparent caretaking, at-home father caretaking, or at-home mother caretaking). The parents of these children were scattered across different provinces, most having migrated to economically developed neighboring provinces such as Zhejiang, Guangdong, or Fujian or megacities (e.g., Chongqing and Wuhan) in inland provinces. The interview schedule focused on major domains of the children's lives and was designed to elicit information on family dynamics (e.g., children's interactions with at-home caretakers and migrant parents), peer networks, school attachment and performance, and daily routine activities as well as parental migration histories. In addition, some questions about emotional difficulties and future plans were included, as I hypothesized that parental migration and prolonged separation may have a long-lasting effect on children's psychological well-being. All the interviews were conducted during my visits to children's homes, with parents or guardians requested not to be present in the room to avoid potential interference and student discomfort. The length of the interviews ranged from half an hour to about one hour.

Additional qualitative data were collected through my interviews with primary caretakers of these children, including grandparents (twenty-two), at-home fathers (four), and at-home mothers (four). All the interviews were conducted at the home of the interviewees, with most of them occurring before the child interview. The interview schedule of adult caretakers focused on caretakers' relationships with left-behind children, communication with migrant parents, challenges of raising children with one or two parents chronically absent, and financial situations such as remittance and the expenditure on food, housing, and children's education. These interviews generally took longer than the children's interviews, ranging from one to two hours.

To include the perspective of migrant parents in my data, I supplemented the child and caretaker interviews with in-depth interviews of twenty-five migrant parents. Through personal connections, I visited two small companies—one toy manufacturer and one cell-phone screen manufacturer—in Baoan, Shenzhen city, during the summers of 2017 and 2018. The founders of these two factories were from Peace County and had maintained strong connections with their hometowns, recruiting many staff members and workers from Peace County each year. Surprisingly, most of the employees I interviewed came from different provinces, adding significant heterogeneity to my data and inspiring me to understand this issue from a wider and national angle. Among the twenty-five migrant parents interviewed, five had specialized/technical school educations and worked as technicians or in managerial positions, while the other twenty worked on the assembly lines.

While the formal in-depth interviews occurred only during the summers of 2017 and 2018, I started my fieldwork and informal data collection two to three years before the formal interview process, having informal and unstructured conversations with various stakeholders such as grandparent caretakers, remaining at-home parents, returning migrant parents, and schoolteachers. Our conversations included many topics, including but not limited to migration in the local community, *dagong* experiences, caretaking arrangements for left-behind children, and whether and how these experiences potentially shaped children's physical and psychological development. These data guided my initial development of interview schedules and questionnaires and were included in the final data analyses.

Organization of the Book

As noted, this book attempts to explore whether and how children's left-behind status—largely shaped by China's unique structural and cultural characteristics—impacts children's general well-being, including school performance, problematic behaviors, feelings of ambiguous loss, and emotional well-being. Specifically, this book aims to investigate how reconfigured family structures, induced by parental migration, shape dynamic relationships in translocal households and how these relationships influence children's behavioral and psychological outcomes (see fig. 1.1). Theoretically elaborating and empirically testing the role of contexts at multiple levels—and the dynamic social processes embedded in these contexts—this book illuminates not only whether LBC status is associated with a myriad of developmental outcomes but also both how this status is influenced by the larger social context and to what extent it influences children's development, directly and indirectly, through immediate social processes.

My investigation begins by studying the reconfigured family structure, alternative caretaking arrangements, and respective caretaking practices after parental migration. In chapter 2, I test the first part of the overarching theoretical model—childcare arrangements and the theoretically relevant individual, family, and structural factors associated with decisions regarding these arrangements. Albeit a critical component of the migration decision-making process, caretaking arrangement is a surprisingly under-researched topic. Utilizing both qualitative and quantitative data, this chapter highlights various caretaking arrangement trajectories—some stable and others characterized by instability and change over time. Furthermore, this chapter aims to identify potential individual, familial, situational, social, and cultural factors contributing to the decision regarding caretaking arrangements. Importantly, I find that structural factors, particularly the rural–urban income gap and the *hukou* system, significantly increase rural-to-urban migration and the probability of children being left behind. At the household level, the availability of mentally and physically healthy grandparents substantially increases parental migration, confirming the significance of intergenerational support in internal migration in rural China.

Chapter 3 extends previous research by empirically investigating different types of caretaking practice provided by at-home caretakers (e.g., at-home parents or grandparents), focusing on caretaker monitoring and supervision, caretaker–child bonding, and caretaker harsh discipline. In this chapter, I ask two research questions: (1) Do alternative caretaking arrangements (e.g., grandparenting or one-parent caretaking) differ substantially from normative two-parent families in the realm of caregiving practices? And (2) within these alternative arrangements, are there any significant differences in the forms and quality of child-rearing practice? In particular, I critically engage in the discussion of grandparenting—a common yet culturally unique arrangement in translocal families in rural China—by focusing on its prevalence and cultural, economic, and situational drivers. In my exploration of the heterogeneity within grandparent caretaking arrangements and caregiving practices, I debunk the myth that one-parent caretaking (i.e., caretaking by one left-behind mother or father)—an arrangement strongly promoted by the academic community and local and central governments—is superior to grandparenting in rural China. Rather, the data paint a quite complicated picture regarding caretaking practices, highlighting the nuanced, dynamic, and multidimensional relationships between left-behind children, migrant parents, at-home parents, and grandparents.

Chapter 4 taps into another critical but often neglected dimension of caretaking among translocal families in rural China: long-distance parenting. Long-distance parenting—a topic increasingly acknowledged in transnational migration literature—has yet to be systematically addressed by Chinese internal migration scholarship. Extending previous literature, the chapter investigates three primary strategies employed by migrant parents to perform traditional parenting duties: mobile parenting via modern information and communication technology (ICT), short visits to children and family members, and children's visits to host cities of migrant parents during summer breaks or other holidays. The last strategy—although commonplace in rural China—is largely ignored by prior scholarship. Using survey and in-depth interview data, this chapter describes how long-distance parenting is performed by migrant parents, assesses the frequency of visits between migrant parents and children, and identifies potential predictive structural and situational factors associated with the adoption of these strategies. The data reveal that migrant parents often strive to perform conventional parental duties from afar; these endeavors, however, are frequently undermined by numerous barriers at the structural, familial, and individual levels.

Having examined caretaking arrangements and practices both at children's everyday location and with their long-distance parent(s), I shift my focus to children's behavioral and psychological outcomes, investigating the underlying social processes linking parental migration to these outcomes. Chapter 5 explores the relationships between parental migration/caretaking arrangements and children's schooling, focusing on students' academic performance, school bonding, and desire to drop out of school. Situating children and caretakers within the context of China's "education fever" culture, chapter 5 analyzes how different childcare arrangements influence children's educational outcomes, both directly and indirectly, through varying caretaking practices. In addition, I investigate prevailing sentiments regarding the "deleterious" effects of grandparenting on children's academic performance, exploring both whether these sentiments are valid and how they can be strategically addressed. The results reveal that children's school involvement is substantially weakened when a mother migrates (and the father remains at home) or when both parents migrate and the child is cared for by one grandparent. Nevertheless, these effects are largely indirect, mediated by caretaking practices such as physical and emotional support, discipline, and monitoring and supervision provided by caretakers.

Chapter 6 continues to explore the associations between LBC status and children's behavioral outcomes, focusing on involvement in deviant or delinquent behaviors, including affiliation with deviant peers, involvement in delinquency, and engagement in deviant behaviors. Providing further support for chapter 5, chapter 6 reveals that caretaking arrangements, not left-behind status per se, influence children's deviance and delinquency involvement. I further establish that caretaking practices and school bonding are key social processes linking parental migration to children's deviance and delinquency. Finally, this chapter highlights the direct and conditional effects of other individual and household characteristics, including children's gender and parental marital status.

Chapter 7 turns to the associations between LBC status and children's psychological well-being, focusing on children's feelings of ambiguous loss toward temporally and spatially separated parents and whether and how these feelings are reciprocally associated with dimensions of psychological well-being such as symptoms of social withdrawal, social and physical anxiety, and self-harm. Adopting the ambiguous loss lens, I establish that left-behind children regularly exhibit ambivalent feelings toward their migrant parents and parental migration. Children left behind generally understand the economic justification of parental migration and chronic absence but are simultaneously burdened by both its disruption to family life and a lack of intimacy with parents. In addition, based on findings from in-depth interviews, I develop a scale to quantitatively measure children's feelings of ambiguous loss and test its reliability and predictive validity. As will be evident from chapter 7, the concept of ambiguous loss has theoretical and practical significance in China's LBC research. I find that ambiguous loss has consistent and robust effects on children's psychological well-being, transcending the joint influence of critical risk and protective factors such as caretaking practices and long-distance parenting.

Finally, chapter 8 concludes by summarizing major empirical findings from previous chapters and investigating a critical dimension associated with the left-behind experiences—the development of resiliency through early independence, intimacy with grandparents, and deep appreciation of the sacrifices of migrant parents and grandparents. Furthermore, this chapter concludes by exploring policy implications for future work with left-behind children and programs at institutional and familial levels, particularly programs targeting intervening mechanisms derived from the key findings.

2

Who Leaves and Who Stays?

Factors Associated with Parental Migration and Caretaking Arrangements

> Nowadays, if there are ten children, nine of them are raised by grandma. Parents are all working outside.
>
> —at-home father Lu

The decision for rural parents to migrate to urban areas entails a series of intricately linked calculations and continuing negotiations within the extended household—a process that often includes not only weighing expected financial costs against potential returns but also reallocating resources toward migration, subsistence farming, childcare, and eldercare. A fundamental question that must be answered by parents and extended household members is: How should resources be reallocated to achieve maximum utility? More precisely, who should stay and who should migrate to maximize the productivity of an intralocal family, such as household income, children's educational achievement, and, ultimately, the family's intergenerational mobility? For example, should children migrate with parents to destination cities to achieve better educational outcomes? Or, if children stay behind, which family members are ideal primary caretakers? Internal migration in China is often motivated by an increasingly deep rural–urban income gap, as demonstrated within this chapter as well as numerous other studies; however, a myriad of factors at macrostructural and micro-individual levels collectively shape and determine parents' decisions regarding both migration itself and the allocation of caretaking resources.

This chapter investigates parental decision-making regarding childcare arrangements—a critical but often neglected component of the migration decision process—focusing on types of arrangements, their stability and change over time, and underlying individual, familial, and macrostructural correlates. First, using data collected from the student survey, I examine whether children's demographic characteristics and familial backgrounds (e.g., family socioeconomic status) are associated with parents' decisions on caretaking arrangements post-migration.

Second, I explore how the macrostructural context of migration is manifested locally and is interpreted by parents, caretakers, and children left behind. Finally, given the prevalence of grandparenting (i.e., grandparents serving as surrogate parents for an extended period) in rural China, I highlight how grandparenting transforms from a social-cultural role within the private family sphere to a prominent sociopolitical role within the public space.

The discussion in this chapter proceeds as follows. First, guided by the theoretical model presented in chapter 1, I briefly review the prior literature linking individual, familial, and macrostructural factors to the reassignment of childcare responsibilities. Following that, I use quantitative and qualitative data to understand the varying types of caretaking arrangements and how situational, individual, familial, and structural factors influence the stability and fluidity of these arrangements over time. In the third section, I test the validity of the theoretical model by using quantitative data to explore the influences of individual and family factors as well as interview and field observation data to identify the effect of macrostructural constraints and individual and familial correlates.

Predictors of Parental Migration and Caretaking Arrangements: A Brief Literature Review

Numerous studies have attempted to theorize and identify predictors of rural-to-urban migration at structural, community, familial, and individual levels. At the macrostructural level, this literature focuses on the salient influence of a rural–urban income gap and regional economic inequality as critical "push-pull" factors of migration (L. Ma et al., 2019; Todaro, 1969). The steadily increasing rural–urban income gap in China during the last several decades (X. Ma et al., 2018)—with urbanites earning about 2.56 times as much as rural residents in 2020 (National Bureau of Statistics, 2020)—is one of the deciding factors of internal migration. An equally critical "push-pull" factor is regional economic inequality characterized by an ever-widening trend of coastal–inland divide in the last three decades. As such, coastal provinces such as Guangdong, Zhejiang, and Jiangsu and megacities such as Shanghai, Beijing, Guangzhou, and Shenzhen have witnessed the highest net migrant inflow, while central and western provinces such as Sichuan, Anhui, and Guizhou have recorded the largest net migrant outflow in the last several decades (Chan & Ren, 2018; Shi et al., 2020).

The literature on the decision of migrant parents on caretaking arrangement is much more limited. Unequivocally, the same host of macrostructural factors associated with parental migration influences the decision on childcare arrangements. As discussed in chapter 1, the deciding contributor of the left-behind children phenomenon is China's *hukou* system and, more broadly, a dual rural–urban social-economic system, which prevents rural migrants and their children from accessing state-sponsored social welfare programs (e.g., quality public education) in host cities (Mallee, 1995). As a result, about two-thirds of the children are left behind in migrant origin communities, with one parent or grandparents serving as primary caregivers (Chan & Ren, 2018).

The variation of local employment opportunities and regional economic inequality is another influential factor. In more developed rural areas in China, young parents may decide to leave one parent at home to look after children and seek local employment opportunities. In less developed regions where the opportunity cost of having one parent staying behind is substantially higher, this strategy may not be rational or practical, leading to two-parent migration and grandparents or other extended family members serving as primary caretakers. Finally, certain industry sections may require workers with specific physical strength, skills, and other traits. The lack of labor in caring sectors in developed countries, for example, spurs a wave of female migration from developing countries (e.g., the Philippines), with most of the women working as caregivers such as nannies, eldercare workers, and domestic workers. As a result, men and husbands are increasingly left behind and undertake caring or nurturing tasks vacated by absent mothers (Parreñas, 2005a, 2009). In the same vein, many rural-to-urban migrants in China in the early 1990s were female workers, working primarily in the domestic sphere (e.g., domestic workers or nannies), labor-intensive factories, or the service sector such as restaurants, hotels, and retail stores (Gaetano & Jacka, 2004).

The theory of neoclassical economics shifts research focus from macrostructural aspects to the influence of subjective dimensions, proposing that migration is the outcome of family members weighing the perceived costs and benefits of migration (Stark & Bloom, 1985). According to this theory, the family becomes the basic social unit that decides who migrates and works where, who stays behind, and the primary responsibilities of each household member (e.g., farming, childrearing, and eldercare). In general, young, and relatively more educated males are more likely to migrate, leaving older, female, and less educated rural residents to stay behind (Fan, 1999). Researchers also point out that strong and weak social ties between migrants and nonmigrants decrease the risk and uncertainty of the migration process (e.g., costs of traveling and income level in destination areas), precipitating the massive flow of labor from rural to urban and inland to coastal provinces in China (Chan & Ren, 2018; Massey et al., 1994).

To date, few studies have attempted to investigate factors associated with caretaking arrangements at family and individual levels. The limited literature indicates that the decision of sole migration, couple migration, or family migration is the outcome of migrant parents actively rearranging household labor to achieve maximum earnings from urban work opportunities. As such, children's ages and the availability of intergenerational support are the most critical factors (Fan et al., 2011; Fang & Shi, 2018). Newborn children who need intensive childcare, for example, tend to live with their mother in migrant origin communities. When children grow up and become more independent, they are more likely to migrate with their parents to host cities. Around the time of high school, however, they often return to migrant-origin communities, reflecting the rigidity of *hukou*-based curriculum

(Chan & Ren, 2018). Characteristics of parents, including age, education levels, and migration history, also play a pivotal role in shaping migrant parents' decision to leave children behind or bring them along. Nevertheless, some recent studies observe that the practice of "economic rationality" has been on the decline, as migrants with higher socioeconomic status actively choose household reunion in cities compared to solely focusing on maximizing household income (H. Chen et al., 2020).

Integrating insights from prominent theories of migration and empirical research in left-behind children, I hypothesize that the characteristics of children (age, gender, living on campus) and parents (parental education, marital status of biological parents), availability of intergenerational support, and household socioeconomic status are associated with types of caretaking arrangements. In addition, I explore how macrostructural barriers are experienced and interpreted by rural parents and members of the intralocal households, which directly influences the outcome variable studied in this chapter.

Child Caretaking Arrangement: Types, Change, and Stability

The Prevalent Types of Child Caretaking Arrangement

The first goal of this chapter is to identify types of child caretaking arrangements observed among rural parents at the research sites as well as potential social, cultural, and demographic factors associated with such arrangements. The variable caretaking arrangements was assessed by asking children whether their parents migrated to other cities over the last twelve months and subsequently asking them who acted as their main caretakers. Figure 2.1 shows the distribution of caretaking arrangements among the sampled students in Peace County, Jiangxi province. Overall, about half of the children (49%) reported that at least one parent had migrated and that they were being raised by a remaining parent, grandparents, or

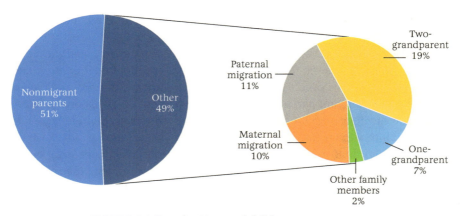

FIGURE 2.1 Prevalent types of childcare arrangement.

other relatives or were living independently. These results are largely consistent with previous research. According to 2010 census data (ACWF, 2013), the percentage of left-behind children in Jiangxi province was slightly over 50 percent, comparable to the estimation (49%) in our sample.

In terms of specific caretaking arrangements, a quarter of children reported living in skipped generation families (primarily cared for by grandparents), with 19 percent (n = 223) being attended to by two grandparents and 7 percent (n = 86) by sole-grandparent caretakers. The prevalence of skipped-generation households in this sample is similar to findings from recently collected nationally representative datasets, which reported that approximately 50 percent of left-behind children were cared for by grandparents (ACWF, 2013; Lu et al., 2019a). In fact, in some parts of Jiangxi province, the percentage of skipped-generation households has been found to be as high as 90 percent (Xu et al., 2014). In addition, approximately one out of five children reported they were cared for by one-parent caretakers, with sole-mother caretakers consisting of 11 percent (n = 136) and sole-father caretakers 10 percent (n = 115). The prevalence of maternal migration in this sample appears to be higher than that in data collected at the national level (Chan & Ren, 2018), likely due to an overall higher prevalence of rural-to-urban migration in Jiangxi province. Finally, 2 percent of the children surveyed (n = 20) reported that they were living with other extended family members (not grandparents) or were living independently at the time of the interview.

It should be noted that while caretaking arrangement decisions are often shaped by a myriad of factors at individual and familial levels, the influence of structural and cultural factors cannot be overstated. An important finding regarding caretaking in rural China is that most grandparent caretakers are paternal, rather than maternal, grandparents. In my sample, approximately 85 percent of children left behind by two migrant parents reported that they were attended by paternal grandparents, while only 15 percent were raised by maternal grandparents, reflecting the dominant influence of the patriarchal and patrilinear family values in rural China. These results sharply contrast with findings from research conducted in major migrant-sending countries in East Asia or Latin America (Hoang et al., 2015; Oliveira, 2018; Parreñas, 2005b). Hoang and colleagues (2015) investigated the caretaking arrangements of dual-parent-migrant households in Vietnam, Indonesia, Thailand, and the Philippines and found that only 26 percent of left-behind children in Indonesia and the Philippines and 38 percent in Thailand were cared for by paternal family members. In contrast, 73 percent of children left behind by two migrant parents in Vietnam were attended by paternal family members. Although the measures of caretaking arrangements utilized among these studies are slightly different—for example, Hoang et al. (2015) included caretakers from extended family members (e.g., aunts and uncles), and my study only includes paternal and maternal grandparents—these results nevertheless demonstrate the deep and lasting effects of social institutions and cultural norms on households and parents' adaptive strategies post–parental migration.

The Fluidity of Caretaking Arrangements

The survey data provide a snapshot of the prevalence of certain caretaking arrangements; however, it should be noted that these data cannot capture temporary variations in caretaking over time. The interview data reveal that caretaking arrangements were in constant flux, constrained and shaped by a matrix of structural and situational factors. Among these, the most cited factors were a child's developmental stage and its temporal implications (e.g., intensive care during early age and education of school-aged children), the availability and health of caretakers, the relationship between migrant parents and other members in the extended family, household income, and housing conditions in host cities. Grandpa Longda and his wife, parents to two adult migrant daughters, illustrated how these factors collectively shaped the household's decision-making regarding the temporal and spatial arrangement of childcare. When interviewed in 2018, grandpa Longda and his wife were raising two of their grandchildren, the fifteen-year-old son of their older daughter and the baby son of their younger daughter. When I walked into grandpa Longda's house, his wife had just traveled to Jiangsu province, escorting the baby grandson back to his migrant parents. When asked about caretaking decisions regarding the baby, grandpa Longda commented:

> He [son-in-law] had a bad relationship with his mother.... The son and the mom did not have a good relationship. At first, they [paternal grandparents] were happy to death, only one son, now one grandson. Yeye [paternal grandpa] was cooking dishes when he first heard the news, he poured oil onto his hand! That's how happy he was! ... But the two had a broken relationship, totally broken. He [son-in-law] was so mad, so he sent the baby to us. Then I said you could send him to us, that's about it, you know? They were reluctant to send the baby to us at the beginning. They did not even come and visit us during the Spring Festival [after the child was born]!

Concerned with a lack of medical facilities and sanitation in rural areas, grandpa Longda's son-in-law was initially hesitant to leave his son with them but ultimately chose to do so due to the conflict with his parents. Nevertheless, after only a few months, grandpa Longda decided to send the baby back to his parents in Jiangsu because of health concerns. He said,

> The baby boy was born on August 20 [in 2017], we took care of the boy for a few months, and then he [son-in-law] took him back. After a few months, they sent the child back to us. The baby was not healthy, [my wife] took him back [to Jiangsu province]. My wife will [stay there and] help take care of the child until school winter break, then she will take the older one back. She will go to school here. They take care of one [the baby boy] and we take care of one [the older five-year-old granddaughter]. We rented an apartment in Meitang [the town near the school], my wife will be there....

Grandpa Longda's case demonstrates that caretaking arrangements are often fluid, shaped by an interplay between macrostructural conditions (e.g., the rural–urban gap of medical facilities and limited school options for migrant children) and individual or situational factors (e.g., familial conflict, children's health status, and parents' and grandparents' ability to take care of children). In one year, grandpa Longda's newborn grandson cycled through multiple caretaking arrangements including at-home mother/maternal grandparent caretaking in the village, migrant parent caretaking (with potential assistance of paternal grandparents) in the host city, maternal grandparent caretaking in the village, migrant parents/maternal grandmother caretaking in the destination city, and, finally, migrant parent caretaking in the city. Each of these caretaking arrangements was temporally and spatially determined by the dynamic interplay between structural constraints and cultural and material resources available to the translocal family.

Fluidity and change in caretaking arrangements are often found to be the norm and not the exception for most translocal households, particularly during the first few years after a child's birth. These arrangements nevertheless become more or less stable when the need for intensive childcare diminishes and/or when children reach school age. In his detailed description of the caretaking arrangements of his two grandchildren, grandpa Longer highlighted moments of stability rather than change over the years. At the time of the interview, grandpa Longer and his wife were raising two paternal grandchildren, a fourteen-year-old girl and a ten-year-old boy. In the interview, I asked him about the caretaking arrangement:

INTERVIEWER: From when did you start to take care of your grandchildren?

GRANDPA LONGER: They [grandchildren] were cared for by us from being little ones. From when they fell onto the ground, they were left here. . . . The baby was born in Jiangsu province. They [migrant parents] were working there. My wife went there to take care of the baby, so I say it has been this side [grandparents] since the baby was born. It has always been this side.

INTERVIEWER: So your wife was not here?

GRANDPA LONGER: No, not here. So, I would say, it's always us. The two [grandchildren] were raised by us all the way to this big. She [daughter-in-law] was just pregnant for a few months, going through her belly. After that, it has always been my wife. . . . They went to school here. They went to school there [Jiangsu province] for a while, then they came back and never went there again. They went to pre-care there [the host city], and then came back, still in pre-care.

In grandpa Longer's case, while there was some change in the spatial dimension in caretaking arrangement over time, the two grandchildren were primarily attended to by his wife from "when they fell onto the ground." Moreover, they were sent back to the countryside since preschool and "never went there again." This type of caretaking arrangement appears to be prevalent among these translocal families. From the first few months until toddlerhood, children are often jointly cared for by grandparents (mostly the grandmother) and one migrant or left-behind parent. Around one to three years old, when the intensity of childcare declines and children are ready for preschool, the caretaking arrangement often transitions to solo caretaking, with either migrant parents or grandparents being fully in charge. These temporal and spatial transitions in caretaking largely depend on migrant parents' financial status, which determines their own housing conditions as well as their willingness to pay for their children's higher caretaking and educational costs in destination cities. Grandpa Longer's wife, for example, co-lived with his son and daughter-in-law in receiving cities for a few years because his son worked as a businessman and was able and willing to pay the substantially higher costs of childrearing in urban areas. Grandpa Longda, in contrast, planned to raise his baby grandchild in the village because of financial constraints. Moreover, despite parental economic status, the interview data revealed that when children reached school age (about five to six years old), most of them came back or stayed with grandparents in rural areas because of the difficulty in accessing public schools or the excessively high tuition costs of private schools in host cities.

Individual, Familial, and Structural Factors Associated with Caretaking Arrangements

Individual and Familial Characteristics Associated with Caretaking Arrangements

In this section, I turn to our quantitative data and use multinomial regression models to investigate whether children's demographic characteristics and familial backgrounds predict types of childcare arrangement (table 2.1). I used three variables to assess children's characteristics. Children's age and gender (male = 1, female = 0) were straightforward measures like those utilized in previous literature. A contextually sensitive measure, living in a school dorm (1 = yes, 0 = no), was also included as a control variable. I controlled this variable because I observed that some middle schoolers lived on campus due to the distance between their residence and the school. This condition lessened caretakers' childcare duties but imposed an extra financial burden (e.g., food and housing costs) on parents. For familial background, I included family socioeconomic status such as father's and mother's education levels, a child's perceived family economic status in his or her village (ranging from the highest = 1 to the lowest = 5), and number of household properties. Number of household properties was a count measure of three items: ownership of a car, a truck, or a two- or more than two-story house. I believe that these three indicators are better indicators of family socioeconomic status in rural China than household income—which is unlikely to be accurately reported by adolescents—and are more relevant to a family's migration decision-making (McKenzie, 2005). Finally, I included the number of siblings, availability of grandparents, and marital status of biological parents. Previous literature has

TABLE 2.1
Multinomial logistic regression models predicting alternative caretaking arrangements versus nonmigration

	Maternal migration versus nonmigration exp(b)	Paternal migration versus nonmigration exp(b)	Two-grandparent caretaking versus nonmigration exp(b)	One-grandparent caretaking versus nonmigration exp(b)
Male[a]	1.16	0.80	0.94	0.57*
Age	1.07	1.10	1.21	1.36+
Living in a school dorm[b]	1.05	1.11	1.26	0.73
Father's education	0.97	1.10	1.09	0.73**
Mother's education	1.00	0.99	1.04	1.24*
Household property	1.12	0.80	0.87	0.71+
Perceived family economic status	1.03	0.87	1.04	0.83
Marital status of biological parents[c]	0.05**	0.20**	0.08**	0.10**
Number of siblings	0.89	1.24*	1.23**	0.97
Grandparent availability[d]	2.92**	1.23	12.38**	14.23**

Note: $p < 0.10$; *$p < 0.05$; **$p < 0.01$; $N = 1{,}210$.

[a] Female as the reference category.

[b] Living at home as the reference group.

[c] Divorced or separated as the reference group.

[d] Not living with grandparents together as a reference group.

demonstrated that these factors are associated with parental migration status in rural China (Fan & Li, 2020; Fan et al., 2011; Fang & Shi, 2018). Because the sample size of children living with other family members (i.e., children living with extended family members other than grandparents or living independently) is too small ($n = 20$), I excluded this group from the multinomial regression analysis.

Using nonmigrant parents as a reference group, table 2.1 indicates that, overall, children's characteristics and familial factors had differential effects on parents' caretaking arrangement strategies. Children's individual traits (age, gender, and whether living in a school dorm) did not appear to impact choices between maternal migration, paternal migration, two-grandparent caretaking, and nonmigration. In contrast, children's demographic characteristics such as sex (exp(b) = 0.57) and age (exp(b) = 1.36) significantly impacted the choice between one-grandparent caretaking and nonparental migration, with girls and older children more likely to be cared for by one-grandparent caretakers. Understandably, parents likely feel more comfortable leaving older children to one-grandparent caretakers, as they are more independent and need less intensive childcare. The gender effect is more complex and requires additional explanation. It is possible that parents in rural Jiangxi value boys more than girls, as reflected by the preferred treatment of migrating with boys rather than girls to host cities documented in prior research (ACWF, 2013; Wang, 2005). This finding may also reflect the stereotypes of parents and grandparents regarding gender differences, as girls are considered less "wild" and more introverted and thus can be managed by an aged sole-caretaker grandparent. In addition, girls left behind may be more "suited" for the companionship role for sole-caretaker grandparents and can even function as caretakers of elders, reversing caretaking roles (Jingzhong & Lu, 2011).

Among familial factors, the marital status of children's biological parents was the only factor consistently associated with each of the four alternative caretaking arrangements. Children with married biological parents had decreased odds of maternal migration versus nonmigration by 95 percent, decreased odds of paternal migration versus nonmigration by 80 percent, decreased odds of two-grandparent caretaking versus nonmigration by 90 percent, and decreased odds of one-grandparent caretaking versus nonmigration by 92 percent. Further data analysis showed that about one-fifth of children of migrant parents reported that their biological parents were divorced or separated (19.4%), ten times higher than that of children of nonmigrant parents (1.9%). This correlation can be attributed to two factors (S. Hu, 2018; W. Li, 2018). First, young migrant parents in receiving cities, predominantly working in factories or the service industry, are exposed to more liberal social values and attitudes promoting an egalitarian marital relationship. When new expectations derived from these liberal values and attitudes are not met, marital dissolution may occur. Female migration, in particular, potentially reconfigures gender roles and improves women's earning potential and economic independence (W. Li, 2018), leading to an altered relationship between husbands and wives and mutual expectations. Second, migrant parents often live apart from each other, with most seeing each other a few times a year if one is left behind (Jingzhong, 2011). Even when both parents migrate, many do not live in the same city or the same place. The long-term separation inevitably leads to a lack of satisfaction of basic physical and emotional needs, including desires for companionship, care, daily intimacy, and sexual lives, increasing emotional estrangement between spouses and declining commitment to the union. Indeed, a national survey conducted in 2010 showed that about a quarter of migrant workers had participated in extramarital sex, about two to three times higher than rural residents (9.1%) and about 50 percent higher than urban residents (15.7% to 19.1%; Pan, Parish, & Huang, 2011). Finally, the consistent effect of biological parents' marital status may also reflect the necessity of migration after divorce, either because divorced parents feel the need to avoid a negative label at home or to address financial problems due to lost labor in the family.

The second familial factor, the number of siblings in the household, had differential effects on a household's decision-making regarding caretaking arrangements. Having more children in a family increased paternal migration ($\exp(b)$ = 1.24) and dual-parent migration ($\exp(b)$ = 1.23). Conversely, the number of siblings decreased maternal migration ($\exp(b)$ = 0.89) and one-grandparent caretaking ($\exp(b)$ = 0.97), although these two associations were not statistically significant. These results highlight the salience of traditional gender norms in shaping the decision of parental migration and caretaking arrangements in rural China, with the father taking primary responsibility for financially supporting the family and the mother becoming an unpaid caretaker. Overall, these results suggest that when a rural family has more children, the family often resorts to paternal migration or, if intergenerational support is available, dual-parent migration to ease the added financial burden. The decision between single versus dual-parent migration largely depends on whether grandparents (particularly two grandparents) are available at home for childcare.

Finally, the availability of grandparents plays a significant role in shaping a household's decisions regarding migration and caretaking arrangements, increasing the odds of dual-grandparent caretaking versus nonmigration by twelve times ($\exp(b)$ = 12.38) and single-grandparent caretaking by fourteen times ($\exp(b)$ = 14.23). As multiple studies have documented, intergenerational support is critical for facilitating parental migration due to institutional discrimination against migrant workers and their children, particularly the lack of access to public schools for migrant children in receiving cities (Chan & Ren, 2018; Fan & Li, 2020). Interestingly, the effect of grandparent availability on paternal migration was not statistically significant ($\exp(b)$ = 1.23, $p > 0.05$) but was highly significant for maternal migration ($\exp(b)$ = 2.92, $p < 0.05$), suggesting that a father's decision to migrate was not dependent on whether intergenerational support was available, in sharp contrast with a mother's decision to migrate. These findings, while underscoring the influence of traditional gender roles in shaping a household's decision to migrate and to adopt specific caretaking strategies, reveal how rural parents adapt to dramatic social changes under structural and cultural constraints. Specifically, a mother is often left behind to take care of children when no grandparent support is available but may actively seek to migrate by herself or with her spouse when intergenerational support for childcare is provided.

Overall, the multivariate regression analyses provide important insights on the identification of individual and household factors associated with caretaking arrangements. Among children's characteristics, sex and age were significantly associated with a specific caretaking arrangement, with girls and older children being more likely to be cared for by a single caretaker grandparent versus nonmigrant parents. Among familial background factors, the marital status of a child's biological parents was consistently associated with parental migration, perhaps reflecting the unintended consequences of migration on marital stability and the devastating impact of marital dissolution on a household's economic status in the context of rural China. Moreover, the number of children and the availability of grandparents were found to be powerful predictors of parental migration, with the number of children increasing both paternal migration and dual-parent migration and the availability of grandparents strengthening the likelihood of dual-parent migration and maternal migration.

Why Are Children Left Behind? Accounts of Migrant Parents and Grandparents

In this section, I turn to the qualitative data to further the understanding of how structural, familial, and individual factors interact with each other and shape parents' decisions on childcare arrangements. I focus on parents' and grandparents' accounts of why one or both parents migrate while children are being left behind, the prevalence of grandparenting and related sociocultural factors, and sole-parent caretaking.

In the previous section, I established that rural–urban income disparity is the primary pushing and pulling factor influencing parents' decisions to migrate. A parent's (or parents') decision concerning whether to bring children to receiving cities or leave them behind, however, is more than a purely economic decision. Rather, as demonstrated in previous research and delineated in the qualitative data that follow, this decision is shaped by a dynamic interplay among three intermediate environmental factors—the costs of raising children in receiving cities (e.g., education), a lack of childcare, and urban housing conditions/availability—all of which are shaped by governmental policies and other structural forces typically beyond individual and family control. These three factors, often intrinsically intertwined, collectively shape parents' decisions regarding childcare arrangements. Grandpa Longer's comments on his wife's decision to return home with their grandchildren illustrated the situational complexity:

> It's hard to say. . . . It's better to be at home, the cost is less. It's better for him [his son] to leave them [grandchildren] here. If he has money, he gives some money. If not, he does not pay a penny, right? This is being honest. . . . Going to school there is not as good as going to school at home. It's better to have children to go to school here. Someone will watch them if children study here, outside [host city] no one watches them. Most of the time, my son is not at home, he travels everywhere. Sometimes at night, he is already so far away, traveling all the time. He does not stay at the factory much.

As grandpa Longer pointed out, the advantage of leaving children behind was obvious: saving childcare costs and the presence of a caring guardian when parents are not available. Although childcare institutions thrive in urban China, due to concerns of costs, quality of caring, and security as well as young parents' busy working and social schedules, parents often prefer grandparents as primary caretakers. Using the China Health and Nutrition Survey, Chen, Liu, and Mair (2011) found that coresidential grandparents spent more time on childcare than mothers, except when children were younger than one year old. Moreover, nonresidential grandparents were also actively involved in childcare, taking care of grandchildren in their own homes during after-school hours or on weekends (F. Chen et al., 2011). The spatial separation between rural grandparents and migrant parents, however, makes this prevailing care arrangement in urban China infeasible for intralocal households, facilitating their decision to leave children behind. When asked why children did not migrate with them, one migrant mother responded matter-of-factly, "Who is going to watch the children?"

The alternative option, migrating with children and grandparents, is often a short-term solution to temporary events such as caring for newborn babies or physically sick migrant parents or children because this arrangement substantially increases housing and other living costs, adding much financial stress and conflict within these intralocal families. Urban housing in China—particularly in megacities such as Beijing, Shenzhen, Guangzhou, and Shanghai, all destination cities for migrant parents—is already overcrowded, with even more substandard conditions for rural-to-urban migrants. Many unmarried migrant workers live in factory dorms, often sharing one small room with three to four coworkers. Married couples often rent one-room apartments in migrant-concentrated neighborhoods (e.g., urban villages). Although the cost of rent is substantially lower in these neighborhoods, it is still disproportionately high relative to a migrant parent's income. For example, the cost of renting one small room in urban villages in Shenzhen in 2018 was about 500 to 800 yuan, about one-fourth to one-third of a migrant's monthly income. In my interviews, migrant parents, children, and grandparents all cited poor urban housing conditions as a critical factor contributing to children being left behind. When asked whether they had thought about bringing children to Shenzhen, migrant mother Xue Gang, who left two teenage children behind, responded:

> We thought about this before. In the beginning, we were not together, it was not convenient to bring children with us. Then grandparents came, they came to help us. [But] they were not used to it, and would not come here again no matter what.... The main reason is the housing conditions. At home, it is so spacious, and here it is such a small room. They were not used to it at all. Also, in the countryside, the cost is lower. You can grow vegetables there, right? Here, the costs are everywhere. You need to buy everything, even water, right?

As suggested in Xue Gang's comments, a lack of affordable housing for migrant parents and the substantially higher costs of daily living are two critical factors contributing to grandparents and children being left behind in migrant-sending communities.

Another deciding factor is the difficulty of accessing state-funded public schools and the prohibitive cost of attending private schools. Although the 2006 Compulsory Education Law stipulated that local governments should provide compulsory education to all children, children of migrants generally face many institutional and unofficial obstacles that prevent their access to state-funded public schools in receiving cities, leading their families to either pay a substantially higher cost to attend private schools or choose to send them to low-quality and unlicensed migrant children schools (Holdaway, 2018; Xiong, 2015). One migrant parent whom I interviewed in Shenzhen, for example, stated that the tuition fee for his son's private elementary school was more than 10,000 yuan each semester, not including the costs of lunch and other school-related expenses. As a result, migrant children often return to rural areas to attend elementary school or, at most, wait until junior high school to take advantage of the nine-year compulsory education system. Most migrant parents, however, do not even consider the option of bringing children to host cities, understanding that the cost of education in receiving cities is substantially higher compared with that of leaving children behind.

The Prevalence of Grandparenting: Economic and Cultural Factors

The survey data reveal that more than half of children left behind are primarily cared for by grandparents; this finding is further validated by interview and field observations. Indeed, grandparenting—in which grandparents replace parents as primary caretakers for an extended period—has become a prominent social and cultural phenomenon in rural China, increasingly accepted by migrant parents, grandparents, and even left-behind children themselves. Xiaolian, for example, left her six children (five girls and one boy) with grandparents to work in a cell phone manufacturing factory in Shenzhen. We asked Xiaolian whether the grandparents felt it was too great a burden caring for six children and whether they complained about it:

INTERVIEWER: Did they say anything, like us taking care of your kids?

XIAOLIAN: No, they didn't say anything. Their (adult) children, sometimes they said things. We just pretended that we didn't hear anything. Right? It's all like this here, what can you do?

INTERVIEWER: You said their sons said things?

XIAOLIAN: Yes, sometimes their sons say things. The two [grandparents] did not say anything.

INTERVIEWER: Why their sons, they are not married and do not have children?

XIAOLIAN: How do I know? So, it's like this. A very strange one even said, from when my third daughter was born, he said, you guys working outside and Mom taking care of your kids, Mom is working too hard.

INTERVIEWER: Yeah?

XIAOLIAN: Yes, she works hard, but she still has to do it. It's like this. It's not only us, but every family is like this.

In this conversation, Xiaolian acknowledged that it was indeed physically and mentally challenging for grandparents to care for six children; however, she astutely pointed out that her case was far from being unique, instead maintaining "she still has to do it" because "it's not only us, but every family is like this." Interestingly, her in-laws agreed with her. Because "it's all like this here," grandparents are obligated to be the primary caretakers of grandchildren. This sentiment was echoed by other grandparent caretakers. Grandfather Xiao, who was looking after two grandchildren with his wife when interviewed, acutely observed that grandparenting was not a localized phenomenon but was likely prevalent throughout rural China. He commented:

> Although I cannot see too far away, it's all the same around me. What can you do? It's possible that what is beyond my surroundings is still the same, it's probably the same, not only in our Jiangxi province.

Indeed, rural grandparents serving as surrogate parents is not a localized phenomenon only found in Peace County. The National Bureau of Statistics (2016) reported that at the national level, 43.4 percent of left-behind children with both parents having migrated were cared for by grandparents or other family members in 2010; this number increased to 45.8 percent in the year 2015. The prevalence of grandparenting is even higher in major migrant-sending provinces such as Jiangxi province, which sees more than half of children left behind cared for by grandparents (ACWF, 2013). The critical question here is why grandparenting in rural China has been dramatically transformed from a social-cultural role in the private family sphere to a sociopolitical role in the public space. In the following sections using interview data, I highlight the role of grandparenting as both a cultural adaptation and a practical solution to the structural constraints placed upon China's multilocal families.

ECONOMIC INCENTIVE. The economic factors driving this sharp rise in grandparenting are readily apparent. The "new economics of labor migration" posits that migration is a household rather than an individual decision, with its primary motivator being the maximization of utility within a household through the allocation of certain tasks to specific spaces and roles (Lucas, 1997; J. Shen, 2013; Taylor et al., 2003). Grandparenting, or a childcare arrangement in which both parents have migrated and left children behind with their grandparents, maximizes a multilocal household's earning potential while simultaneously minimizing its total living cost. This arrangement enables both parents to migrate and to devote all their time and energy to the provision of financial support and grandparents, whose economic value in the labor market is substantially reduced, to continue farming less productive land and simultaneously provide essential childcare. In my interviews with migrant parents and grandparents, most respondents, including those left behind, made it clear that such an arrangement was the optimal choice available to them. Migrant mother Xue Gang, who migrated with her husband to work in Shenzhen, recalled the incident when grandparents asked one of them to return:

> Yeye [grandpa] Nainai [grandma] once asked, this was when the children were in elementary school, they asked us to have one person back to take care of the children. We told them, it was okay to go back and take care of the children, it would be a little bit easier for you. But money, the money side, I said we would not have enough to eat, not enough for expenses, not to mention saving some. Grandparents did not say anything further, they then helped us raise the children, they did not say anything more. . . . Too much life pressure. In our place we use coal [to heat], we use coal in the winter, and even coal costs a few thousand yuan a year.

GRANDPARENTING AS A CULTURAL ADAPTATION. While the basic neoclassical migration model can well explain the financial incentive of grandparenting, this theory fails to capture the impacts of cultural norms and values on decisions made related to caretaking arrangements. In particular, this perspective fails to explain why grandparents, who presumably occupy the highest position within a rural Chinese household, would choose to sacrifice themselves and undertake such an exhausting surrogate parent role. Shared parenting, particularly occasional childcare assistance from grandparents, is prevalent among rural and urban young parents (Y. Hu & Scott, 2016; Logan & Bian, 1999). Young parents, due to their heavy work schedule and other daily obligations, often seek childcare assistance from grandparents during their children's early years. However, this cultural practice of shared parenting differs significantly from grandparenting due to rural-to-urban migration. When parents migrate, grandparents become the primary caretakers and often replace parents as "other-mothers" (or "other-fathers") for an extended period (Parreñas, 2005a; Ye & Lu, 2011). Conversely, when both parents remain present, grandparents occupy a secondary role, and their assistance is perceived by both parties as supplemental and temporary.

This shift, while somewhat puzzling, is not entirely unexpected, nor is it inconsistent with China's "filial piety" (*xiao*), the social norm structuring and governing intergenerational relationships. While filial piety emphasizes the virtue of respect for parents, elders, and ancestors as well as the importance of establishing harmonious and benevolent familial and societal relations, this concept has been reformulated and redefined in recent years, underscoring key elements such as mutual caring and affection—elements largely dismissed in previous traditional interpretations. In other words, whereas the traditional version of *xiao* emphasizes a compulsory quality such as obligation, duty, and total obedience from children, this new version highlights the reciprocal relationship between children and parents. As such, grandparenting is not a violation of the modified "filial piety"; rather, it is understood as "part of a lifelong intergenerational exchange, by which parents and children provide for each other's needs in anticipation of reciprocity when they need help" (Logan & Bian, 1999, p. 1254). Such a modified definition appears to be wholeheartedly embraced by migrant parents and grandparents, as exemplified in my interview with grandpa Longer, who was raising two of his grandchildren when I interviewed him. When asked whether his son ever paid him for the care of the grandchildren, he responded:

GRANDPA LONGER: I help raise the little ones. Eating, drinking, it's all mine. When my son [came to visit and] went back [to the host city], his car was filled up with all kinds of stuff, oil was tens of kilograms, meat, tens of kilograms, fish, eggs, chickens. Chickens, every time, at least ten chickens.

INTERVIEWER: Does he give you some money for childcare?

GRANDPA LONGER: I don't take it. En, when I cannot move, cannot do anything, you can give me money. Now I can still make money, I can still do it, I don't need it. I ask them to use the money for themselves.

In grandpa Longer's case, the payback will occur in the future, when he is much older and "cannot move, cannot do anything." While the long-term intergenerational agreement has not yet been fulfilled for young grandparents such as grandpa Longer, we did observe such an exchange in other cases, particularly when grandparents are older and migrant parents have greater financial stability. Grandpa Xiao and his wife, who raised two same-aged grandchildren for fifteen years, commented on the financial exchange over the years:

INTERVIEWER: How did the childcare affect your farming?

GRANDPA XIAO: We did not do any farming in the first two, three years, could not do it.

GRANDMA XIAO: Little children, a bunch of stuff.

INTERVIEWER: Did they give you any money?

GRANDPA XIAO: They gave us some money. At that time, they did not have much, each year they gave us a little bit more than 1,000 yuan for living costs. Children's milk powder, visiting doctors, they paid those costs. They gave us 1,500 yuan each year in the first few years. They did not have much money. At that time the salary was low. The first few years I used my savings, slowly used up all my savings. It was until the last two to three years that the financial situation was better, children were older, but more places for expenses. Now they give me a little bit more money, and I am older and cannot farm anymore.

In grandpa Xiao's case, he and his wife had to stop farming in the first two to three years to raise the two grandchildren, with only marginal monetary and/or material support from their migrant sons. They depleted all their hard-earned savings within the first few years. When his physical health deteriorated and his two sons' financial situations improved, grandpa Xiao began to receive more stable financial support. He later admitted that each of his sons gave him about 10,000 yuan a year in addition to the living costs (school and other expenses) of the grandchildren, which could be considered a decent living in rural Jiangxi province. This case illustrated how the intergenerational agreement is fulfilled, with grandparents initially providing material resources and labor and migrant children committed to future reciprocity.

It should be noted that while the modified version of filial piety emphasizes a reciprocal relationship between parents and children, grandparents do fully understand the inherent uncertainty of the future commitment (e.g., eldercare), given the potential of permanent spatial separation in the future. In fact, for many grandparents, grandparenting is simply an altruistic behavior that benefits the multilocal household, exemplified by the "striving team" concept coined by sociologist Rachel Murphy (2020). In this spatially dispersed "striving team," each member strives to perform a certain role with the goal of maximizing children's educational mobility and intergenerational socioeconomic mobility. Specifically, migrant parents work tirelessly and work overtime in host cities to provide for the full household, grandparents sweat on their small piece of land to supplement the household income and provide nurturing for grandchildren in origin communities, and children study hard to obtain good academic standing in schools. Thus, grandparents are simply "doing their job," endeavoring to support migrant children and grandchildren to move up the social and economic ladder. As such, the contract of intergenerational exchange between grandparents and migrant children is often implicit and unwritten—interpreted and reinforced by a localized definition of filial piety. Grandpa Nongsan, who was raising a two-year-old granddaughter when interviewed, commented on the informal nature of the arrangement between him and his migrant son:

GRANDPA NONGSAN: Snack, food, diapers, it's all on us. Not to mention diapers, snacks, this morning's snack cost me four, five yuan. It cost me five yuan. Ice pops, she ate four or five. And watermelon, we already bought a few watermelons to eat. What else? She does not eat apples much, all left in the fridge, there are four apples left.

INTERVIEWER: That means you need to pay the expenses?

GRANDPA NONGSAN: Yeah, we pay the expenses. We can afford it. If we cannot afford it, then there are no other ways.

INTERVIEWER: Do they give you any money?

GRANDPA NONGSAN: During the Spring Festival, they will give some money. If he has money, he will give a little bit. What does 1,000 yuan do? A thousand yuan! But I did not ask my son and daughter-in-law for money. I did not even talk about money with them. Whatever amount he makes is his money. If we can afford it, we will do it. If we cannot afford it, he will still give us some money. Now I can still afford it. I never asked, whatever he gave. [He said] he needs to buy a house after being married. I said when you were married, I did not buy you a house. We will buy you a car. You are married, you make your own money, you go to buy a house yourself. The child, we will help you raise her. [My wife] cannot do anything, basically a full-time caretaker. We have several people here; I still have a daughter who will go to school soon.

In grandpa Nongsan's case, because he can "afford it" and his son "needs to buy a house after being married," he only received a symbolic childcare payment during Chinese Spring Festivals. The implicit understanding is that "if we cannot afford it, he will still give us some money" or, as grandpa Longer said before, "when I cannot move, cannot do anything, you can give me money." Such an informal and unwritten arrangement is quite common in these multilocal families. Although I observed several cases in which migrant parents remitted a fixed amount regularly, this occurred only when grandparents did not have a stable source of income and were fully dependent on migrant children. For most of these families, the amount and frequency of remittance were not formally established and were conditional on grandparents' financial security, children's needs, and specific life stages of migrant parents and grandparents. For example, migrant mother Xiaolu sent money to her parents-in-law "when sometimes you want to send some money, and they will not ask you for money if you don't remit" because her parents-in-law owned a small business previously and were still farming. For grandpa Jingpin, the amount of remittance he received reflected his son's financial status in host cities as well as grandpa Jingpin's physical health status. In the early years when he and his wife were working, his son sent him 3,000 yuan a year, which increased to 5,000 yuan and finally to 10,000 yuan in the last two years.

SOLE-GRANDPARENT CARETAKING. The expectation that "when I cannot move, cannot do anything, you can give me money" also implies that the sole-grandparent caretaking arrangement is inconsistent with local social norms. Both the classical and the modified version of filial piety posit that adult children are fully responsible for parents' eldercare, which is of critical importance because of a lack of state-funded safety net measures in rural China. As such, when one grandparent passes away and particularly when the remaining grandparent is not in a good physical condition, at least one of the migrant parents is expected to return, providing both child- and eldercare. For example, father Lu, who migrated to Shantou in Guangdong province with his wife, returned a few years ago after his father passed away. The return migration, however, is not plausible when a multilocal household's financial situation is dire, compelling the migrant parents to stay within an urban area and the remaining grandparent to serve as the sole caretaker. The case of grandma Ren, who helped raise six grandchildren through the years, is a typical example of a sole-grandparent caretaker.

I first interviewed grandma Ren in the year 2012 when she was sixty-two years old. When I walked into her front yard on a hot summer day, I was surprised to see that most of the front yard was occupied by blossoming cotton plants, a sign that the household was using every possible way to make some extra cash. The house was a two-story house built in the late 1980s, with the outside visibly dilapidated and needing significant repair. Grandma Ren raised two sons and two daughters with her husband. Her husband died in 2008 following a tragic motorcycle accident in which he was riding a motorcycle while drunk and drowned in a narrow canal. The family, however, was plagued by misfortunes even before her husband's tragic death. Their eldest son, Ming, remained a fugitive for more than a decade after stealing underground cable lines and could only secretly visit his family from time to time. (Ming finally turned himself in to the police in 2013 and was sentenced to two years in prison.) In addition, grandma Ren's older daughter, Xiang, was widowed. Xiang's husband passed away due to lung cancer at the age of thirty-four, leaving two young daughters and one son behind. The misfortunes led both families to be the most impoverished families in each of their local villages, eligible for and receiving rural low-income household government assistance, roughly 1,500 yuan a year. This amount of money, although appreciated by grandma Ren, was not sufficient to put enough food on the table, pressuring her daughter and daughter-in-law to migrate to support the family. After her husband's death, grandma Ren became the sole caretaker of her grandchildren for more than ten years. She was the primary caretaker of three girls and two boys when I first interviewed her, caring for these children independently, except for when the children were less than two years old, during which time her daughter or daughter-in-law would stay at home to assist. In 2018, the last time I interviewed her, these children were all old enough to work, and she was living with a five-year-old granddaughter, the younger daughter of her second son.

Grandma Ren's case, while extraordinary, reflects the typical factors contributing to sole-grandparent caregiving at the research sites. All sole-grandparent-caretaking households interviewed shared a common characteristic: extreme poverty resulting from a single or a combination of many misfortunes, including household members' severe illness and death, marital dissolution, and/or a large debts due to these misfortunes. The lack of sufficient government-funded social security measures in rural China dictates that any crisis, particularly a household member's severe illness and large medical bills, will devastate the foundation of a relatively financially stable family. Indeed, each of the sole-grandparent caretakers discussed these misfortunes, as well as their own physical and mental inability to fully meet their grandchildren's physical and emotional needs. While my interviews with dual-grandparent caretakers often went smoothly and were filled with warm greetings and laughter (with some notable exceptions), my conversations with one-grandparent caretakers were often characterized by emotional outbursts and sad personal stories. Borrowing the concept of "reactionary" coping used by Baker and Silverstein (2012, p. 66), we can surmise that two-grandparent caretakers enjoy better psychological well-being than one-grandparent caretakers because one-grandparent caretaking is mostly a "reactionary" arrangement due to a past crisis in the household, while two-grandparent caretaking is typically a planned arrangement oriented toward providing both children and the family with future success and stability.

Importantly, these findings are consistent with my quantitative findings on one-grandparent caretaking, which indicate that a higher level of household socioeconomic status (e.g., a father's education level and the amount of household property) was associated with a lower likelihood of one-grandparent caretaking (see table 2.1). The interview data also help one better understand why girls and older children are more likely to be left behind to sole-grandparent caretakers than boys and younger children. Whereas migrant parents are compelled to remain as migrant workers due to poverty and thus cannot fulfill their obligations of eldercare, they still attempt to minimize grandparents' workload by leaving their elder children and girls behind and taking younger children and boys—who are perceived to require more intensive caretaking—with them to host cities.

Sole-Parent Caretaking: Familial and Situational Factors

I have established in previous sections that the grandparenting arrangement—with both parents migrated to urban areas and grandparents and children left behind in rural communities—achieves maximum financial returns for multilocal households at the research site. Solo-parent migration, thus, is often an involuntary decision shaped by a myriad of familial and individual factors, particularly the absence of intergenerational support (Fan et al., 2011). Recall that in the quantitative data (table 2.1), the availability of grandparents was a deciding factor in parents' decision to migrate, increasing the odds of dual-parent migration more than twelve times and maternal migration almost two times. This finding is further substantiated by interview data; in fact, none of the left-behind parents interviewed (n = 8) reported receiving any intergenerational assistance in childcare. Seven of them reported deceased paternal grandparents, while the remaining parent reported a single grandparent with dementia who needed intensive care from her adult children. In a casual conversation, one left-behind mother aptly pointed out, "I don't have parents to take care of my kids. Both passed away a few years ago. Otherwise, I would have migrated to cities a long time ago."

The second theme emerging from the interview data on sole-parent caretaking is that parents return for child- and eldercare, particularly when elders are in poor physical and mental condition. As aforementioned, both the traditional and the modified versions of filial piety prescribe a reciprocal relationship between migrant parents and grandparents, with grandparents providing childcare early on and migrant parents offering eldercare when needed in later years. Migrant father Wei's wife, who previously worked in a cell-phone factory in Shenzhen, recently returned to Guangxi province due to his father-in-law's physical illness. Wei said:

> My wife stays at home because my little child is at home, yeye and nainai are at home too. My father was sick some time ago, he has not fully recovered yet. So, my wife just quit her job, going back to take care of the child. Before, my dad was the one to take care of the child. . . . So, she now stays at home taking care of the children.

This reciprocal relationship, particularly the provision of eldercare by adult children, is culturally promoted and thus expected, even given intense financial constraints and long-distance spatial separation. To be able to manage these obligations, adult migrant children sometimes negotiate with each other and pool resources from the extended household to cover child- and eldercare. Left-behind mother Dai, for example, returned to take care of her two children, an eighth grader and four-year-old girl, two years ago when her mother-in-law had dementia. To fully take advantage of her time at home and salvage some extra income, Dai developed an informal agreement with her brother-in-law, arranging to simultaneously care for the two nephews, a thirteen-year-old boy and three-year-old boy. While Dai did not provide details of the arrangement, it is common for each migrant adult to take turns providing child- and eldercare or to assign one person to be the primary caretaker and compensate that person for the loss of income. For example, grandparents Zhu, a couple in their late eighties, had been cared for by their four migrant sons, with each returning for three months each year.

A central question that draws much research interest is if one parent is pressured to stay at home or return, how does the family decide who migrates and who stays behind (Parreñas, 2005b, 2009)? In general, the husband, who assumes the role of breadwinner in a typical nuclear family, is expected to work outside, illustrated by the old Chinese saying "male leading outside, female leading inside." Indeed, while none of the four mothers felt the need to explain why they stayed at home, the left-behind fathers did. Laojiu, a left-behind father, made the effort to explain why he stayed at home and his wife worked in cities. Laojiu claimed:

LAOJIU: There are no other ways. There is no money to use [if she doesn't work outside]. She can make some money if going outside. And, she is not very healthy. She had two surgeries. Her uterus was cut off, and she had gallstones. She cannot do stuff here; we can only let her go outside to make some money. I do some farming at home. She cannot do anything, cannot do anything here. This year she helped seedling for half of a day, then she felt painful here (pointing to his stomach). Working as a housekeeper she can make several thousand yuan, make about 4,000 yuan [a month].

INTERVIEWER: How much land do you farm right now?

LAOJIU: I have nineteen *mu* of double-crop early rice, nineteen *mu* of double-crop, that is thirty-eight *mu* a year. I also have seven to eight *mu* one-crop rice. To be honest, you are a man; you cannot use her money. Last year I also saved about 30,000 yuan working at home. This time, if I sell my crop, I can get about 20,000 to 30,000 yuan. Subtracting the cost, what is left is all mine.

While Laojiu was pressured to work on the farmland and some odd jobs at home and made less money than his wife, he made it clear that he did this for the sake of his wife's physical health and the family. In addition, since "you are a man; you cannot use her money," he worked tirelessly on his farmland and was proud that he made a decent amount of money while simultaneously caring for his children. In this way, the prescribed gender norms were not violated, and his masculinity and the status of being the provider of the family remained intact.

Conclusion

The chapter intends to identify macro-institutional and micro-individual factors associated with parental migration and childcare arrangements in rural China. Utilizing quantitative and qualitative data collected from Peace County, Jiangxi province, I find that at the macrostructural level, both the rural–urban income gap and the *hukou* system significantly influence rural-to-urban migration at the research sites. At the micro level, the availability of grandparents increases parental migration significantly, confirming the prominent role of intergenerational support in internal migration in China. Moreover, the marital status of biological parents is significantly associated with parental migration. Although the causal direction of this association is less clear, it appears that parental divorce is likely to be the result of or is at least facilitated by migration-related experiences.

In terms of caretaking arrangements, grandparenting, a condition in which both parents have migrated and left children and grandparents behind in rural areas, is the most prevalent type of childcare arrangement at the research sites, followed by individual paternal migration and maternal migration. In general, a family's childcare arrangement, including who the primary caretakers are and the physical location of the family member, is constantly changing during children's early ages, reflecting migrant parents' struggles to cope with institutional constraints and to mobilize limited cultural and material resources. Barring significant changes (e.g., parental divorce and death of caretakers), caretaking arrangements, however, become more or less stable after children reach the school age, with most children at this developmental stage cared for by grandparents or sole-parent caretakers within origin communities.

A household's caretaking arrangement decisions are shaped by a combination of factors at macro-institutional and micro-individual levels. In general, children are left behind because the long-lasting *hukou* system institutionally discriminates against rural-to-urban migrants and migrant children, limiting or denying their access to affordable housing, public school education, and state-funded medical insurance. As a result, migrant parents often depend on grandparents to provide childcare in the countryside. The prevalence of grandparenting can be attributed to both economic and cultural factors. From an economic perspective, grandparenting is the most cost-effective arrangement, as dual-parent migration, under the institutional constraints, minimizes educational and living costs while maximizing a household's financial returns. Culturally, the prevalence of grandparenting is underpinned by a modified version of filial piety, which emphasizes migrant parents' and grandparents' commitments to a lifelong intergenerational exchange in which grandparents provide initial childcare and migrant parents offer eldercare in later years.

The total dependence on assistance from extended family members coupled with a severe lack of governmental support leaves some rural households disadvantaged and vulnerable. In particular, the one-grandparent caretaking arrangement appears to be an involuntary decision based on unfortunate circumstances. Households with these arrangements are characterized by low socioeconomic status, directly resulting from or at the very least exacerbated by exposure to misfortunes such as the severe illness and/or death of family members or marital dissolution. This personal misfortune-driven financial burden forces parents to migrate rather than providing expected child- and eldercare at home. Along the same vein, sole-parent migration appears to be largely an involuntary decision at the research sites. Because these households lack critical intergenerational support, one parent is often pressured to either return to or remain in the countryside to provide child- and/or eldercare.

How do these caretaking arrangements influence childcare quality? For example, do grandparents, most of them in their fifties to seventies, illiterate or with little education, have what it takes to raise and nurture a new generation of children in modern China? Do caretaking practices differ between paternal- and maternal-migration families? How do types of caretaking arrangement interact with macro and micro factors to shape caretaking practices? In the next two chapters, I delve into these questions by investigating the caretaking practices of primary caretakers living together with children as well as the distant parenting of migrant parents living apart.

3

Caretaking at Home

Grandparenting and One-Parent Caretaking

> Children nowadays, it's not easy to raise them well if society continues like this. Because (when) grandparents raise them, it doesn't matter how you raise them, they do not listen to you, they do not listen. . . . It's not appropriate for grandparents to beat them up [laughing]. If we were parents, we could just spank their ass when they don't listen to us.
>
> —grandpa Jingpin, 2017

At that time of our first interview in 2012, grandpa Jingpin and his wife Mianlin had lived in small Hongguang village for most of their lives. The couple had two adult children—one son and one daughter—both migrated and *dagong* in coastal cities in Southeast China. A few years after arriving in Shenzhen, where she migrated after junior high school, their daughter Xin married a Hong Kong truck driver and gave birth to a boy. Jingpin's wife Mianlin traveled to Hong Kong occasionally to assist with childcare, particularly during the first few years after the child's birth. While Xin's life was considered more or less successful by the standards of local villagers, the story of Jingpin and Mianlin's son Ping was not viewed in such a positive light. Ping, father to a twelve-year-old daughter and a five-year-old son, had recently been divorced. Ping's daughter was now in the custody of the mother and living with her maternal grandparents, while his son was in the custody of the father and living with grandpa Jingpin and Mianlin. Grandpa Jingpin often became furious when discussing his son's divorce, attributing much of the family's hardship to the failure of his son's marriage:

> It's all for the son, for the daughter-in-law. We got killed by the daughter-in-law. It was better if not buying the f-cking house for them at Daping [a nearby town]. To buy that house, we spent 280,000 yuan. They did not have any money, and we owed others more than 100,000 yuan. Need to work really hard [to pay the debt]. It doesn't work. . . . We need to buy that house for them, and not for long, she wanted to divorce.

Shortly after the divorce, Mianlin went to Nanchang, the capital city of Jiangxi province, to work as a housekeeper—in part to make extra money to pay for the debt and in part to escape the stress of her son's divorce. Mianlin's exit left grandpa Jingpin as the only adult at home, responsible for raising a five-year-old grandson with seemingly boundless energy. At the same time, he had nearly twenty mu of land to cultivate, a heavy workload even for a young couple in the village. In our first interview, the fifty-five-year-old grandfather described in detail the challenges of watching and monitoring his five-year-old grandson:

INTERVIEWER: How do you raise the child by yourself?

GRANDPA JINGPIN: [sarcastically] How do I raise him? It is okay if he is in school, it doesn't matter. Now, he is in someone else's house.

INTERVIEWER: He is playing outside?

GRANDPA JINGPIN: Yeah, I often need to go out to find him when it is time to eat. He is now playing in someone's house. He doesn't know he needs to come back when it is lunchtime. I need to shout out. [He is] often eating in others' houses. It annoys other people.

INTERVIEWER: He is only five. How can he know?

GRANDPA JINGPIN: Yeah, the little one doesn't understand. He is okay with it. . . . He doesn't stay at home, always eating in other people's houses. It doesn't seem to be all right . . .

Five years later, I interviewed grandpa Jingpin again. At this time, the boy was almost ten years old and undoubtedly equipped with vastly improved physical and cognitive abilities to navigate the surrounding world. Grandpa Jingpin gave an almost identical description of his grandson's behavioral pattern:

> Usually . . . he is staying at home today . . . but usually during weekends, you cannot even find him. He rides a bike . . . he now has a cell phone, his dad got him a cell phone during last year's Spring Festival . . . before that when I tried to find him, sometimes I went to school, I went to Majiazue [a nearby village], I went everywhere to look for him. Riding a bicycle and going everywhere . . . you cannot find him. He does not come back to eat lunch, sometimes he eats at other people's houses, and sometimes he does not eat at all.

The caretaking example of grandpa Jingpin—characterized by a severe lack of monitoring and supervision that could be marginally defined as child neglect and abuse—is not an exception in rural China. Indeed, one of the greatest concerns of migrant parents is that grandparents are not adequately equipped with the appropriate attitudes, knowledge, and skills necessary to monitor children's daily activities and to discipline deviant and wayward behaviors when necessary (X. Chen, 2017; X. Chen & Jiang, 2019; Huang et al., 2023b; Ye & Murray 2005; X. Zhao et al., 2014). Although these concerns are often conveyed by migrant parents in private settings and extensively discussed in public spaces (e.g., local, and national news media), surprisingly, little empirical research has investigated the forms and quality of caregiving by at-home caretakers—even as caregiving remains a key component intrinsically impacting migrant parents, caretakers at home, and children's physical, mental, and social development. As a result, we do not know if grandpa Jingpin's case is as prevalent as many have speculated or whether it is an exception occurring due to an unfortunate interplay of individual personalities, caretaking arrangements, poverty, and misfortune (e.g., divorce).

In this chapter, I address this research gap by empirically investigating multiple dimensions of caretaking practices provided by at-home caretakers, including caretaker monitoring and supervision, child–caretaker bonding, and caretaker harsh discipline. At-home caretakers here are defined as caretakers who choose to or are pressured to stay in their home communities and are the designated primary caretakers of children. These include nonmigrant dual-caretaker parents, sole at-home parents, grandparents, and other adult caretakers. Specifically, I intend to investigate two research questions frequently asked by migrant parents and the larger society. First, do alternative caretaking arrangements (e.g., grandparenting and one-parent caretaking) differ substantially from the normative two-parent family in the realm of caretaking practices such as monitoring, supervision, and discipline? Second, within these alternative arrangements (e.g., maternal migration versus paternal migration), are there any significant differences in the quality of child-rearing practices? In the following sections, I first provide a brief review of the existing research on parental migration and caretaking practices and on which I build a theoretical model that guides the empirical analyses. I then investigate differences in the three dimensions of caretaking—caretaker monitoring and supervision, child–caretaker bonding, and caretaker harsh discipline and punishment—across a variety of living arrangements. As in chapter 2, I use survey data to investigate whether there is a statistically significant association between caretaking arrangements and caretaking practices, and then I compare the quantitative findings with analyses from more nuanced and richer in-depth interview data.

Parental Migration and Caretaking Practices: The Theoretical Model

Do parental migration and alternative caretaking arrangements influence the quality of caretaking practices, and if so, how do they operate? As briefly discussed in chapter 1, I utilize the family process theory—which contends that a family is a system in which each member has specific roles and obligations prescribed by social and cultural norms (Broderick, 1993)—to understand how parental migration shapes differential caretaking practices. In a typical family embedded within the patriarchal system in rural China, the husband is prescribed as the backbone and the breadwinner, and the wife normally serves as the homemaker and occupies a less prominent role. Although this traditional ideology was temporarily replaced by state feminism during the Maoist era (1949–1976), it has never been seriously challenged, and a marginally modified version gradually reemerged after the 1980s (Hu & Scott, 2016). This neotraditional version slightly alters the traditional ideology of male providers and female homemakers, framing the husband as the main provider and the wife as the main homemaker (Zuo & Bian, 2001). Grandparents, as indispensable members of extended families, often serve as primary or secondary caretakers when living under the same roof or being geographically close (e.g., living in the same village). These prescribed roles and obligations provide culturally established codes for family members to interact with one another, shaping hierarchical positions and interactional patterns within the family. A family is thus a system in which members are interdependent, and their behaviors reflect and are profoundly influenced by other members' actions, thoughts, and feelings. A change in one person's role in the family, therefore, is predictably followed by reciprocal changes in others, leading to an imbalance in the system or a shift toward a different equilibrium. The imbalance or the new equilibrium, however, may lead to dysfunction if the changes cannot be maintained over a long period (Broderick, 1993).

Based on the propositions of the family process theory, one can expect that parental migration may lead to substantial changes and adaptations in caretaking roles undertaken by adults and children within a multilocal family, directly and indirectly influencing caretaking practices at or away from home. A migrant mother, for example, is still expected by family members and the larger society to maintain a traditional nurturing identity, even though she may struggle to meet these expectations and to perform sufficient "mothering" from a distance. Also, maternal migration imposes enormous pressure on the at-home father to adapt to this care reconfiguration, including assuming maternal duties and performing "emotional work" (Lam & Yeoh, 2018; Parreñas, 2008; Wen & Lin, 2012). The role of grandparents also changes when one or both parents migrate, as they often become primary caretakers and replace parents as "other mothers" (or "other fathers") for an extended period (X. Chen & Jiang, 2019; Parreñas, 2005a; Ye & Murray, 2005). Children, especially girls, may also experience substantial changes in roles and expectations, as they are often required to assume more house chores (H. Chang et al., 2011) or even become primary caretakers of elders in the family (Ye & Lu, 2011).

The recent China Family Panel Studies (CFPS) project is probably one of the few that directly investigates the effects of parental migration on caretaking practices in rural China (L. Chen et al., 2015). Compared with parents in nonmigrant families, caretakers in left-behind children's families are found to be less involved in children's learning and education (e.g., reading to children and supervising and tutoring homework), have less interaction with children, and provide a less stimulating home environment (L. Chen et al., 2015). As a result, left-behind children, in general, report a higher level of conflict and a lower level of intimacy with adult caregivers (Ye & Murray, 2005). This line of research also finds that a caretaker's parenting practices and children's expectations are heavily shaped by the gender of a caretaker (Lam & Yeoh, 2018; Parreñas, 2008). Maternal migration, for example, has been found to impact children's development more negatively than paternal migration (Parreñas, 2008, 2009; Wen & Lin, 2012). Children cared for by an at-home father, for instance, report a significantly lower level of family cohesion and support compared with those cared for by an at-home mother (Wen & Lin 2012). These negative family dynamics, then, have a significant adverse impact on children's psychological and behavioral outcomes (Dittman, 2018).

Based on the previous literature, I have developed a theoretical model—a subset of the model presented in chapter 1 (fig. 1.1)—to guide the analyses in this chapter. Specifically, I hypothesize that the characteristics of children (age, gender, living on campus), parental characteristics (parental education, marital status of biological parents), and household socioeconomic status are associated with parental decisions on migration and caretaking arrangements, which, in turn, influence varying dimensions of caretaking practices. Because the part of the model regarding the predictors of parental migration and caretaking arrangement has been extensively discussed in chapter 2, I focus on caretaking practices as the dependent variables and investigate the effects of their precursors at individual and familial levels in this chapter. Moreover, because the survey data were collected from one county and lack variations at the macrostructural level, the theoretical model does not consider the structural constraints at the macro level (e.g., rural–urban income gap).

Parental Migration and Caretaking Practices: Caretaker Monitoring and Supervision

I first investigate the empirical association between parental migration and caretaker monitoring and supervision. Strict caretaker monitoring and supervision occupy a unique position in the Chinese culture, as the Chinese proverb "a strict father gives birth to a filial son, and a loving mother often loses" (yan fu chu xiao zi, chi mu do bai er) demonstrates. Indeed, when left-behind children complain about being "abandoned" by migrant parents; the words they often use are "my mom does not *guang* me anymore." The term *guang*, while imbued with many different emotions, literally means monitoring and supervision in Chinese. In other words, monitoring and supervision are perceived as an essential component of parenting by adults and children alike in Chinese culture. As such, strict caretaker monitoring and supervision play a critical role in structuring caretaker–child relationships and shaping children's cognitive, psychological, and behavioral outcomes.

Multivariate Quantitative Analyses

I conducted multivariate regression models to examine the association between parental migration/caretaking arrangement status and caretaker monitoring and supervision. The measure of parental migration and caretaking arrangements, as fully described in chapter 2, classifies respondents into six groups: nonmigrant family, paternal migration and children primarily cared for by an at-home mother, maternal migration and children primarily cared for by an at-home father, two-grandparent-caretaking with both parents having migrated, one-grandparent-caretaking with both parents having migrated, and children living with other extended family members or neighbors or even by themselves with both parents having migrated. As discussed in chapter 2, the last group was excluded from the quantitative analysis due to its small sample size. In the multivariate regression model, the group of children of nonmigrant parents was used as the reference group. The outcome variable caretaker monitoring and supervision consists of five items: (1) my parents/caretakers know where I am after school; (2) I tell my parents/caretakers whom I am with when I go out; (3) when I go out at night, my parents/caretakers know where I am; (4) when I go out, my parents/caretakers will ask where I go; and (5) if I get home late, my parents/caretakers would expect me to call to let them know in advance (X. Li et al., 2000). The composite score of the caretaker monitoring and supervision was created by averaging the five individual items (alpha = 0.77). Finally, I used the same familial and individual background variables used in previous analyses as control variables in the model, which were fully described in chapter 2: age, gender (male = 1, female = 0), living in a school dorm (yes = 1, no = 0), marital status of biological parents, number of siblings, perceived family economic status, parental education, and number of household properties.

The multivariate analysis (table 3.1) shows that overall, all groups of left-behind children reported lower levels of caretaker monitoring compared with the reference group (children of nonmigrant parents). Particularly, one-grandparent caretakers ($b = -0.40$, $p < 0.01$) and left-behind fathers ($b = -0.27$, $p < 0.01$) exercised significantly lower levels of monitoring and supervision on their children's daily activities. In contrast, two-grandparent caretaking ($b = -0.05$, $p > 0.05$) and paternal migration ($b = -0.08$, $p > 0.05$) did not differ in the levels of monitoring compared with the reference group. Additionally, a test of the linear combination of coefficients (Gordon, 2015) revealed a significant amount of heterogeneity among the left-behind child population. One-grandparent caretaking and maternal migration appeared to have the most deleterious effects on monitoring and supervising children's activities. Children from one-grandparent caretaking households had a significant lower level of monitoring than children of two-grandparent caretaking ($b = -0.35$, $p < 0.01$) and those of paternal migration ($b = -0.32$, $p < 0.01$). Likewise, children living with an at-home father reported a significantly lower score than children of two-grandparent caretakers ($b = -0.22$, $p < 0.05$).

In summary, the quantitative data demonstrate that caretaking arrangements are significantly related to the variation of caretaker monitoring and supervision. Particularly, maternal migration and one-grandparent caretaking imposed more detrimental effects on the levels of caretaker monitoring and supervision than other caretaking arrangements. However, it is not clear why these two types of

TABLE 3.1
Regression model predicting caretaker monitoring/supervision and caretaker–child bonding

	Caretaker monitoring/ supervision B	SE	Caretaker–child bonding B	SE
Intercept	5.96**	0.56	4.87**	0.68
Two-grandparent caretaking[a]	−0.05	0.08	−0.03	0.08
One-grandparent caretaking	−0.40**	0.12	−0.10	0.12
Maternal migration	−0.27**	0.10	−0.14	0.11
Paternal migration	−0.08	0.09	−0.05	0.10
Male[b]	−0.33**	0.06	−0.22**	0.06
Age	−0.19**	0.04	−0.18**	0.04
Living in a school dorm[c]	0.06	0.09	0.13	0.09
Parental education	0.08**	0.02	0.07**	0.03
Household property	0.05*	0.03	0.05	0.03
Perceived family economic status	0.05	0.05	0.01	0.05
Marital status of biological parents[d]	0.00	0.10	0.08	0.11
Number of siblings	0.04	0.03	0.01	0.04
R^2	0.10		0.05	

Note: *$p < 0.05$; **$p < 0.01$; B = unstandardized regression coefficient; $N = 1{,}177$; SE = standard error.

[a] Children of nonmigrant parents as the reference group.

[b] Female as the reference category.

[c] Living at home as the reference group.

[d] Divorced or separated as the reference group.

caretaking arrangement stood out. To answer this question, I turn to in-depth interview and field observation data, which enumerate cultural, social, and situational factors undergirding such differences. In the next two subsections, I aim to explore why monitoring and supervision of one-grandparent caretakers and left-behind fathers differed from other types of caretaking arrangements at the research sites.

One-Grandparent Caretaking: It Would Be Much Better If There Were Two People at Home

The case of grandpa Jingpin described at the beginning of the chapter exemplifies challenges faced by one-grandparent caretakers. Although he is not widowed, grandpa Jingpin's wife, Mianlin, rarely returned home after "going out to *dagong*." This arrangement left him as the only adult to attend to a five-year-old boy while also keeping up with often grueling farming obligations. Grandpa Jingpin complained when asked whether it was difficult to raise the grandchild all by himself:

INTERVIEWER: Is it difficult to raise him all by yourself?

GRANDPA JINGPIN: Every day you need to do something, cleaning him, feeding him, washing clothes. . . . Every day you have a bunch of things to do. . . . Not only taking care of children but also doing something, having more than ten *mu* of land.

INTERVIEWER: You grow cotton?

GRANDPA JINGPIN: Five *mu* cotton. . . . Eight *mu* of single-crop late rice and four and a half double-crop early rice. . . . Adding cotton, that is sixteen, seventeen *mu* of rice or cotton.

The case of grandpa Jingpin clearly illustrates that, in a one-grandparent caretaking household, the sole grandparent caretaker simply does not have enough time, energy, and physical and mental strength to monitor and supervise young grandchildren. This situation is further exacerbated by poverty, which is also one of the driving factors of parental migration and the alternative caretaking arrangements, as discussed in chapter 2. In grandpa Jingpin's case, he was responsible for a larger piece of farmland than most younger couples I interviewed in the villages, likely because of his investment in the house and the debt owed to others. While his son was outside *dagong*, "messing around" (getting divorced), and having a relatively "easy" job, grandpa Jingpin was "dead tired" due to his backbreaking farming and childcare responsibilities. As a result, grandpa Jingpin could barely provide basic caretaking (e.g., food and clothes) for the boy and often did not have time and energy to monitor his whereabouts and other activities, particularly during weekends and holidays.

The finding that one-grandparent caretaking was associated with a lack of close monitoring and strict supervision was also corroborated by grandchildren's reports. An eighth-grade boy, Xiaowei, primarily cared for by his grandmother due to his grandfather's chronic physical and mental illness and a need for long-term intensive care, described how he sneaked out to play with his friends on weekends without his grandma's permission. He said, "[on weekends], I watch TV, going out to play, and do a little bit of homework. . . . I go out to play in my classmates' houses . . . she [grandma] does not know. If I tell her, she will definitely not let me go . . . anyway, it does not affect my study . . . I only go out to play on Saturdays and Sundays."

As I discussed in chapter 2, a myriad of factors, including economic and contextual factors (e.g., household poverty), precipitate the single-grandparent caretaking arrangement in the first place. While these risk factors continue to affect sole grandparent caretakers' caretaking capabilities, a unique post-migration change—the need for one-grandparent caretakers to perform caretaking roles beyond gendered boundaries—further aggravates the situation. For example, grandpa Jingpin complained that the tasks such as "cleaning him, feeding him, and washing clothes" were not "what a man should do." Grandma Ren, who endured chronic financial hardship after her husband's tragic motorcycle accident (the story was first introduced in chapter 2), described in detail how seemingly minor tasks such as riding a motorcycle to pick up children from school or grocery shopping in nearby small towns became substantially complicated for aged female caretakers. In the interview, I asked what transportation method her granddaughter used for school:

INTERVIEWER: Your younger one [the youngest grandchild] is in the first grade. The school is pretty far away. Does she know how to ride a bicycle?

GRANDMA REN: No, she doesn't. I ask Mr. Jingpin to take her to the school, a few hundred RMBs a year. I don't know how to ride a motorcycle. How can I ride it? It's difficult for me to walk her to school. It's early [in the morning], three times every day [morning, lunchtime, and afternoon]. Mr. Jingpin needs to take his own grandson to school, so he will help me take her [granddaughter]. A few times a day! . . . When she grows up a little bit, if she knows how to ride a bicycle, she will ride a bicycle. . . . It would be much better if there were two people at home. Now it all depends on me. I cannot even buy stuff. If she [the granddaughter] wants to eat something, we don't have a motorcycle, we can only walk. Sometimes there is no ride to DaPing [the nearby town]! For example, she wants to eat an ice pop. She becomes so annoying after a while! I have to ask my nephew to buy a box of ice pop back . . . I can only walk and cannot carry them back. They will melt into water if I am the one to take them back. How can you eat that?

As grandma Ren commented, "It would be much better if there were two people at home." This statement can be construed in two ways. First, a household with two grandparents is better simply because there is one more person to share the burden of farming and childcare as well as to support one another emotionally and physically—this is of critical importance given aging grandparents' rapidly deteriorating health and heavy farming workload. Secondly, in households with both grandparents, work duties are often conveniently split along gender lines, with the grandmother taking care of children full time and working domestically and the grandfather primarily working on farming land or business while providing occasional childcare assistance (e.g., driving children to school). This gender-aligned work division not only reduces grandparents' workload; more importantly, it increases grandparents' feeling of comfort and security and perceived contribution to the household as a member of the unified "striving team." This gender-based labor division, unfortunately, is not plausible for sole-grandparent caretakers, who are often forced to engage in activities beyond gender boundaries (e.g., riding a motorcycle for a grandma and washing children's clothes for a grandpa), adding even more difficulties to their daily lives and an accumulation of chronic stress over time. Indeed, we observed that in dual-grandparent caretaker households, even though most also had their own piece of land to cultivate or a small business to run, grandparents felt comfortable and were often happy with both their reconfigured roles and the quality of caretaking. Grandpa LongDa, who had two migrant daughters, anticipated how he and his wife would split the labor when his granddaughter came to live with them in the spring:

GRANDPA LONGDA: She (the older girl) will go to school here. . . . We rented a house in the town, [my wife] will stay there, [the girl] will study there. I am the only one who eats a lot of bitterness [laughing]. I have forty to fifty pigs, more than ten *mu* of double-crop early rice. Nowadays I go out every day . . .

INTERVIEWER: So you are able to manage it?

GRANDPA LONGDA: Well, I just do it. Every Monday to Friday I also need to go to restaurants to collect leftover food to feed the pigs. I go there every day.

As detailed in chapter 2, a household's collective decision regarding caretaking arrangements depends on the interplay of multiple factors at structural, familial, and individual levels, among which (and of critical importance) are household income and the health of grandparents and parents. Sole-grandparent caretaking is often the direct result of household poverty, which necessitates the migration of both parents to make ends meet rather than having at least one parent at home and helping raise children with the grandparent—a more "filial" and locally accepted approach. Nevertheless, a major difference between one-grandparent and two-grandparent caretaking is that, while all rural households strive to adapt their family structure and caretaking strategies to dramatic social changes in contemporary rural China, two-grandparent caretakers have the luxury of sharing the burden and aligning their workloads along gendered line, assuming roles consistent with the traditional gender norms. Alternatively, sole-grandparent caretakers shoulder a heavier burden of both household and caretaking responsibilities and often are forced to venture into unfamiliar caretaking and other roles beyond gendered boundaries.

Maternal Migration and At-Home Father Caretaking

The second key finding from the quantitative analysis is that when only one parent migrates, the gender of the migrant parent matters. Specifically, maternal migration is significantly associated with a lower level of parental monitoring and supervision. This finding is consistent with research in transnational migration in Southeast Asian countries (Asis, 2006; Graham & Jordan, 2011; Parreñas, 2008,

2009) and much work in rural China (e.g., Murphy, 2020; Wen & Lin, 2012; Yue et al., 2016). In a series of articles and books, Rhacel Salazar Parreñas documents that left-behind children in the Philippines feel more comfortable with sole-father migration than sole-mother migration, since the latter engenders a violation of widely accepted gender roles (e.g., Parreñas, 2005a, 2008, 2009). When a mother migrates, children left behind report "minimized mothering" from the migrant mother and a lack of caretaking from the stay-at-home father, who is often unwilling to traverse gender boundaries and to provide "emotional work" traditionally reserved for the mother. These same findings are replicated in the body of research on internal migration in China, with studies showing that maternal migration leads to more injurious effects on children's development than paternal migration, including behavioral outcomes such as school engagement, healthy behaviors, and children's life satisfaction (Wen & Lin, 2012; Yue et al., 2016).

The lone-migrant mother families were relatively rare in the two villages in which I conducted my field observation, and I only interviewed four of these families. When interviewed, all of them, unprompted, pointed out their immense sacrifices for the family as well as their economic contributions. Laojiu—whose story was discussed in chapter 2—for example, revealed that he was forced to stay behind because his wife's physical health did not allow her to stay at home and farm. Rather than depending on his wife's urban income, Laojiu farmed more than nineteen *mu* of double-crop early rice, all while working additional odd jobs and caring for his younger son, a sixth grader. Although his wife, working as a housekeeper in Nanchang (the capital city of Jiangxi province), made more money than him, LaoJiu remained proud of his financial contribution to the family, given the constraints of rural–urban income disparity. Indeed, his industriousness was recognized and highly admired by peer villagers.

Another at-home father, Lu, whose wife worked as a migrant worker in a shoe manufacturing company, proudly showed me his apple orchard when I interviewed him. Although the apple orchard was relatively small—only dozens of apple trees with most having yet to bear fruit—Lu was proud of this orchard and talked at length about his efforts and ultimate success in planting these apple trees in the southern part of China. Claiming that the orchard would produce a large number of organic apples that were never produced in the South before, Lu was optimistic that he would make a good fortune in the near future. In this way, both at-home fathers sent a strong message to their children, spouses, extended kin, and peer villagers that they were still the providers of the family and should not be evaluated based on their temporary undertaking of domestic roles in the multilocal household.

The interview data thus provide indirect support for the quantitative findings. Like their counterparts in developing countries such as the Philippines and Indonesia (Lam & Yeoh, 2018; Parreñas, 2005a), at-home fathers in rural China perceive maternal migration and the potential reversal in parents' gender roles as a threat to their gender identity. Past research indicates that fathers manage this situation by employing a number of coping strategies, including dependence on female adults or older female children at home, increased alcohol and drug use, and the redefinition of "provider" and "fathering" (Lam & Yeoh, 2018; Murphy, 2020). Consistent with this body of research, one salient strategy used by at-home fathers in Peace County was the maintenance of "productive selves," which helped justify their lack of involvement in childrearing and retain their masculinity.

Parental Migration and Caretaking Practices: Caretaker–Child Bonding

In this section, I turn the attention to the second dimension of caretaking practices: caretaker–child bonding. The scale of perceived caretaker–child bonding was measured by five items asking respondents how often they communicated with primary caretakers about their daily lives and problems (Whitbeck et al., 1993). These items include how often children talk with their caretakers about their feelings and what happened in their lives as well as how often children solve problems with and receive encouragement/praise from caretakers. The aggregated score of caretaker–child bonding was calculated by averaging the original scores of the five items (alpha = 0.76).

Multivariate Regression Analyses

Table 3.1 provides the multivariate analyses of the associations between caretaking arrangements and caretaker–child bonding. Compared to children living with nonmigrant parents, those living with two-grandparent caretakers ($b = -0.03$), left-behind mothers ($b = -0.05$), one-grandparent caretakers ($b = -0.10$), and left-behind fathers ($b = -0.14$) all reported lower levels of bonding with caretakers. These regression coefficients, however, were not statistically significant at the 0.05 level, indicating that there was much within-group heterogeneity and caretaking arrangement was not the deciding factor for the development of caretaker–child bonding and intimacy. Nevertheless, the magnitude of these regression coefficients suggests that children living with a left-behind father and those cared for by a sole-grandparent caretaker were relatively disadvantaged. Finally, although not of focal importance, the results reveal that among control variables, children's gender and age were significant predictors, with boys and older children reporting lower levels of perceived caretaker–child bonding than girls and younger children ($b = -0.22$, $p < 0.01$, and $b = -0.18$, $p < 0.01$, respectively). Moreover, a higher level of parental education was associated with stronger caretaker–child bonding ($b = 0.07$, $p < 0.05$).

Respect Toward Caretakers and Guang

The in-depth interview data appear to provide support for the quantitative findings, suggesting that left-behind children in Peace County had lower levels of communication with caretakers and received less emotional support and encouragement. Indeed, many at-home caretakers, particularly grandparents, expressed concerns that their children did not communicate with them frequently enough. Xiaowei's grandma commented:

> My grandson is a little bit strange. Like he did something in school, he did not communicate with us, not talking much with me. Like sometimes there were school activities, he did not talk with us much. Something happened in school, when he came back, he did not talk with us much. Exams, except when he got a score of one hundred or got the first place, or he got a trophy or some monetary award, usually he did not talk with us about them. He did not talk with us at home, not communicating with us.

Apparently, Xiaowei did not consider it necessary to communicate with his grandma about school and other daily activities, except for praiseworthy items. The same interactional pattern was observed by grandma and grandpa Ping, who took care of two grandchildren, a thirteen-year-old granddaughter and a ten-year-old grandson. They observed that while the two children developed a strong bond with each other, they rarely interacted with their grandparents and other adults.

> We have two children, one grandson, and one granddaughter. They don't talk with us too much. They don't talk too much with yeye (grandpa) and nainai (grandma), they don't talk much with their parents either. There is no solution here. When it's time to eat, you ask them to eat, it's like you are begging them. If you don't ask them, they two will eat together (upstairs).... They two talk with each other, they just don't talk with us. They siblings do talk, laughing and playing. They two have no problems with each other, they just don't talk with us.

The lack of communication between children and caretakers could be normative given that the sample children were seventh and eighth graders, venturing into puberty and eager to explore boundaries beyond the sphere of family. A large amount of research has conclusively demonstrated that children at this developmental stage become more independent and self-assertive and less emotionally connected to parents while simultaneously becoming more invested in social interactions with peers and friends (e.g., Branje, 2018; Fuligni, 1998). Nevertheless, the chronic temporal and spatial distance between children and one or both parents aggravates the already tenuous caretaker–child connection during this particular life stage, leaving children to pull even further away from caretakers and become more invested in peer/friend relationships.

An alternative explanation is that the low level of caretaker–child bonding and the nonsignificant associations observed within the quantitative data may be due to the cultural bias of the measure. The scale of caretaker–child bonding, while widely used in the literature, may not be culturally sensitive and therefore may not fully capture caretaker–child bonding in the context of rural China. For example, Chinese parents are typically more restrained in physically and emotionally demonstrating their warmth and affection toward children; rather, care and love are characterized by parental devotion and sacrifice toward children's education, success, and other future opportunities (C. Wu & Chao, 2017). As a result, scholars have emphasized the use of indigenous concepts and measures (R. K. Chao, 1994; R. Chao & Tseng, 2002), suggesting that other dimensions such as children's respect toward parents and caretakers are more culturally sensitive indicators of caretaker–child bonding.

Indeed, many grandparents shared stories about emotional intimacies developed over time, particularly when children were younger. Grandpa Xiao, who raised two grandchildren, Ziyang and Ziming, from when they were infants, vividly recalled how his two grandchildren worshiped him during their childhood and early adolescence. Although a farmer his whole life, grandpa Xiao was also a leader of the local religious association and actively participated in community affairs; as such, he was highly regarded by local peasants and schoolteachers. He recalled:

> My two grandchildren, they lived in the house of their home teacher [during junior high school years]. The home teacher said, he told Ziyang and Ziming, he said you need to learn from your grandpa. It will be good if you learn from your grandpa, you can make progress. You know what they said to Teacher Yan? Teacher Yan told me later, he said, "I told them that they need to learn from you. If you don't learn from your grandpa, you are not going to be good. They said, 'How are we able to learn from him? My grandpa is such a great person.' That's what they said" [laughing].

Grandma Ming told a similar story from when her grandson was a first grader. She said:

> My grandson, he was doing his homework there. He said, "Grandma, I don't know how to do this, come and take a look." I said, "Don't you say you are smart, how come you don't know how to do this?" he said, "Grandma is smarter." ... We spent ten yuan and bought a sugar can, then he added some Sprite into it. His mother drank it and felt that the taste was not right. I said it must be that your son poured some liquid into it. I said it must be Sprite. He said, "Grandma is so awesome! How do you know I put some Sprite in?"

In these two cases, children developed respect toward their grandparents not because of the demand of the patriarchal social norms or the pressure of hierarchical structure in the household but because they closely witnessed grandparents' contribution, sacrifice, and positive influence in the community on a daily basis. At other times, children—even at early ages—noticed the struggle and hardship of grandparent caretakers and developed a camaraderie with them. Grandma Ren, a sole-grandparent caretaker introduced in chapter 2, described why her six-year-old granddaughter was determined to stay with her rather than visiting her parents during summer breaks:

> The little granddaughter, she used to stay with me. She was raised by me when she was little. During a summer break, she said she wanted to be my

companion. I am the only one here. The little granddaughter said she wanted to be my companion. When Grandpa was here, he would take two children to go together [to visit their parents]. Now Grandpa is gone, she wants to be my companion. Sometimes she would say, "Mom said you need to go out to take a sun bath."

Another indigenous concept related to Chinese parenting practices is *guang*, literally translated as "to govern" or "to supervise." The term, however, is much more encompassing and ambiguous, as it carries other positive connotations and can mean "to care for" or "to love." The multidimensionality of this concept suggests that in Chinese culture, parental affection, love, and involvement are intrinsically entangled with firm parental control and governance (R. Chao & Tseng, 2002). Indeed, previous research has found that, compared to parents and children in American or European countries, Chinese parents and children construe the meaning of parental control quite differently (R. K. Chao, 1994). For example, parental control is associated with perceived parental hostility and rejection in Caucasian families, whereas similar parenting practices are perceived as a sign of parental warmth and acceptance by Chinese adolescents (R. K. Chao, 1994; R. Chao & Tseng, 2002).

Strict control, as a means to reduce opportunities for victimization and to improve school success, was a practice commonly employed by rural caretakers in Peace County—particularly by two-grandparent caretakers, who had more human capital and other resources to enforce strict rules than sole caretakers. As a result, I often saw close if not excessive control over children in two-grandparent households, especially for girls. A seventh-grade girl, MiaoMiao, described in detail her grandparents' strict monitoring over her time spent with friends. In our interview, I asked her about the caretaking of her grandparents:

INTERVIEWER: Are your grandparents strict with you?

MIAOMIAO: Well, it's okay. It depends. . . . They are strict in some areas, but not in others. . . . For example, school, because they don't really know, they cannot be very strict with it.

INTERVIEWER: How about your social life?

MIAOMIAO: They control *everything*! For example, I need to tell them every time before I go out; I cannot go out when there are only two girls; [they need to know] whom I go with; I cannot be too far away.

INTERVIEWER: That means you need to go out with boys?

MIAOMIAO: No, they don't allow me to go out with boys. It means there should be at least three girls together. I feel, er, they just don't like me to go out. . . . We rarely go out to play.

It should be noted that when it comes to two-grandparent caretaking, not only girls reported such close watching and monitoring. Boys were also prohibited from going out to play and were encouraged to stay at home to study. Many boys under two-grandparent care described the same level of control and supervision, reporting that, even during weekends, they rarely went out and often stayed at home watching TV or playing on their cell phones. Jiahui's grandparents described their grandson in this way when asked whether he ever argued with them: "No, he doesn't. When I chastise him, he doesn't talk back. He is a good kid. He does not go out." A seventh-grade girl mentioned that she rarely went out on weekends; instead, she "watched TV" at home and "played at home" by herself and "didn't go out on Saturdays and Sundays."

The lack of social activities with peers did not appear to bother grandparents in Peace County; rather, this behavior was encouraged and even complimented. As we can see in the comments of Jiahui's grandma, "he does not go out" was matter-of-factly a compliment instead of a concern, and "not staying at home" was very much frowned upon by every grandparent. This may reflect migrant parents' and grandparents' acute concerns about children's safety, particularly the possibility of traffic accidents and drowning during summertime floods. Moreover, this may reflect the spread of the so-called "education fever"—referring to Chinese parents' intensive involvement in children's education and high expectations for children's academic performance—from urban middle class to rural areas of China in recent years (Y. Chen et al., 2021). Because rural grandparents do not have the luxury to invest the same level of human capital (e.g., parents' education) and financial capital into children's schooling as their urban and middle-class counterparts do, grandparents and parents in rural China often keep their children at home, with a slim hope that children will spend more time on homework and improve their school performance. Importantly, while children more or less resist excessive control, they also understand the underlying good intentions and thus comply with grandparents' demands, displaying little deliberate resistance. In fact, some children, particularly those left behind by both parents, express jealousy that they don't have parents to "*guang*" them in their daily lives (Murphy, 2020).

Parental Migration and Caretaking Practices: Caretaker–Child Conflict and Harsh Discipline

Conflict between caretakers and children and harsh disciplinary practices have been found to have unique effects beyond positive parenting (e.g., caretaker monitoring and supervision)—these effects are often expressed through a child's negative psychological and behavioral outcomes, such as delinquency and depression (Klahr et al., 2011; Lewis et al., 2014). How and in what way do caretaker–child conflict and disciplining practices manifest in the context of rural-to-urban mass migration? In this section, I examine the differences in caretaker–child conflict and harsh discipline across the five types of caretaking arrangements. Caretaker–child conflict was measured by asking adolescents how often during the last month (1) they were criticized, (2) they were shouted or yelled at by their caretakers,

(3) their caretakers were angry with them, and (4) they argued/fought with their caretakers (Conger et al., 1994). The final scale of caretaker–child conflict was created by averaging the four items (alpha = 0.77). Moreover, we asked children whether their parents/caretakers ever hit, kicked, or used other methods to physically punish them in the past twelve months. Because of its relative infrequency, this variable, use of harsh discipline, was dummy coded, with 1 = yes and 0 = no.

Multivariate Quantitative Analyses

Table 3.2 provides a summary of the multivariate regression analyses focusing on the relation between caretaking arrangements and caretaker–child conflict. After eliminating the effects of the control variables, the results suggest that children living with two grandparents reported the lowest level of conflict, significantly lower than that of nonmigrant children ($b = -0.15$, $p < 0.05$). While not reaching statistical significance, children cared for by sole-grandparent caretakers ($b = -0.13$, $p > 0.05$) also reported a lower level of conflict. The difference between children of maternal migration and nonmigration was small and nonsignificant ($b = -0.03$, $p > 0.05$). Surprisingly, although nonsignificant, children with paternal migration (i.e., primarily cared for by sole-mother caretakers) reported the highest level of conflict ($b = 0.07$, $p < 0.05$). Further analysis shows that this group also had a significantly higher level of conflict compared with those living with two-grandparent caretakers ($b = 0.22$, $p < 0.05$). In summary, these findings reveal that children cared for by grandparent caretakers had a more or less harmonious relationship with their caretakers, while children living with sole stay-at-home mothers reported the highest level of conflict.

The measure use of harsh discipline asked children whether their caretakers ever hit, kicked, or used other methods to physically punish them in the past twelve months. The association between this measure and type of parental migration/caretaking arrangement was highly significant (chi-square = 19.47, $p < 0.01$). A logistic regression model was conducted to investigate whether this bivariate association was robust after controlling for confounding factors. The logistic regression model provides nearly identical findings (table 3.2). The odds of using corporal punishment against children of two-grandparent caretakers ($\exp(b) = 0.49$, $p < 0.01$) and one-grandparent caretakers ($\exp(b) = 0.57$, $p < 0.05$) were about half compared with those living with nonmigrant parents. In addition, further analyses indicate that compared with at-home-father or at-home-mother caretakers, grandparent caretakers were significantly less likely to use corporal punishment. There was no difference between the two types of grandparent caretakers nor any difference between the three types of parental caretakers.

Grandparenting: The Dilemma between Spoiling and Strict Supervision

The quantitative data overall reveal that compared to at-home parents, grandparent caretakers were far less likely to express hostility (e.g., criticizing, shouting, and yelling) or exercise corporal punishment (e.g., hitting, kicking, or other

TABLE 3.2
Multivariate regression model predicting caretaker–child conflict and harsh discipline

	Caretaker–child conflict		Harsh discipline	
	B	SE	exp(b)	SE
Intercept	2.06**	0.48		
Two-grandparent caretaking[a]	−0.15*	0.07	0.49**	0.21
One-grandparent caretaking	−0.13	0.10	0.57*	0.31
Maternal migration	−0.05	0.09	1.18	0.23
Paternal migration	0.07	0.08	1.09	0.21
Male[b]	0.06	0.05	1.55**	0.14
Age	0.05	0.03	0.86	0.09
Living in a school dorm[c]	0.10	0.08	1.10	0.21
Parental education	0.03	0.02	0.95	0.06
Household property	0.01	0.02	1.01	0.06
Perceived family economic status	−0.10*	0.05	0.76*	0.12
Marital status of biological parents[d]	−0.27*	0.09	0.97	0.25
Number of siblings	0.03	0.03	1.02	0.08
Pseudo R^2	0.03		0.06	

Note: *$p < 0.05$; **$p < 0.01$; B = unstandardized regression coefficient; N = 1,177; SE = standard error.

[a] Children of nonmigrant parents as the reference group.

[b] Female as the reference category.

[c] Living at home as the reference group.

[d] Divorced or separated as the reference group.

physical punishment), therefore maintaining a more or less harmonious relationship with their grandchildren. These numerical data are validated by children's, migrant parents', and grandparents' own accounts. Children, for example, often expressed their sincere appreciation for grandparents' sacrifice but sometimes felt uncomfortable or embarrassed since grandparents had done too much for them. Xiaowei, a fourteen-year-old eighth grader, commented on his grandmother's caretaking style and, as a result, his own lack of independence.

> I know she spoils me. Although I know it, it's difficult to change, although I know it. I feel that sometimes I am just being lazy, then I will just do what she asked me to do. Like sometimes I am watching TV, she will prepare me a bowl of face-washing water. She has been doing that for many years. I, sometimes, know I should do it myself, and I said it a few times but sometimes I am just being lazy ... I don't feel that it is all right. Although I did it myself a few times. I only did it a few times, then she did it for me again and I did not say anything.

Like Xiaowei's grandma, it was not uncommon that grandparents in Peace County took care of everything for children and only required them to study hard and achieve good academic standing. This kind of caretaking practice worries migrant parents and the larger society, who criticize grandparents for being too lenient and failing to provide and enforce clear rules and structures for children. The interview results reflect this widespread sentiment, with migrant parents often complaining that grandparents rarely used corporal punishment, a disciplinary method still perceived as effective and legitimate in rural China. Rather than employing "real" punishment, grandparents were said to resort to empty threats and verbal chastisement, which became increasingly ineffective when children gradually realized that these threats would never be fully enforced. These sentiments were exemplified in my interview with Xiaoshu, a twenty-one-year-old migrant mother with two children. She commented on her parents-in-law's discipline strategies:

> When they raise children, they often spoil and pamper little ones. If we parents were there, if we saw anything not right, anything too much, if they did anything wrong, we would just spank them. ... Grandparents, when they are really angry, they may slap them on the wrist. Most of the time, in my mother-in-law's words, they just try to scare them. My five-year-old daughter, when others asked her, said, "My grandma just tries to scare me a little bit." ... Because grandparents often love their grandchildren so much, they are so reluctant to punish them. Except when they are so angry, getting extremely frustrated, they will then give them a slap. When I call back, saying if children don't listen, you can spank them. Grandma often says, you cannot just slap them around, scolding them will be enough.

In her comments, Xiaoshu stressed the clear distinction between the disciplinary practices of grandparents and parents. Parents were often ready to employ corporal punishment while grandparents often resorted to verbal threats, which became increasingly ineffective over time. Interestingly, grandparent caretakers themselves agreed with the observations of both children and migrant parents, acknowledging that they spoiled their grandchildren too much. In a casual conversation, grandpa Xiao (who raised two grandsons from babies to teenagers alongside his wife) reflected on the differences between raising his grandsons and raising his two sons thirty years before.

Grandparents just spoil their children more [than parents]. They are not like parents. What the reasons are, I am not quite sure. Like me, my two sons, Ping, and Bo, when they were in middle school, we were building a house.... Now Ziyang [grandson] is an 8th grader, we are building the house again, adding a section on the other side. They are all 8th graders. I then remember, I said [to my son], when I built the house and you were an 8th grader, I thought you were a grown-up, an adult, I did not treat you like a child. Right? Whatever it was, I considered your thoughts to be the same as those of us grownups. [I thought] you were mature. But now, again, I am the one to lead building the house.... You guys pay the money, but it's us to take the lead, and I think they [grandchildren] are little kids knowing nothing.... When they are walking on the bank of a pond, we even say, "Be careful, don't fall into the pond." We even have those concerns! It looks like we become more naive when we get older. You say it is like this?

The preceding cases demonstrate that grandparents are, indeed, more likely to "spoil" their grandchildren than parents are. The spoiling can be manifested in multiple forms, including cooking children's favorite food, providing luxury material goods, and, most importantly, the reluctance or inability to establish and enforce specified rules and to set boundaries. As in the case of grandpa Xiao, although he treated his teenage sons as adults and expected mature behavior from them some thirty years before, he now considered his teenage grandchildren as babies—even concerned that they might fall into a pond while walking nearby. While grandparents themselves were sometimes befuddled by this differential treatment, prior research suggests that traditional cultural norms in China, which stipulate the role of grandparents and parents in extended households, contribute to this discrepancy. Traditionally, grandparents are cast as providers of affection, as the Chinese old saying "keep maltose in the mouth and play with grandson (han yi nong sun)" demonstrates. Conversely, parents—particularly fathers—are rule creators and enforcers (F. Chen et al., 2011). In the context of mass migration, although grandparents often replace migrant parents as surrogate parents, most are still ambiguous about the role change and are reluctant to take full responsibility and adopt the traditional parental disciplinary role.

Maternal Migration and Paternal Migration Households: Love Needs to Be in Your Heart, Not in Your Eyes

In sharp contrast to grandparents, left-behind parents, regardless of whether they are at-home fathers or mothers, frequently use harsh disciplinary strategies. The example of Laojiu, a fifty-year-old father with two children, embodied this type of parenting practice. When Laojiu was interviewed in 2018, his elder son had already migrated with his mother to Nanchang, the capital city of Jiangxi province, to *dagong*. Laojiu was living with the younger child, a twelve-year-old boy at the time.

He explained in detail his philosophy about discipline and other parenting practices.

> We say we all have children. Raising a child, it is not like you don't love him. Love needs to be in your heart, not in your eyes. You need to strictly discipline him at this time, so you can spare others the trouble of doing it for you in the future. Like if he goes out and steals or robs someone, when the government catches him, they will treat him like a human being? They will beat him up! It will hurt you more than using a bamboo stick does . . . I normally don't beat my children, not often. I don't scold them much either. If I do, I will do it all in one time . . . I say get down on your knees there. He kneels on the ground there, in the dining room. I say have you thought this over? If he says he does, he will get up, if not he will continue kneeling over there. When my elder son was in middle school, he wanted to run. I said, dare you move your feet? I saw he moved his feet, and then quickly took them back.

In at-home father Laojiu's opinion, strict or tough parenting is an expression of love that instills traditional moral ethics in children. These authoritarian/authoritative parenting styles—often referred to as "tough love" and commonly used by low- and working-class or minority parents in the United States (Krisberg, 2017)—are widely adopted by at-home fathers and mothers in rural China. When asked whether her children argued and fought with her at home, DaSheng, a forty-five-year-old at-home mother with one fully grown migrant worker daughter and another in high school, emphatically stated that she held full authority at home.

INTERVIEWER: When little ones are at home, do they argue with you?

DASHENG: They don't argue with me.

INTERVIEWER: So they listen to you?

DASHENG: They listen to me. They do not argue with me. That is simply atrocious. . . . They don't argue with me. My two daughters, they don't argue with me.

INTERVIEWER: So your two daughters, whatever you say, they will do it?

DASHENG: Right, they don't fight with me. You ask them to do their homework, they will do their homework. I don't ask, they will sit in front of the desk, they will do their homework.

As demonstrated in these cases, children of sole-migrant parents were demanded to show respect and obedience by parents at home, and strict and harsh disciplinary practices were occasionally used to effectively control children's wayward behaviors. The differential rates of the use of discipline and harsh caretaking practices between parents and grandparent caretakers can be explained by the apparent ambiguity of social norms regarding the role of grandparents. In general, societal expectations of grandparenting in rural China focus upon roles where grandparents serve as secondary caretakers and are less developed in situations where grandparents essentially become surrogate parents in skipped-generation families. It is possible that grandparents, particularly younger generations with higher education levels, can adapt to these dramatic social changes and renegotiate their roles and identities within the multilocal household. Studies in Indonesia and the Philippines, for example, show that since female labor migration has become so common in the past several decades, fathering practices have been gradually redefined and now encompass providing "moral, emotional and physical care" and acting as "both 'father' and 'mother' to their children" (Lam & Yeoh, 2018, p. 111). Whether and how at-home grandparents in rural China can reimagine their roles and successfully adapt to these changes in both family configuration and the larger society, however, needs to be further investigated.

Conclusion

In this chapter, I investigated differences in caretaking practices across various caretaking arrangements in rural China. The quantitative and qualitative data together paint a quite complicated picture—highlighting the nuanced and multidimensional relationships between left-behind children, migrant and at-home parents, and grandparents. While the analyses reject any simple or homogeneous finding, I am tasked with developing conclusions about the research questions proposed at the beginning of the chapter. That is, do alternative caretaking arrangements (e.g., grandparenting) differ significantly from the normative two-parent childrearing/caretaking practices, and if so, to what degree do the alternative caretaking arrangements differ?

I investigated three dimensions of childrearing practices: caretaker monitoring and supervision, caretaker–child bonding, and caretaker harsh discipline. The analyses demonstrate that there is much heterogeneity in these caretaking practices among at-home parents and grandparent caretakers, with two major findings standing out. First, the analyses show that the effects of grandparenting on caretaking quality are complicated and multidimensional. Whereas the previous literature and public discourse often draw a highly pessimistic picture regarding grandparenting, overall, children cared for by two grandparents provided positive feedback about their life experiences. Compared with their counterparts in non-migrant households, children cared for by two-grandparent caretakers reported a similar level of monitoring and supervision and a comparable level of caretaker–child bonding. This is in direct contrast to reports from children of one-grandparent-caretaking households, who reported the lowest levels of caretaker monitoring/supervision and the weakest child–caretaker bonding. Due to the joint effect of household poverty, aging, deteriorating health, and the backbreaking farming workload, the sole-caretaker grandparents appeared physically and emotionally overwhelmed, leading to the adoption of a largely responsive rather than proactive caretaking style.

Interestingly, children of grandparent caretakers, whether sole-grandparent or two-grandparent caretakers, exhibited the lowest level of caretaker–child conflict. The harmonious caretaker–child relationship may suggest that grandparents and children develop a strong and affectionate bond over time, but it may also reflect grandparents' ambivalence about their changing roles and an unwillingness or inability to discipline their grandchildren when conflict arises. Consistent with widely held public opinion, most grandparents do appear to spoil grandchildren and are not equipped with appropriate attitudes, knowledge, and tools to control children's wayward behaviors when necessary. In contrast, left-behind fathers or mothers are not hesitant to use harsh discipline or corporal punishment when these methods are deemed necessary; however, the effects of these harsh parenting practices are debatable, and no definitive conclusions have been drawn as to their efficacy within the context of rural China.

Second, the results reveal that in the scenario of sole-parent migration, the gender of the stay-at-home parent has an impact. Maternal migration, as suggested by numerous previous studies (e.g., Parreñas, 2009; Wen & Lin, 2012), imposes more damaging effects on children's development than paternal migration. Stay-at-home fathers are often reluctant to cross gender boundaries and perform the role of "mothering," thus failing to monitor children's daily activities and provide consistent emotional support. To maintain their gendered identities, left-behind fathers often present a front of "productive selves," working tirelessly on their farmland or other small businesses. Paternal migration, although resulting in fewer deleterious effects, does appear to have its disadvantages. There is quantitative evidence that left-behind mothers' agency as rule enforcers is often challenged by left-behind children, creating a long-lasting and strained relationship. In other words, left-behind parents, whether at-home fathers or mothers, face severe challenges in expanding social roles across gender boundaries; additionally, these role adjustments are often criticized by left-behind children and the larger society, adding further difficulties to quality caretaking and children's normative development.

4

Parenting from Afar

Long-Distance Parenting and Short Visits

> Because now it is all video. When you have video, it's like your mom is right there with you, right? Now Internet is so prevalent. Normally we use video chat, even telephone [voice-only] chat is rarely used.
>
> —migrant mother Rongmei

In chapter 3, I explored varying dimensions of caretaking practices by copresent caretakers (i.e., left-behind fathers, mothers, and grandparents), focusing on dynamic intrafamilial interactions between at-home caretakers and children left behind (e.g., bonding and support, conflict and tension, and supervision and monitoring of children's conventional and wayward behaviors). For multilocal families, however, caretaking by at-home parents or other primary caretakers (e.g., grandparents) is only one side of the story. Another critical dimension of caretaking, which has drawn growing attention in recent years, is parenting from afar (Cotton & Beguy, 2021; Madianou & Miller, 2013; Parreñas, 2009). Separated by hundreds or even thousands of miles, migrant parents (migrant mothers in particular) genuinely expect—and are widely relied on by children, family members, and society as a whole—to perform traditional parenting duties. Migrant parents strive to meet these expectations in multiple ways, including long-distance parenting or mobile parenting via modern information and communication technology (ICT), short visits to children and family members, and children's visits to parents' host cities during summer breaks or holidays (Alinejad, 2019; Cotton & Beguy, 2021; Ho & Chiang, 2017; Madianou & Miller, 2011; R. Zhou et al., 2017).

I examine these three dimensions of long-distance parenting in this chapter. First, I focus on long-distance or mobile parenting; due to chronic spatial separation, this has become the primary method for migrant parents to perform parental duties. Specifically, I analyze how long-distance parenting is performed by migrant parents, focusing on the types of media used by parents and children, the frequency of communication, and primary conversation topics. Second, I observe that, unlike their transnational counterparts, many children in rural China regularly visit parents in their host cities, particularly during summer breaks or other holidays. In the following section, I explore the prevalence of these visits, how long children stay, and both contributing factors promoting and barriers potentially reducing these visits. Finally, migrant parents regularly pay visits to children and family members. In the last section, I explore the frequency of these visits; potential tension between migrant parents, copresent caretakers, and children during their time together; and both risk and protective factors that may influence these interactions.

Long-Distance Parenting: Choice of Medium Use, Frequency, and Conversation Content

The rapid development of new ICTs in recent years has precipitated mobile devices (e.g., smartphones and tablets) becoming more accessible and affordable; as such, these have increasingly become primary tools for everyday communication for Chinese people. As of May 2021, the number of smartphone users in China reached 970 million—more than all users combined from the United States, Brazil, and Indonesia (Slotta, 2022). WeChat, an instant messaging, social media, and mobile payment app, became the world's largest standalone mobile app in 2018, with more than a billion monthly active users. Besides traditional functions such as sending instant text message, images, audio messages, and short videos, the app provides live audio and video streaming, a function utilized by many migrant parents. Moreover, WeChat users can post text, images, video clips, and articles on an embedded social networking site—a crucial way for spatially and temporally separated family members to share life experiences with one another (Ho & Chiang, 2017; R. Zhou et al., 2017).

The means by which migrant parents, left-behind children, and caretakers exploit these newly developed ICTs have increasingly drawn academic attention (P. L. Liu & Leung, 2017; Wong-Villacres & Bardzell, 2011; R. Zhou et al., 2017). Previous studies have generally found that geographically separated parents and children often take full advantage of advances in technology, regularly video chatting and using social media sites (e.g., Facebook) to develop and maintain emotional intimacy. Additionally, how parents and children negotiate and present themselves has been found to influence their app and platform choices (Alinejad, 2019; Pan et al., 2013; R. Zhou et al., 2017). In other words, media users often purposively choose one or several forms of communication via particular social media platforms based on how comfortable they are sharing information with distant family members—these disclosures may include revealing personal information, sharing particular facets of their own personalities, or other expressions of intimacy. A long-distance relationship thus becomes a relationship that is mediated by technology, to the extent that relationships depend "often entirely, on communication technologies" (Madianou & Miller, 2011, p. 141). As Marshall McLuhan, the author of the book *Understanding Media: The Extension of Man* (1964), famously claimed: "The medium is the message."

Although strongly endorsed by local governments and telecommunication corporations, the effects of distance or mobile parenting on children's short- and long-term development have not yet been fully investigated or understood. We know very little regarding the types of media that migrant parents and children select, the underlying factors contributing to these decisions, the frequency of long-distance communication, and the information that parents and children choose to exchange. In this section, I first investigate how migrant parents and children take advantage of modern ICTs and newly developed social media platforms such as WeChat. That is, which communication methods do migrant parents and children prefer, and why? Second, I explore how often migrant parents and left-behind children communicate with each other and identify social and individual factors contributing to this rate of communication. Finally, I investigate the main topics discussed by parents and children during long-distance conversations and how the use of a particular medium might promote the discussion of certain topics while discouraging others.

Primary Media for Long-Distance Communication and Parenting

I asked children which media they used to communicate with migrant parents over the previous twelve months. The quantitative data indicated that migrant parents and children utilized multiple media, including voice-based phone calls (91%), audio (79%) or video chats (79%) embedded in WeChat, and texting (75%). The interview data provide further empirical support for these quantitative findings. The following excerpts from interview quotes suggest that the most frequently used methods were audio and video calls:

> Phone calls. We make phone calls. . . . About more than half an hour, once a week.
>
> —migrant mother Xiaolu

> We make phone calls. Because grandparents, they don't know how to use video chats, sometimes little children know [how to use it]. You gave them a cell phone, they know how to use them, better than aged grandparents. [But] getting used to using a cell phone is not good, affecting school grades.
>
> —migrant mother Song

> Video chatting and phone calls. The older one knows how to use it, the older one, because she is going to be a fourth grader next semester.
>
> —migrant mother Chunyan

> In the past we did not install Internet cable, now we installed it, and they often video chat. When we had no internet, they often called back.
>
> —grandpa Yubao

Madianou and Miller (2012) find that families utilize three primary communication methods: voice-based communication (i.e., phone calls and calling cards); text-based communication such as texting, email, and instant messaging; and multimedia communication, including social network sites (e.g., Facebook), blogging, video chatting, and videoconferencing (using a desktop or laptop computer). Given the prevalence of mobile phones (particularly smartphones) in rural China, it is not surprising that migrant parents and children used phone and video calls as the primary means of communication (Liu & Leung, 2017; Pan et al., 2013). Interestingly, text-based methods such as email and multimedia communications (e.g., using social networking sites and/or videoconferencing via a desktop or laptop computer) were rarely mentioned in interview data, although they are regularly used by transnational families (Alinejad, 2019; R. Zhou et al., 2017). We speculate that affordability and media literary—highly associated with one another—are the primary factors contributing to such a choice. Compared with those who migrate transnationally (Alinejad, 2019; R. Zhou et al., 2017), migrant parents in rural China have much lower levels of education, socioeconomic status, and media literacy. Indeed, when interviewing students and grandparents at their homes, I noticed that none of the families had a desktop or a laptop computer; at the same time, all migrant parents, at-home caretakers, and some children had a cell phone.

Corroborating prior research (Alinejad, 2019; R. Zhou et al., 2017), the data indicate that long-distance communication exceeds the simple flow of information (e.g., physical health and school grades of children), and its form, frequency, and interactional dynamics are imbued with actively imputed social meanings. Children's active participation in long-distance communication, for example, was considered an indicator of "good parenting" and robust parent–child bonding—particularly by migrant mothers. Xiaolu, a thirty-year-old migrant mother of a three-year-old and a five-year-old, described how warmhearted her children were each time she called them:

> Phone calls. We make phone calls. . . . About more than half an hour, once a week. Because I want to call when there are more people [at home]. It has become a habit now, once a week, about half an hour each time. Kids, they are so warmhearted. He is really willing to talk with me. Then he says, Mom, I miss you so much. I say, eh, when Mom makes more money, I will be back (laughing).

In addition to voice-based phone calls, video chatting—a feature of WeChat offering synchronous audio and video communication—has increasingly become a popular choice for migrant parents and children at home. Video chatting provides migrant parents and children with an opportunity to interact face-to-face regardless of distance—this creates a surreal sense of physical presence, mitigating feelings of strangeness and awkwardness that may occur due to protracted physical and temporal separation. Additionally, young migrant parents utilize this opportunity to observe the ambient condition around children as well as their short- and long-term physical and mental growth. Through video chatting, migrant parents can partially fulfill their parental obligations despite the spatial distance, lessening feelings of guilt regarding "abandoning" children for household economic gains and perhaps even managing to feel like "good parents." Migrant mother Rongmei, a forty-year-old migrant mother of a six-year-old son and a seventeen-year-old daughter, explained that although she had migrated to Shenzhen two years prior and only visited home once a year, she maintained a good relationship with her son, who loved to talk with her every time she called. She explained:

> Because now it is all video. When you have video, it's like your mom is right there with you, right? Now Internet is so prevalent. Normally we use video chat, even telephone [voice-only] chat is rarely used.

Twenty-one-year-old migrant mother Xiaoshu concurred with Rongmei. In our interview, she detailed using video chatting to build intimacy with her two small children, aged one and three.

> The older one is willing [to talk]. The little one, she doesn't even know how to talk, she does not understand. The older one, every time we send a video chat, or call, she picks it up. . . . [We] ask her whether she goes to school, how school goes, she will talk to you. She is willing to answer. . . . Video chat, [in the last] two days there were sixty, seventy minutes. There are also phone calls. Because we call them almost every day. Because they are still young, [so] we call every day. The little one, we just see what she looks like, have her watch the video with us. That's it. You ask her to say Mommy and Daddy, and she doesn't even know how to say it. She is only one year old, not yet to talk.

The preceding interview quote reveals that migrant parents—particularly parents with young children—perceive video chatting as a part of "intensive distance parenting." As explained by Xiaoshu, "because they are still young, [so] we call every day." In addition, just by seeing "what she looks like" and having "her watch the video with us," video chatting gives migrant parents a sense of fulfillment and gratification. Migrant parents—particularly mothers—thus experience the sense of an intact family ("it is like Mom is right there with you"), even as they may be physically separated from children by hundreds or even thousands of miles.

Conversely, the influence of video chatting on developing and maintaining emotional intimacy appears to be more limited when considering older children. Grandma Xiao and her husband—the primary caretakers of two grandchildren over the previous fifteen years—detailed an incident when one of her grandsons felt uneasy when video chatting with his migrant mother, who had been *dagong* in Zhejiang province since the child was one year old.

> Like our oldest grandson, he had no emotional connection with his parents, no connection. His mom video-called him a few days ago, he did not even face the camera. His mom said, Son, why did you not let me see you? He did not video call her. There is no emotional connection. Right?

As in the previous example, while many migrant parents prefer video chatting to achieve the feeling of physical presence, children sometimes feel uncomfortable and may not reciprocate affection at the same level. In fact, the teenager in this example "did not even face the camera," a response distinctively different from that of younger children such as Xiaoshu's daughters. The differential responses may be attributed to the cohort effect. Smartphones have only become affordable and prevalent in rural China over the past decade, so while younger children have been routinely exposed to video chatting since birth, older children have only been exposed since early or middle childhood—a critical period for parent–child bonding. For older children, it appears the sustained emotional detachment due to a lack of parent–child communication during early childhood may not be easily mended.

Despite witnessing the occasional reluctance of children to interact with migrant parents, grandparents generally embraced the convenience and other positive attributes of multimedia and other ICTs, including their potential to develop and maintain emotional intimacy. Commenting on the lack of communication in the "old days" compared with the widespread use of smartphones today, grandparents in Peace County expressed optimism at how advanced technologies can facilitate long-distance parent–child bonding:

> Now it is a little bit better. Now there are cellphones, before there were no cellphones or other stuff, could not connect to him [the migrant parent] from the beginning to the end of a year. In the past there were not many off days either, like my son, he was in Zhejiang province. His boss was very inflexible. Even during the Spring Festival, only ten days, and he kept pushing him [to come back to work]. Now we can video chat, we can call each other.
>
> —grandpa Xiao

Frequency of Long-Distance Communication

In our interviews, parents often claimed they "always" called or video chatted with both children left behind and at-home caretakers. The quantitative data, however, reveal that the frequency of these long-distance communications was, at best, modest. The mode of the frequency of long-distance communication was one or two times a week (47.2% for migrant fathers and 43.3% for migrant mothers), with once every one or two days followed (21.6% for migrant fathers and 28.2% for migrant mothers). Moreover, about one-third of the students reported that their migrant parents called one or two times a month or even less. Surprisingly, the difference in the communication frequency between migrant fathers and migrant mothers was small, although the latter were more likely to communicate every one or two days than the former.

A small number of studies—albeit published about a decade ago—explored this topic and found that the frequency of parent–child long distance communication was relatively low, with children reporting around once a week or lower (L. Chen et al., n.d.; Pan et al., 2013). When comparing this literature with my own study, it appears that the frequency of parent–child communication has increased moderately over time, potentially reflecting the increased use of smartphones and advanced ICTs over the past decade. Meanwhile, the study indicates that while significant progress has been achieved, distance parenting through high-technology apps such as WeChat is hardly a replacement for traditional parenting. After all, a phone call or video chat once a week is unlikely to sufficiently address the emotional costs elicited by chronic spatial and temporal separations, let alone build strong parent–child emotional intimacy. Indeed, migrant parents were fully aware of the limitations of these highly touted communication tools. Migrant mother Chen commented on her interaction with her now-ten-year-old twin daughters, whom she left when they were one and a half years old:

> We communicate by phone calls. Absolutely, there is a little bit of distance. Our conversation is a little bit short. It's not like at home. We talk a little bit more there. . . . Well, we have been away for such a long time. It's better when there is a little bit more familiarity. Like now, they will feel a little bit strange. If you ask, they will answer. If you do not, they do not say anything. The communication is short.

Caretakers at home, including remaining parents and grandparent caretakers, echoed this sentiment. At-home mother Dasheng commented that her daughter rarely talked to her migrant father but had an intimate relationship with the older sister, who lived with them but went to an eastern coast region to *dagong* two years ago:

> The girl does not say anything to her dad, talking very little. Sometimes her dad calls, and she will say a little bit, but they rarely call each other. . . . She will say a few words when her dad calls. She has time, but she does not call her dad. She calls her older sister a lot, like buying something or needing something for school supplies, she will find her sister, she will call her.

The interview data with migrant parents provide some explanation for the infrequency of child–parent long distance communication. Migrant parents generally worked long hours (nine to ten hours each day) and six days a week, which consumed most of their energy and substantially reduced their availability for long-distance communication. This problem is further exacerbated by different daily routines and specific accommodations for children of different ages. For example, young children often go to bed early, long before their parents finish work and other essential activities. Children in junior and senior high schools, particularly those attending boarding schools, were generally prohibited from using cell phones on weekdays and could only communicate with parents on weekends or during a small gap between night self-study classes and bedtime. Migrant mother Ganxue described the difficulties of contacting her two high schoolers—a sixteen-year-old boy and an eighteen-year-old girl, both studying in boarding schools:

> I call them on Sundays, on Sundays. Call them at weekends. Sometimes you want to call them, [but] they have night self-study classes, ending at 10:30 P.M. Sometimes I want to give them a call, and it's like, okay, don't bother them [after 10:30 P.M.]. They take a shower and are ready to go to bed, so it can only be on Sundays.

Migrant mother Rongmei concurred with Ganxue, describing how the contrasting daily schedules of her two children influenced the frequency of mother–child communication. Her seventeen-year-old daughter visited home once a month from boarding school, while her six-year-old son lived with his father and two grandparents at home. She said:

> On average, I call them two or three times a week, at least. My daughter, it can only be once a week because she has her cellphone [back] only on Sundays. Her teacher helps keep the cellphone.... The younger one, there is no restriction. You can call as many times as you want. For my daughter, it has to be on weekends. The rule is already established. We have already paid her living costs, so there is nothing to worry about. After all, [she] is in a small local county seat, not too much complicated stuff.

While these long-distance conversations were generally infrequent, their intensity varied across children's age and gender subgroups. Although migrant parents tend to perform more intensive long-distance parenting when children are young—particularly when they are enrolled in pre-care or elementary schools—this intensity fades as children enter junior and senior high schools. Thirty-year-old migrant mother Chunyan described how her two children, a nine-year-old and a six-year-old, were eager to video chat when returning from their boarding school:

> We video chat with each other. Every time it's them [to initiate the call], sometimes I am very busy, working overtime on Sundays, they call for a video chat.... The older one knows how to use it. The older one, he knows, he will be in fourth grade next semester. Both attend the same boarding school, and they go home every two weeks. When they get home, they will turn on the video chat. Sometimes in school, the teacher will say, "Let me give you a video chat [with your parents]."

This age disparity in children's willingness to communicate with physically distant parents may reflect different levels of independence and maturity; however, this finding may also suggest that advanced ICTs such as live video chat may indeed diminish the impact of both physical and emotional distance. When children regularly see their parents' faces, expressions, and overall virtual presence from an early age, feelings of emotional detachment may be alleviated, and strong bonds can be developed despite chronic physical separation.

Another salient demographic factor associated with children's willingness to communicate is gender—especially for teenage boys and girls. Social norms and expectations dictate that girls are more familial and relationally oriented, while boys are expected to be independent and less communicative (Chen & Liu, 2012). This difference is potentially exacerbated by chronic parent–child separation, as demonstrated by the following quotes:

> My oldest son communicates with me less. You call him, he does not talk much. He does not say more than a few words. My daughter, when you talk to her, you cannot hang up in an hour. Very good talk. My son, very few words. My son talks a little bit more with my husband, with me, very little. The conversation is often short.
>
> —migrant mother Xue.

> Girls are overall better. I am more worried about my son, not too much about my daughter. . . . When he gets older, he says, "I am not a little boy anymore, you don't need to say it, I understand." . . . He is a grown-up, asking me not to say [those things] anymore. [You] talking a little bit more then he becomes annoyed, saying I cannot stop talking about the same thing.
>
> —migrant mother Rongmei

Another aspect of parent–child long-distance communication—one often taken for granted by all parties but that could still play a crucial role in shaping the frequency and nature of this interaction—is the asymmetrical relationship between parents and children. Pan and colleagues (2013) found that only 14 percent of students left behind initiated phone calls to their parents, 54 percent waited for calls from parents, and the remainder (31%) talked to parents only after parents finished discussing various issues with at-home guardians. Although I did not ask specifically who initiated phone calls or video chatting in my interviews, the interview data aptly demonstrate that parent–child long-distance communications were asymmetrical. Chunyan, for example, specifically pointed out that her children were the ones to initiate phone calls, implying that this behavior was uncommon. "Every time it's them [to initiate the call], sometimes I am very busy, working overtime on Sundays, they call for a video chat . . ."

A combination of cultural and contextual factors may contribute to the unidirectional communication. First, the hierarchical structure of power distribution shapes communication styles in a traditional Chinese rural household, in which parents bearing higher levels of family responsibility given their need to care for children's well-being. Second, most children in rural China do not have their own smartphones—a result largely due to parents' concerns regarding children's addiction to games. Indeed, Pan and colleagues (2013) found that only 20 percent of children left behind had their own cell phones, and most used the cell phones of their guardians when communicating with parents. While the number of children with cell phones has gradually increased in recent years, most are not allowed to use them during weekdays, thus substantially reducing time availability to interact with migrant parents.

The remaining factor influencing both frequency and intensity of parent–child long-term communication is the unconventional working schedule of migrant parents. Migrant parents often work extended hours and at irregular times (e.g., night shifts), leading to an unstable pattern in parent–child communication. Grandpa Longshang, a fifty-five-year-old living with his wife, a thirteen-year-old daughter, and a two-year-old granddaughter at the time of the interview, explained this kind of communication pattern:

> When he [the father] is in the mood, he will do it [audio and video chat], [if he is] not in the mood, then no. Sometimes they do it every day, once each day, sometimes once a few days. He will not [video chat] when he is busy. When he is free, he misses his daughter and he will send a video chat, having a little bit of conversation. When he is busy, he cannot remember these things.

Topics of Long-Distance Conversation

Finally, I asked our respondents—both students and migrant parents—what these long-distance conversations were about. Echoing previous research (L. Chen et al., n.d.; Murphy, 2014; Pan et al., 2013), children in the survey reported that their conversation generally revolved around three topics: children's academic performance, physical health, and personal safety. Migrant parents were mostly concerned about children's academic performance, with 93 percent reporting that their parents were very concerned or concerned about grades. Children's physical health was ranked the second, with 90 percent reporting that parents were very concerned or concerned. A similar percentage of children (88%) reported that parents were also very concerned or concerned about their personal safety. Other topics such as friends, moral character development, food, and children's psychological health were discussed less frequently.

Our in-depth interviews with children and migrant parents reveal the same pattern. Children almost universally reported that health and schooling were the most discussed topics. Jingwen, a seventh grader who was living with a younger brother and two grandparents at the time of the interview, succinctly recounted her conversation with migrant parents: "That is, sometimes there is an exam, I will tell her afterward. Sometimes my brother has a fever, catching a cold, I will tell her that." Chuangqi, a twelve-year-old boy living with a younger sister and grandparents, provided more detail:

> We just talked about school and daily activities. For instance, my grandma was sick; For instance, I took an exam, if I got a good grade (laughing). . . . They will say I need to work hard. If my English is not very good, then I need to get up early in the morning and read the English textbook, do a little bit more homework. If my math is not very good, do some extra homework. And I need to read more broadly.

Migrant parents provided similar comments, stressing that schooling was the most important—and many times the only—topic of a conversation. Chunyan, a migrant mother of three, explained, "We did not talk about anything (laughing). . . . Just asking them about school. Not too much to talk about." Since migrant parents lacked the opportunity to help with children's studies or participate in school-related activities, they used these conversations to encourage and implore children to study harder and to promise that they would do anything possible to support children's future education. Ganxue, who had two high schoolers—one eighteen and one sixteen—said:

> I chat with them, basically, asking them to study hard. I say if you study hard, if you do well, [even if] I don't have money, I can take a loan, it's okay to take a loan. I say if you can study [well], if you can [do well], even I don't have money, I will support you [going to college] through a loan.

As the narratives above indicate, schooling and education occupy a central position in long-distance conversations between children and migrant parents, a reflection of the increasing impact of "education fever" in every corner of Chinese society (Y. Chen et al., 2021; Murphy, 2014). Originating from middle-class members of urbanites, "education fever" is characterized by parents' unrealistic expectations of children's academic performance and the enormous pressure placed on children to pursue higher education. A study conducted by China Youth and Children Research Center (2001) aptly reflected this social phenomenon, revealing that 97.1 percent of parents expected children to have at least two years of college, more than two-thirds (70.5%) expected a master's degree, close to half (44.5%) at least a doctoral degree, and one-quarter (23.5%) postdoctoral education. While this study was conducted among urban parents, the preceding data suggest that "education fever" may have also spread to rural China. Such high expectations, unfortunately, sharply contrast with reality for many children. The 2020 census data, for example, reveal that the average education level of Chinese people over fifteen years old was 9.08 years (i.e., roughly junior high graduation); in addition, only 15.5 percent had a college-level of education (National Bureau of Statistics of China, 2021).

While the spread of "education fever" in rural areas may have positive influences (e.g., may facilitate more investment in children's education), it discourages children—particularly those with poor grades—from discussing their academic struggles with parents, adding further conflict to an already tenuous child–parent relationship (Murphy, 2014). Grandpa LongEr—who was raising two grandchildren, a fourteen-year-old and an eleven-year-old, when interviewed—described the tension between his daughter-in-law and grandchildren over school-related conversations:

INTERVIEWER: Do the kids have a good relationship with their parents?

GRANDPA LONGER: Not very good with their mom. The reason for that is, every time their mom calls, she asks them about their grades on the last exam ... that is, whenever she calls, there is nothing else, nothing else. . . . My daughter-in-law, she is a bookworm, you know? She is just a bookworm, all books. She reads when she comes home too, she doesn't come out. She just stays upstairs and reads. A book costing more than 1,000 RMB, she bought it. Always reading. . . . Her children resent it, saying that when Mom calls, it's always about school, nothing else.

INTERVIEWER: You are talking about the older daughter?

GRANDPA LONGER: No, the older daughter and the son all said this. They just don't want to talk to their mom, she is only about grades.

Additionally, the centrality of schooling and education precludes discussion related to other important topics, such as children's daily difficulties and struggles. In fact, the data indicate that these topics were rarely discussed in these long-distance conversations. In addition to the emphasis placed on education, I speculate that—due to chronic spatial and temporal separation—migrant parents find it difficult to identify and engage in more nuanced and sensitive topics, leading to primarily superficial conversations with children (Liu & Leung, 2017; Pan et al., 2013). Moreover, a child may choose to actively construct a positive image as a good student or an "obedient child," selectively disclosing information to parents. In their study of Chinese students studying abroad, R. Zhou and colleagues (2017) found that a principle followed by these children was to report "only the good but not the bad." The same strategy appears to be adopted by children left behind (Pan et al., 2013). Many children left behind only report pleasant things to parents (e.g., "For instance, I took an exam, if I got a good grade"), thus avoiding personal embarrassment or lessening parental concerns regarding their physical or psychological well-being.

Children's Visits to Host Cities of Migrant Parents

In addition to long-distance communication, another key bonding strategy for migrant parents is to bring children to host cities where they work. These visits typically occur during summer breaks, which start at the beginning of July and end on August 30. Migrant parents, particularly those who have crossed provincial boarders, consider this a valued opportunity to interact and bond with children, display affection and commitment, and develop emotional intimacy. Moreover, children's visits are deemed by parents and peer villagers to be an indicator of "good parenting." As such, migrant parents often manage to bring children to visit despite many financial and situational barriers. Left-behind children, as well as grandparent caretakers and migrant parents, confirmed these visits in our in-depth interviews:

> In summer breaks I went to Guangdong province, and to my maternal grandma [waipo] in Hunan province. . . . Close to one month with my waipo, and more than one month in Guangdong.
>
> —Jiahui

> They went there [Guangdong province] every summer break, probably skipped just one year. . . . We picked them up when it was close to school time.
>
> —grandpa Chen

> When I was little, we went there [Shanghai] every summer. During winter breaks, sometimes we went there, sometimes we didn't. We would stay there for two months during summer breaks.
>
> —Jingwen

> I went there four, five times. . . . Came back when it was time to report to school. Almost the whole summer I was there.
>
> —Daping

> They came here to visit, playing for two months and then went back. In summer breaks, all three kids came.
>
> —migrant parent Chunyan

These narratives indicate that migrant parents frequently bring children to host cities for an extended period, particularly for those who cross provinces. Consistent with these data, the survey reveals that a significant percentage of left-behind children visited their parents regularly. Among children whose parents lived away when interviewed, close to one-third never visited (31.6%) or visited only once every two or three years (9.2%); however, the majority (59.3%) visited at least once a year, a number largely consistent with what I observed in the qualitative data. Specifically, one-third (35.2%) visited migrant parents once a year, and a quarter (24.1%) visited at least two times a year. These findings suggest that migrant parents fully recognize the importance of spending time and bonding with children and manage to create parent–child interactional opportunities despite many financial and situational barriers.

Utilizing data from the currently left-behind children, we ran a multivariate ordinal regression model to identify individual and family variables associated with children's visits to migrant parents (table 4.1). The dependent variable, the frequency of children's visits, was grouped into four categories: never, once every two or three years, once every year, and two or more times a year. The results indicate that the frequency of children's visits was shaped primarily by three factors: household socioeconomic status, types of parental migration and caretaking

TABLE 4.1
Ordinal regression model predicting children's visits to migrant parents

	B	SE	Significance level
Threshold			
Never	−0.52	0.78	
Once every two or three years	0.04	0.77	
Once every year	1.67	0.78	*
One-grandparent caretaking[a]	0.38	0.31	
Maternal migration	−1.20	0.31	**
paternal migration	−1.25	0.29	**
Male[b]	0.43	0.22	*
Age	−0.18	0.14	
Living in a school dorm[c]	0.23	0.31	
Parental education	0.14	0.09	
Household property	0.33	0.16	*
Perceived family economic status	0.10	0.17	
Marital status of biological parents[d]	0.10	0.29	
Number of siblings	−0.11	0.12	
Inter-province migration	−0.10	0.13	
Pseudo R^2		0.15	

Note: $*p < 0.05$; $**p < 0.01$; B = unstandardized regression coefficient; $N = 305$; SE = standard error.

[a] Children of dual-migrant parents as the reference group.

[b] Female as the reference category.

[c] Living at home as the reference group.

[d] Divorced or separated as the reference group.

arrangements, and a child's sex. First, household socioeconomic status was a critical factor contributing to the frequency of children's visits, with a higher number of household properties positively associated with visiting frequency ($b = 0.33$, $p < 0.05$). Understandably, parents who can afford the costs of transportation and living expenses are more likely to bring children to host cities. In particular, children's visits (sometimes accompanied by grandparent caretakers) exacerbate the meager living conditions of migrant parents, as most live in dormitories shared with coworkers or rent a small and poorly furnished apartment. While relishing time spent with parents and shared activities such as visiting zoos, parks, and cinemas, children quickly find out that living space in urban areas is extremely limited and their daily activities are constrained in a small space during weekdays, or even during weekends when parents need to work overtime.

My interview with grandpa Miao reveals the difficulties of living arrangements when children visit parents:

INTERVIEWER: Do they [migrant parents] come back during Spring Festivals?

GRANDPA MIAO: They come back during Spring Festivals, once a year. [They] typically come back during Spring Festivals and summer breaks. During summer breaks, [children] go there and stay for more than one month.

INTERVIEWER: They take all three children with them?

GRANDPA MIAO: Yeah, they take three children with them. They don't have much space. They get another room for MiaoMiao. . . . The little sister sleeps with MiaoMiao, and the youngest one stays with their parents.

INTERVIEWER: They have two rooms?

GRANDPA MIAO: *How could they have two rooms?* His boss, sometimes when you have guests, he will find an extra room for you. The boss. My son has some technical skills. He is in charge of machine repair and maintenance. The boss trusts him.

The case of MiaoMiao and her siblings is far from unique. Among the migrant parents I interviewed, all of them lived either in a factory dormitory or in a one-room apartment, which presents an enormous challenge when children come to visit. In fact, many children, particularly teenagers, are reluctant to visit because of this lack of living space. Qiankun, who hadn't visited his father for at least two to three years, explained, "The major reason is that he does not have space. He lives in a dorm, and he often changes places." Most parents and children, however, manage this situation by using bunk beds or temporarily sleeping on the floor.

Second, the regression model shows that parental migration type, that is, sole- or dual-parent migration, was a statistically significant factor in predicting children's visits. Compared with those cared for by two grandparents, children of maternal migration ($b = -1.20$, $p < 0.01$) and children of paternal migration ($b = -1.25$, $p < 0.01$) were much less likely to visit migrant parents. Indeed, among children cared for by one parent (i.e., sole-parent migration), about half of them (47%) never visited the host cities of migrant parents. By contrast, only a fifth of children (19.3%) with dual-migrant parents never visited their parents.

This pattern—consistent with previous literature (Murphy, 2020)—is probably due to three reasons. First, parental reputation—as loving and supportive parents—may be less threatened when only one parent migrates, as this arrangement—particularly paternal migration—aligns with traditional labor divisions in rural China. By contrast, children of dual-migrant parents often feel "abandoned"; this feeling can be further amplified if migrant parents do not manage to bring children to the host cities. Second, children—due to prolonged temporal and spatial separation from migrant parents—may develop a strong connection with the at-home parent and hence express reluctance to visit a migrant parent during summer breaks or other holidays. Finally, as mentioned previously, migrant parents' extremely limited living space may play a significant role in discouraging children from visiting. Compared with sole-migrant parents who often live in dormitories, most dual-migrant parents have their own small but relatively private space, providing children some stability in terms of living and interacting with parents.

The final significant factor associated with children's visits was a child's gender. Our regression model shows that migrant parents were more likely to bring boys rather than girls to host cities ($b = 0.43$, $p < 0.05$). While traditional social norms and values related to gender have been dramatically transformed in recent years, the effect of the long-established "son preference" remains in rural China, and parents prefer providing more opportunities for boys when resources are limited.

Visits of Migrant Parents to Children and Family Members

The final dimension of long-distance parenting includes the visits of migrant parents to children and family members at home, during which migrant parents provide on-site parenting along with copresent caretakers (such as the at-home parent, grandparents, or other caregivers in the household). Previous studies have concluded that such coparenting practices often entail some inherent risk, creating conflict with copresent caretakers regarding parenting philosophy and practices or tension with children due to changes in rules and expectations (Dittman, 2018). While these conflicts do occur from time to time, my interviews with migrant parents and grandparents indicate that they do not arise frequently; rather, migrant parents often feel at ease to leave parenting to at-home caretakers and to enjoy the short but valued union with family members and friends. When asked whether there was any conflict over shared parenting during these short stays, grandpa Miao said:

> No, not really. It's the same. We are the ones taking care of children. Her parents come back, back with those who migrated together. [Visiting] this family and that family, not at home from morning to night. Only a few days back home, and they have many coworkers. Those coworkers [living] in different places, visit your family once, visit his family once, each visit is for one day. Not at home, coming back very late at night.

Number of Years of Parents Working "Outside"

To understand the development of such child–parent interactions and other family dynamics, I investigate three dimensions of parental visits, including the length

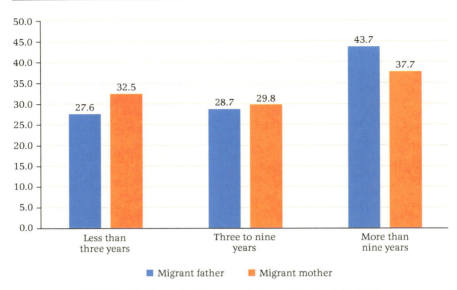

FIGURE 4.1 Time of migrant parents working "outside" (%).

of parental migration, the frequency of parental visits to children and family members, and visit duration. First, I asked children (to the best of their knowledge) how long their fathers and mothers had migrated and worked "outside." This question allowed me to estimate how much time children had spent with parents since birth. For fathers who were working "outside" at the time of the study, an astonishingly high percentage (43.7%) had worked "outside" for more than nine years (fig. 4.1). About a quarter of the fathers had been away for three to nine years (28.7%), and a similar number had worked outside for less than three years (27.6%). In total, about three-quarters of the fathers (72.4%) worked "outside" for at least three years. The data regarding maternal migration provide a similar story. A slightly lower percentage of the mothers, although still more than a third, had worked outside for more than nine years (37.7%). In addition, 29.8 percent of students reported that their mothers worked outside for three to nine years, and close to a third worked outside for less than three years (32.5%). That is, in total, more than two-thirds of the mothers (67.5%) worked outside for more than three years.

Although the survey data already demonstrate a long period of parent–child separation, this number appears to be an underestimation based on my in-depth interviews. While I did not specifically ask migrant parents how long they had worked "outside" in the interviews, migrant parents frequently disclosed that they had already worked outside before they were married or only stayed for one or two years at home after a child was born. Indeed, many parents migrated when they were fifteen to sixteen years old, right after graduating from middle school. These accounts are also supported by interviews with grandparents, who often became primary caretakers when grandchildren reached the age of one to two years old.

The following quotes derived from interviews with migrant parents and grandparents provide strong evidence for the prevalence of chronic parent–child separation:

> My older child, after she was born, I stayed [at home] for half a year. The little one, about one year.
>
> —migrant mother Xiaolu

> Almost everyone went out to work, children were left to elders at home when they reached one year old.
>
> —migrant mother Shu

> I went out to work when the child was a little bit more than two years old. Then it was the second child. I stayed a little bit longer for the second one, [waited until she was] about three to four years old.
>
> —migrant mother Chunyan

> The older one was one year and four-month-old [when his mother migrated], the younger one was ten and a half months old. . . . Before that, it was us too, along with their mother [to take care of the children]. Then their mother left, went out to *dagong*. One year and four-month-old, she went to Shenzhen to *dagong*. The younger one, he was one year old until October, [the mother] left in August. Not even one year old, could not even walk.
>
> —grandpa Xiao

> Three years old, less than three years old [when my daughter-in-law went out to *dagong*]. She went out when the child was one year old, was out for one year, and came back for one year, and then went out again. It has been a few years after that.
>
> —grandparent Chen

These interview data reveal that most parents migrated and worked "outside" before they were married, and the majority of them—primarily the mothers—returned and stayed for one or two years at home on the birth of a child. These findings align with my observation of the demographic composition of the villagers in the last decade. Indeed, during the time I visited (mostly in summer), I could barely find anyone younger than forty-five to fifty years old, except for a small number of parents who were obligated to stay behind due to poor health, a lack of intergenerational support for childcare, or filial obligation to providing eldercare for parents with severe health problems. These observations are also consistent with the national pattern, characterized by a dramatic increase in rural-to-urban migration, particularly in inland provinces such as Jiangxi province in the past two decades (Chan & Ren, 2018; Su et al., 2018). The minor inconsistency between the qualitative data and survey report is likely due to the intermittence of parental migration, as migrant parents sometimes return when they are unemployed, encounter family emergencies, or are in poor health.

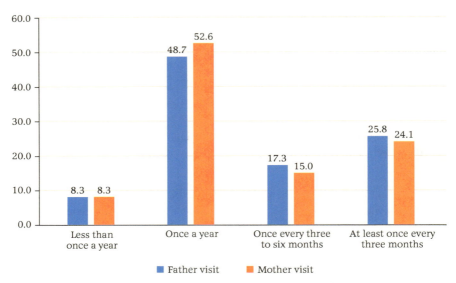

FIGURE 4.2 Time of migrant parents visiting children and family members (%).

Parental Visits to Left-Behind Children and Family

The second question asked how frequently migrant parents visited left-behind children and family members. The survey data indicate that parents, particularly those who migrated interprovincially, visited children and family members rather infrequently (fig. 4.2). For fathers who currently worked outside, a quarter of them (25.8%) visited family members at least once every three months, 17.3% once every three to six months, and almost half of them about once a year (48.7%), and 8.3 percent returned less than once a year. The frequency of maternal visits had a similar distribution. About a quarter of migrant mothers visited at least once every three months (24.1%), 15 percent visited at least once in half a year, slightly more than half paid visits each year (52.6%), and 8.3 percent visited less than once a year. In other words, parental visits were rather infrequent, with the mode of a father's or a mother's visits being once a year.

I used multivariate ordinal regression model to identify individual and familial factors associated with visits of migrant fathers and migrant mothers (table 4.2). The first salient factor was parental migration status. Compared with one-parent migration arrangement, parents of dual-migrant households visited children and family members less frequently, even when migration distance—approximately measured by using inter-province migration—was controlled in the model. Specifically, migrant fathers of dual-grandparent caring families visited children and family members marginally less compared with fathers from paternal migration families ($b = -0.55$, $p < 0.10$)—a finding that may indicate migrant fathers' trust in dual-grandparent caretaking. However, there was no significant difference in a migrant mother's visits to the family across different caretaking arrangements.

TABLE 4.2

Ordinal regression model predicting frequency of parental visits

	Father's visits (N = 236)			Mother's visits (N = 206)		
	B	SE	Significance level	B	SE	Significance level
Threshold						
Less than once a year	−4.84	1.01	***	−4.98	1.05	***
Once every half to one year	−1.51	0.95		−1.60	0.99	
Once every three to six months	−0.31	0.95		−0.78	0.99	
Two-grandparent caretaking[a]	−0.55	0.31	*	−0.38	0.37	
One-grandparent caretaking	−0.10	0.37		−0.45	0.43	
Male[b]	0.08	0.26		−0.07	0.29	
Age	−0.41	0.17	**	−0.51	0.18	***
Living in a school dorm[c]	−0.50	0.37		−0.65	0.44	
Parental education	0.06	0.11		−0.14	0.12	
Household property	−0.06	0.19		0.50	0.22	**
Perceived family economic status	0.08	0.21		−0.12	0.22	
Marital status of biological parents[d]	0.06	0.36		0.93	0.37	**
Number of siblings	−0.01	0.13		−0.24	0.16	
Inter-province migration	−0.90	0.16	***	−0.77	0.16	***
Pseudo R^2	0.23			0.26		

Note: *$p < 0.10$; **$p < 0.05$; ***$p < 0.01$; B = unstandardized regression coefficient; SE = standard error.

[a] Children of dual-migrant parents as the reference group.

[b] Female as the reference category.

[c] Living at home as the reference group.

[d] Divorced or separated as the reference group.

The second significant factor, unsurprisingly, was the spatial distance between the home village and the migration destination city. Since I didn't have a measure that accurately assessed the origin-destination distance, I used inter- versus intra-provincial migration to capture such a measure. This variable was classified into three categories: both parents migrated within the province, one parent migrated across the provincial boarder, and both parents migrated across the provincial boarder. The regression coefficient for either a father's visits ($b = -0.90$, $p < 0.01$) or a mother's visits was highly significant ($b = -0.77$, $p < 0.01$), with parents who migrated across the province visiting family members much less frequently. Specifically, the frequency of visits for within-province migrants ranged from once every two weeks to several times a year. For example, left-behind father Laojiu's wife—who worked as a nanny in Nanchang, the capital city of Jiangxi province—visited home two times a month and often took a leave to help with cooking during harvesting seasons. Migrant parent Pan, who worked in a neighboring city, visited during holidays and significant events such as National Day, Spring Festival, Tomb Sweeping Festival, and birthdays of family members. In sharp contrast, most migrant parents who crossed provincial boarders visited home only once or twice a year, and their visits occurred almost exclusively during China's traditional holiday, the Spring Festival. The following interview quotes, derived from reports of students and grandparents, provide evidence for these findings:

> (Parents visit) once each year, during Spring Festivals.
>
> —student Junhao

> Sometimes there was some business to handle, he would come back for a few days, and then left. But generally speaking, he came back during Spring Festivals and stayed for ten days to half a month.
>
> —student Jingwen

> Once a year. He came back during Spring Festivals for two weeks.
>
> —left-behind mother Dasheng

> (He) came back during the Spring Festival, only during the Spring Festival.
>
> —grandpa Jingpin

> (He) only came back during Spring Festivals. Sometimes children would go there (during summer breaks). One time I escorted them there, their grandma did it once too. My son came back once when his grandma passed away, other times were all during Spring Festivals.
>
> —grandpa Yubao

The third primary factor contributing to the low frequency of parental visits is the marginal socioeconomic status of migrant parents—who are often employed in lowly paid manufacturing or service industries that demand long working hours and rigid working schedules and provide little if any medical, retirement, or other benefits. Indeed, it is common practice for migrant workers to work on weekends or take night shifts when companies receive large orders, and a substantial percentage, as much as 50 percent or more of their salaries, is from working overtime. Visits to children and family members, hence, entail a heavy financial burden for migrant parents due to the resultant loss of salary and potential fines imposed by employers. As such, family socioeconomic status is a significant predictor of the frequency of parental visits, as evidenced in the significant and positive association between the amount of household property and the frequency of maternal visits in the regression analysis ($b = 0.50$, $p < 0.05$). Migrant mother Xue Gang, who migrated from Guizhou province—a southwestern province about twenty-four hours away from the host city Shenzhen—described the dilemma:

> I want to go home often, but financially . . . (laughing). It's not convenient. Definitely want to visit, [but] if you return, the salary for this month will be gone. When you are back you still need to pay rent, and living costs, and now you don't have money. Definitely want to visit. . . . Just think, if you took a ten-day break, then you could not even get the full basic salary, [you can] only make a little bit more than one thousand yuan. It's not even enough for rent and living costs, and you need to borrow money. . . . I visit them every year, every year during the Spring Festival. I have been here for three years; I go back every year. Not at other times, do not go home during other times.

The fourth significant factor associated with parental visits was the age of children. Although the student sample was composed of seventh and eighth graders and thus had a small variation of age, the regression models still revealed that age had a statistically significant effect, with migrant fathers ($b = -0.41$, $p < 0.05$) and mothers ($b = -0.51$, $p < 0.05$) more likely to visit home when their children were younger. The age effect could be more salient when children are in their early childhood, during which children are physically and emotionally more dependent on their parents.

Finally, as noted previously, the marital status of biological parents was a statistically significant factor for maternal visits. Children raised by both biological parents reported that their migrant mothers visited home more frequently ($b = 0.93$, $p < 0.05$). This can be a serious issue as the divorce rate has increased dramatically in rural China in the past several decades (M. Chen et al., 2021; W. Li, 2018) due to social changes such as the rural-to-urban migration, greater autonomy for women, and reduced social stigma. Parental divorce is documented to negatively influence children's emotional and psychological development (C. Zhang, 2020). This effect can be exacerbated for children with migrant parents, when an already limited parent–child interaction time is further reduced or abruptly halted due to custody arrangements. For example, during my interviews in Peace County, I heard several stories recounting how grandparents or parents shielded children under their custody from interacting with the other biological parent, thus creating additional communication barriers between children and parents.

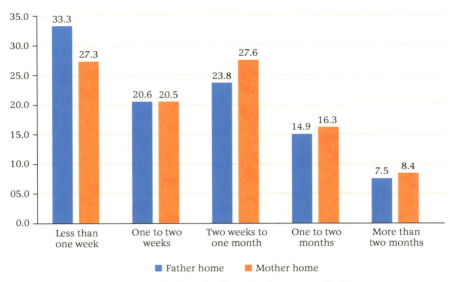

FIGURE 4.3 The length of stay during parental visits.

The Length of Stay during Parental Visits

Finally, I asked children, on average, how long parents stayed at home when they visited (fig. 4.3). For migrant fathers, a third stayed for less than a week (33.3%), one out of five (20.6%) stayed for one to two weeks, slightly less than a quarter (23.8%) for two weeks to one month, 14.9 percent for one to two months, and 7.5 percent for two months and more. The average time of staying was slightly longer for migrant mothers. Specifically, the percentage staying at home for less than a week was substantially lower for migrant mothers compared with migrant fathers (27.3% versus 33.3%). In comparison, the percentage of migrant mothers staying at home for two weeks or more was higher. In summary, the majority of visiting fathers (53.9%) and about half of migrant mothers (47.8%) stayed at home for less than two weeks.

We used ordinal regression models to analyze the associations between the duration of visits and the individual and household characteristics (table 4.3). Interprovince migration was a consistent and significant factor for both migrant fathers and migrant mothers, with inter-province migration predicting a longer stay than those migrating within-province (b = 0.51, p < 0.01 for fathers and b = 0.52, p < 0.01 for mothers, respectively). In other words, migrant parents who crossed provincial borders compensated for less frequent visits with slightly longer stays at home—which almost exclusively occurred during Spring Festivals. A small number of individual- and family-level variables were also marginally significant. The amount of household property, an indicator of household socioeconomic status, was positively associated with a longer stay for both migrant fathers and mothers, although the regression coefficient was only marginally significant

TABLE 4.3

Ordinal regression model predicting the duration of parental visits to children and family

	Father's visits (N = 237)			Mother's visits (N = 204)		
	B	SE	Significance level	B	SE	Significance level
Threshold						
Less than one week	1.53	0.90	*	0.44	0.90	
One to two weeks	2.56	0.91	***	1.56	0.91	*
Half a month to one month	3.77	0.93	***	2.82	0.92	***
One to two months	5.32	0.97	***	4.50	0.97	***
Two-grandparent caretaking[a]	0.18	0.29		−0.62	0.33	*
One-grandparent caretaking	0.49	0.35		−0.14	0.39	
Male[b]	−0.11	0.24		−0.38	0.26	
Age	0.09	0.15		0.26	0.16	*
Living in a school dorm[c]	0.13	0.35		−0.35	0.40	
Parental education	0.06	0.10		−0.06	0.11	
Household property	0.33	0.18	*	0.14	0.20	
Perceived family economic status	0.22	0.19		0.25	0.21	
Marital status of biological parents[d]	0.13	0.34		0.14	0.34	
Number of siblings	0.08	0.12		0.11	0.14	
Inter-province migration	0.51	0.14	***	0.52	0.14	***
Pseudo R^2	0.11			0.13		

Note: *$p < 0.10$; **$p < 0.05$; ***$p < 0.01$; B = unstandardized regression coefficient; SE = standard error.

[a] Children of dual-migrant parents as the reference group.

[b] Female as the reference category.

[c] Living at home as the reference group.

[d] Divorced or separated as the reference group.

for migrant fathers ($b = 0.33$, $p < 0.10$). Finally, migrant mothers stayed at home longer when children were older ($b = 0.26$, $p < 0.10$), and migrant mothers of dual-grandparent caretaking families spent less time at home compared with those of maternal migration households ($b = -0.62$, $p < 0.10$).

Conclusion

In this chapter, I investigated various parenting practices employed by migrant parents, focusing on long-distance or mobile parenting, children's visits to host cities during summer or other holidays, and the visits of migrant parents to family members. Migrant parents, despite a myriad of structural and situational barriers, strive to perform conventional parental duties from afar to create intimacies ostensibly inherent in nuclear families. While these endeavors are commendable and have shown some promise; they are frequently undermined by barriers at the structural, familial, and individual levels—particularly disadvantaged socioeconomic status, chronic spatial and temporal separation, and distance between the migrating parent(s)' rural village and migration destination.

Similar to their transnational counterparts documented in global migration literature (Madianou & Miller, 2011; Oliveira, 2018; Parreñas, 2005a), China's rural-to-urban migrants have increasingly adopted long-distance or mobile parenting due to the recent development of ICTs, the widespread use of smartphones, and the presence of structural barriers preventing permanent family settlement in host cities. While mobile parenting is strongly endorsed by networking companies and local governments, its effects appear to be severely limited. The frequency of such a communication is relatively low, largely due to migrant parents' busy and irregular working schedule (e.g., long working hours and working on weekends), children's conflicting daily schedules, and time zone differences. Specifically, most migrant parents communicate with family members and children through audio or video calls about one or two times a week, which gives parents a window into the daily routines of children but little into children's struggles in other areas. As such, these conversations—often initiated and preferred by migrant parents rather than children—are mainly superficial or routine, centering around topics such as children's academic performance and the physical health of children and caretakers. Nevertheless, migrant parents and grandparent caretakers see a glimpse of hope, as new technologies such as video chats potentially create a sense of physical presence, thus reducing the geographical and psychological distance between migrant parents and children left behind. Whether this glimpse of hope will materialize, however, must be further investigated by data collected from multiple sites and using different methods.

A somewhat surprising finding—which was rarely studied by past research—is that migrant parents perform "responsible parenting" by frequently bringing children to host cities. Many left-behind children, particularly those of dual-migrant parents, visit their parents around once a year and spend at least one month with their parents. This extended period provides a rare opportunity for parents and children to interact with each other and to develop familiarity, bonding, and emotional intimacy. While often embraced by migrant parents and children, these visits can sometimes become compulsory, leading to reluctance from both parents and children. In particular, limited living space, poor living conditions, and a lack of parental care during working days undermine parents' endeavors to develop durable parent–child bonding during these visits. Nevertheless, these findings have important policy and program implications. The few programs targeting left-behind children in China almost exclusively focus on children living in rural areas, who often live remotely and scattered and are difficult for social workers and program volunteers to reach. An innovative strategy is to develop programs for children visiting migrant parents in summer breaks, with the following targets: (1) providing immediate assistance such as housing assistance, city tours, and caretaking and (2) offering parenting courses and psychological counseling to bridge the communication gap and increase bonding between parents and children.

Another important dimension of long-distance parenting is parental visits to family, which exhibit some unique characteristics: (1) chronic separation from children, with many parents (particularly the younger cohorts) spending time with children for only one or two years in total; (2) low frequency of visits, with most parents, particularly interprovincial migrant parents, visiting on average once a year; and (3) short duration of visits, with many parents only being able to afford to return for less than two weeks for each visit. In addition, since most parents can only visit once a year, they almost exclusively return during China's traditional holiday, the Spring Festival. Combined, these unique characteristics establish parameters for how migrant parents perform parenting during these short visits. Specifically, most parents are reluctant to exercise normative authoritarian parenting practices during these visits to avoid or reduce conflict with children and primary caretakers. This laidback approach, on the other hand, may be interpreted by children as a lack of parental involvement, reinforcing the perception of being "abandoned" by migrant parents for economic gains.

In summary, this chapter establishes that migrant parents, despite the presence of numerous barriers, manage to perform parenting duties utilizing a variety of methods including long-distance parenting, children's visits, and parental visits. Whether and to what extent these practices—individually or in tandem with at-home parenting/caretaking—influence children's behavioral and psychological growth is rarely investigated. I address these significant research gaps in the next three chapters. Specifically, I examine how remote parenting—together with at-home caretaking—influences children's educational performance (chapter 5), problematic behaviors (chapter 6), and psychological well-being such as emotional problems and ambivalent feelings toward migrant parents and caregivers (chapter 7).

5

"Have You Finished Your Homework?"

Parental Migration, Caretaking Practices, and Children's Schooling

> [When] grandparents are raising children, it is totally up to the children themselves. Yeye and Nainai cannot help. How can Yeye and Nainai help? Nowadays those in the village, they [grandparents] do not even know how to write their names. Most of them don't know how to write their names. How can they help? What can they do to help?
>
> —grandpa Xiao

Academic performance and intergenerational mobility due to schooling occupy one of the most important positions in both the minds of parents and children in rural China (Y. Chen et al., 2021; Huang et al., 2023a). When asked about motivations of migration, the cost of education is frequently cited by rural parents (S. Hu, 2019; Ye & Murray, 2005). Since 2006, tuition for Chinese students attending public elementary and junior high schools (i.e., first to ninth grades) has been free; however, the expenses of attending senior high schools are prohibitively high and account for approximately a quarter of an average rural Chinese person's annual net income (S. Hu, 2019). The costs of attending private schools—which have become increasingly popular in China—are even greater. Indeed, migrant workers have reported that remittance is regularly used to support children's education, ranking second only to daily financial expenses (F. Hu, 2012; S. Hu, 2019).

Parental migration typically improves a household's financial status and increases investment in children's education (Bai et al., 2018; Lee, 2011); unfortunately, these benefits can also be counteracted by numerous other negative social factors (e.g., weakened parental involvement in children's studies) post-migration. Particularly, parental migration—as grandpa Xiao explained earlier—often predisposes left-behind children to care by grandparents, who are often illiterate or inadequately educated and cannot provide much if any support for children's schooling. Indeed, one of the major concerns of migrant parents is that grandparents are incapable of supervising or tutoring children's study, leading to poor academic performance and negating one of the primary motivators of parental migration.

In this chapter, I investigate the associations between parental migration/caretaking arrangements and children's schooling, focusing on two areas: students' academic performance and school bonding. I employ the student survey data to elucidate the social mechanisms that shape the ways in which caretaking arrangements impact both educational outcomes directly, and indirectly through intervening caretaking practices (e.g., at-home caretaking and long-distance parenting). Moreover, I take advantage of the qualitative data and investigate the prevalent sentiments regarding the deleterious effects of grandparenting on children's education, exploring whether these sentiments are valid and how they can be adequately addressed. Guided by the theoretical model in chapter 1 (fig. 1.1) and the body of literature regarding parental migration and children's educational outcomes, I first present a theoretical model delineating how parental migration influences children's education directly and indirectly through the quality of caretaking practices. Next, I utilize student survey data to empirically test this theoretical model, focusing on caretaking at home and the two school outcome variables—academic performance and school bonding. For each of the outcome variables, I investigate the hypothesized associations using bivariate and multivariate analyses and test whether the hypothesized associations are mediated by the quality of caretaking practices at home. In the next section, I use qualitative and field observation data to complement the quantitative findings in the previous section, focusing on the prevalent sentiments regarding grandparenting and its deleterious effects on children's educational achievement. Finally, I explore whether and to what extent characteristics of long-distance parenting—parent–child communication, the inculcation of the importance of education, and children's visits to parents' host cities—are related to school involvement.

Parental Migration and Children's Schooling: The Theoretical Model

While many studies have investigated the association between parental migration and children's schooling, this relationship remains theoretically and empirically ambiguous. Theoretically, there is no clear linkage between parental migration and children's school success. On one hand, parental migration potentially improves household financial status and increases the consumption capacity of families in rural China, including increased investment in children's education. On the other hand, parental migration decreases parental involvement in children's education and other types of parental care (e.g., parental monitoring and discipline), negatively influencing children's academic performance and other developmental outcomes. For example, children may feel neglected or "abandoned" by their migrant parents, which may lead to anxiety, depression, and withdrawal symptoms (Z. Liu et al., 2009)—factors negatively associated with children's school success. Echoing the theoretical ambiguity, empirical studies provide, to a large extent, mixed findings. While some studies have found positive effects of parental migration on children's education (Bai et al., 2018; Lu, 2012), others have reported null or even negative results (Bai et al., 2020; Y. Dong et al., 2021; S. Hu, 2019; W. Liang et al., 2008; Meng & Yamauchi, 2017; Meyerhoefer & Chen, 2011; W. Shen et al., 2021; S. X. Wang, 2014). Shen, Hu, and Hannum (2021), for example, found that although paternal migration increased family economic capital, it had an overall negative effect on children's education. Similarly, Dong and colleagues (2021) found that the cumulative number of years of parental migration had no significant effect on children's educational performance.

One noticeable finding in this stream of literature is that not only does whether parents migrate matter but who migrates matters (X. Chen et al., 2019; B. Y. Hu et al., 2020; W. Liang et al., 2008; Lu, 2012; M. Zhou et al., 2014). In particular, these studies consistently demonstrate that maternal migration leads to more negative developmental outcomes among children left behind when compared to paternal migration. X. Chen and colleagues (2019) found that maternal migration in rural China decreased left-behind children's academic performance, while paternal migration was positively associated with children's school success. In a similar vein, W. Liang and colleagues (2008) reported that academic outcomes of left-behind children were particularly worrisome when the mother migrated—whether alone or with her husband. A small number of studies also suggest that when both parents migrate, who the caretakers are (e.g., grandparents or aunts/uncles) plays a dominant role in children's development (X. Chen et al., 2019; X. Chen & Jiang, 2019).

Another important finding illuminated in this research is that the effect of parental migration on children's school success is moderated by children's gender, with girls more likely to receive the benefit than boys (B. Y. Hu et al., 2020; W. Liang et al., 2008; Lu, 2012; Meng & Yamauchi, 2017; W. Shen et al., 2021; M. Zhou et al., 2014). Even when a negative association was found (W. Shen et al., 2021), this negative influence was stronger for boys than for girls. For example, using longitudinal data from the China Health and Nutrition Survey, Lu (2012) found that the positive effect of parental migration on education was significantly greater for girls than for boys; additionally, these same findings are largely replicated in research conducted in other migrant-sending developing countries such as Mexico (Antman, 2012) and those in Southeast Asia (Parreñas, 2005a). A viable explanation is that when a family's financial status improves, more resources are invested in girls to alleviate the persistent male–female gap in basic schooling, thus increasing the marginal benefit of educational investment (Antman, 2012; Lu, 2012). However, there are exceptions in this literature. Using the longitudinal Gansu Survey of Children and Families, F. Hu (2013) found that the absence of parents had a larger negative effect on girls' educational performance when compared with boys'.

While this body of literature is generally informative, it has some serious limitations. For example, many studies employ a dichotomized measure of parental migration and fail to address heterogeneity in types of parental migration and caretaking arrangements. In addition, this line of research neglects to acknowledge that caretaking arrangements may differ considerably among children of dual-migrant parents, which influences children's educational trajectories and other developmental outcomes. Although more than half of the left-behind children are primarily cared for by grandparents (ACWF, 2013), research exploring the heterogeneity of grandparenting arrangements—and the resulting empirical implications of these arrangements—is extremely limited. Additionally, few studies have investigated the critical role of caretaking practices, which not only directly influence children's developmental trajectories but also potentially mediate the effects of parental migration and caretaking arrangements on the strength and directions of these trajectories.

I address these issues in this chapter. Guided by the theoretical model presented in chapter 1 (fig. 1.1), I hypothesize that the characteristics of children (age, gender, living on campus), parents (parental education, marital status of biological parents), and the household (family socioeconomic status) are associated with parental decision-making regarding migration and caretaking arrangements. Caretaking arrangements, in turn, impact the quality of caretaking practices at home and long-distance parenting. Finally, the quality of caretaking practices and remote parenting predicts outcomes related to children's schooling, including academic performance and school bonding. In other words, the theoretical model highlights the key mediating role of the quality of caretaking practices and how types of parental migration and caretaking arrangements influence children's schooling both directly and indirectly through the quality of caretaking. While this theoretical model is primarily tested by using student survey data, I complement the quantitative findings with qualitative data and field observations.

Parental Migration/Caretaking Arrangements and Children's School Involvement: Quantitative Analyses

In this section, I employed a three-step procedure to empirically investigate the hypothesized associations presented in the theoretical model utilizing the student survey data. First, I conducted descriptive analyses to explore whether children's schooling differed across types of caretaking arrangement. In the second step, I tested whether the relationships found in descriptive analyses was robust in multivariate regression models when demographic and family background factors were controlled. The third step tested whether caretaking practices of children—supervision and monitoring, caretaker–child bonding, and hostility toward children—mediated the associations between caretaking arrangements and schooling. For this purpose, I conducted stepwise regression analyses to assess whether the associations between caretaking arrangements and school outcome variables observed in baseline models changed significantly in full models with hypothesized mediator variables included (Baron & Kenny, 1986). Finally,

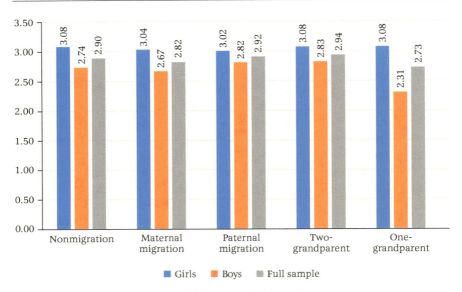

FIGURE 5.1 Children's academic performance.

because children's gender is a salient factor that shapes children's own behavior as well as caretaking arrangements and practices, I conducted gendered subgroup analyses in each of the three steps.

Academic Performance

The first dimension of children's schooling includes their self-reports of academic performance. In the questionnaire, students were asked for their grades in each of three core subjects—English, math, and Chinese—ranked within their classes the prior semester. The response categories were "the upper level = 5," "middle-upper = 4," "middle = 3," "middle-low = 2," and "low = 1." I computed the average of the rankings within the three subjects to capture students' academic performance.

DESCRIPTIVE ANALYSIS. Figure 5.1 depicts the distribution of students' ranking of their academic performance across caretaking arrangements in the full sample and within each gender group. On average, these seventh and eighth graders reported that their academic performance was around the median level (mean = 2.89). Interestingly, children of paternal migration (mean = 2.96) and children of two-grandparent caretakers reported the highest grades (mean = 2.94) and children of nonmigrant parents were in the middle (mean = 2.89), while those of maternal migrants (mean = 2.80) and those cared for by one-grandparent caretakers ranked the lowest (mean = 2.73).

As discussed previously, gender has been found to moderate the association between parental migration and respondents' academic performance (B. Y. Hu et al., 2020; W. Liang et al., 2008; Lu, 2012; W. Shen et al., 2021; M. Zhou et al., 2014).

To investigate this gender effect, I calculated the average school performance across living arrangements by gender. As expected, boys (mean = 2.73) reported a significantly lower level of school performance than girls (mean = 3.07). Moreover, patterns regarding the associations between parental migration/caretaking arrangements and school performance differed distinctively across genders. Among girls, those living with nonmigrant parents and those cared for by one- or two-grandparent caretakers reported the highest levels of school performance (mean = 3.08); conversely, those living with one-parent caretakers reported noticeably lower grades (mean = 3.04 for maternal migration and mean = 3.02 for paternal migration, respectively). In sharp contrast, among boys, those cared for by a left-behind mother (i.e., paternal migration, mean = 2.82) and those cared for by two-grandparent caretakers (i.e., dual-parent migration) reported the best school performance (mean = 2.83), those living with nonmigrant parents fell within the middle (mean = 2.74), and boys living with a left-behind father (i.e., maternal migration, mean = 2.67) and those cared for by one-grandparent caretakers (mean = 2.31) reported the lowest scores. In other words, girls did better in school when both parents migrated and they were cared for by one or both grandparents, and boys fared better when they were cared for by two-grandparent caretakers or when they lived with a left-behind mother.

MULTIVARIATE REGRESSION MODELS. I then investigated whether these patterns remained robust and what underlying social mechanisms explained such patterns in multivariate regression. In model 1, I conducted multivariate regression analysis, with perceived academic performance as the dependent variable, caretaking arrangements as the key independent variable, and child and parental/household characteristics as controls. In model 2, I added caretaking practices as mediators and investigated whether the inclusion of these variables changed the regression coefficients of caretaking arrangements, using children living with nonmigrant parents as the reference group. I ran these models for the full sample and across the gender groups.

Model 1 (table 5.1) indicates that the bivariate association remained robust when a series of demographic and family background variables were controlled. Specifically, children of paternal migration (b = 0.04) and children cared for by two-grandparent caretakers (b = 0.02) reported the highest level of academic performance, and those of maternal migration (b = −0.06) and those cared for by one-grandparent caretakers scored the lowest (b = −0.12). Moreover, these associations changed noticeably when caretaking practices—the hypothesized mediators—were included in the model (model 2, table 5.1). As seen in model 2, caretaker monitoring and supervision had a strong and positive effect on children's academic performance (b = 0.25, p < 0.01). In addition, I observed that the regression coefficient of one-grandparent caretaking reduced from −0.12 in model 1 to −0.02 in model 2, representing an 83 percent decrease. Moreover, the sign of the regression coefficient of maternal migration changed from negative in model 1 (b = −0.06) to

TABLE 5.1

Multivariate regression models predicting children's academic performance (unstandardized regression coefficients)

	Total (n = 1177)		Male (n = 616)		Female (n = 523)	
	Model 1	Model 2	Model 1	Model 2	Model 1	Model 2
Intercept	2.62	1.51	2.34	1.34	2.48	1.21
Two-grandparent caretaking[a]	0.02	0.04	0.06	0.05	−0.02	0.03
One-grandparent caretaking	−0.12	−0.02	−0.28*	−0.12	0.02	0.08
Maternal migration	−0.06	0.01	−0.13	−0.07	0.05	0.18
Paternal migration	0.04	0.06	0.06	0.07	−0.06	−0.02
Caretaker monitoring/supervision		0.25**		0.22**		0.31**
Caretaker hostility		−0.01		0.03		−0.02
Caretaker–child bonding		0.06		0.04		0.07
Age	−0.23**	−0.17**	−0.25**	−0.20**	−0.18**	−0.12
Male[b]	−0.27**	−0.18**				
Living in a school dorm[c]	0.09	0.08	0.15	0.13	0.05	0.03
Parental education	0.12**	0.09**	0.12**	0.10**	0.12**	0.09**
Household property	0.00	−0.02	0.02	0.00	0.01	−0.02
Perceived family economic status	0.15**	0.14**	0.17*	0.16**	0.13	0.09
Marital status of biological parents[d]	0.09	0.08	0.04	0.04	0.13	0.13
Number of siblings	0.08*	0.07*	0.06	0.05	0.09*	0.07
R^2	0.12	0.20	0.11	0.17	0.07	0.20

Note: *$p < 0.05$; **$p < 0.01$.

[a] Children of nonmigrant parents as the reference group.

[b] Female as the reference category.

[c] Living at home as the reference group.

[d] Divorced or separated as the reference group.

positive in model 2 ($b = 0.01$). Although these regression coefficients were not statistically significant, such a dramatic change—coupled with the significant effect of caretaker monitoring and supervision—suggests that strict caretaker monitoring and supervision may explain some of the effects of caretaking arrangements on children's academic success (Baron & Kenny, 1986).

Among control variables, children's age and gender were significant correlates. Older children were more likely to report a lower level of academic performance, suggesting that compared with seventh graders, eighth graders—with only one year left until the critical high school entrance exam—were more likely to negatively evaluate their academic performance. Consistent with prior research (Marc Jackman & Morrain-Webb, 2019), girls reported a higher level of school performance than boys did. With regard to parent and family background variables, two of the three family socioeconomic variables, parental education and perceived family economic status, were consistently and positively associated with children's academic success. Interestingly, the number of siblings was significantly and positively associated with academic success, with children with more siblings reporting a higher level of academic success.

GENDERED ANALYSIS: DOES CHILDREN'S GENDER MAKE A DIFFERENCE? Given the potential of a child's gender in altering the relationship between caretaking arrangements, caretaking practices, and children's academic success, I ran the regression models for each gender group separately. These findings add further insight to the influence of caretaking practices on children's academic performance as well as the "effect pathways" (W. Shen et al., 2021) underlying such associations.

Table 5.1 presents the quantitative findings for the full sample and by gender. The results indicate that boys cared for by one-grandparent caretakers had significantly lower level of academic success ($b = -0.28$, $p < 0.05$) compared with boys living with nonmigrant parents (model 1). This association, however, decreased to nonsignificance ($b = -0.12$, $p > 0.05$) in model 2, when the three measures of caretaking practices were introduced into the regression model. Coupled with the highly significant regression coefficient of caretaker monitoring and supervision ($b = 0.22$, $p < 0.01$), these findings suggest that, among boys, the association between caretaking arrangements and academic success is at least partially explained by the quality of caretaking practices. Similarly, I found that for girls, the associations between caretaking arrangements and children's academic success changed noticeably from model 1 to model 2. For example, the effect of one-grandparent caretaking increased from $b = 0.02$ to $b = 0.08$, and the effect of maternal migration increased from $b = 0.05$ to $b = 0.18$, revealing that the positive effects of parental migration on children's school performance were substantially stronger when the quality of caretaking practices were controlled.

In summary, the quantitative findings indicated that overall, compared to children living with nonmigrant parents, those with migrating mothers and those cared for by one-grandparent caretakers exhibited significantly lower levels of academic success. The effects of other caretaking arrangements (i.e., paternal migration and two-grandparent caretaking), by contrast, did not differ from those of living with nonmigrant parents. Moreover, the significant effects of caretaking arrangements were largely indirect through varying levels of monitoring and supervision of children. Finally, children's gender played a critical role in determining the strength of the associations between caretaking arrangement and academic performance. In particular, boys cared for by a single grandparent experienced a significantly lower level of monitoring and supervision, decreasing their school success. By comparison, maternal migration appeared to indirectly place girls into a more disadvantaged position, as left-behind fathers had a lower level of monitoring and supervision of their daughters, resulting in poor school performance.

School Bonding

In this section, I investigated the second measure of schooling: children's bonding with their school, peer students, and teachers—factors that are strongly associated with students' academic success and other prosocial development (Bryan et al., 2012; X. Chen, 2009). The scale of school bonding consisted of seven items: (1) I like school very much because I have more opportunities to learn many interesting things; (2) It's important for me to have good grades; (3) I feel safe in school; (4) I always finish my homework on time; (5) Education is very important because knowledge is very important to me; (6) School education can change my life; and (7) Compared with life outside, studying in school is a waste of time. The response category for each item ranged from 1 (do not agree at all) to 5 (completely agree). Before the computation of the final scale, I reversed the coding for item 7 so the direction of its coding aligned with the other six items. The final scale, *school bonding*, was computed by averaging the seven items (α = 0.78).

DESCRIPTIVE ANALYSIS. I first conducted descriptive analysis to explore variations in school bonding of children across various caretaking arrangements. Overall, children reported a relatively strong bonding with peer students and schools (mean = 3.92). As figure 5.2 illustrates, there were noticeable differences in children's self-reporting of school bonding across caretaking arrangements. Children living with nonmigrant parents (mean = 3.94) and those cared for by two-grandparent caretakers (mean = 3.94) reported the highest level of school bonding, followed by children of paternal migration (mean = 3.92). Meanwhile, children of maternal migration (mean = 3.86) and children cared for by one-grandparent caretakers reported the lowest scores (mean = 3.84). Although these findings are slightly different from the results regarding children's academic performance in the previous section, it is important to note that the same two groups, children of maternal migration and children cared for by one-grandparent caretakers remain the most disadvantaged groups.

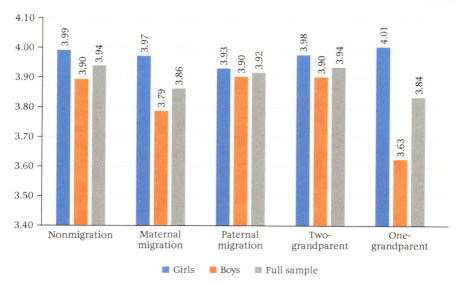

FIGURE 5.2 Children's level of school bonding.

As in the last section, I analyzed whether the relation between caretaking arrangements and school bonding was different across gender groups. Similar to findings in the previous section, boys reported a significantly lower level of bonding with school (mean = 3.87) than girls (mean = 3.98). The associations between caretaking arrangements and school bonding were also different across gender groups (fig. 5.2). Boys of maternal migration (mean = 3.79) and those cared for by one-grandparent caretakers (mean = 3.63) reported the lowest levels of bonding with schools, with the other three groups reporting similar levels of school bonding. By contrast, girls of paternal migration reported the lowest level of school bonding (mean =3.93), with the other four groups reporting similar scores. It should also be noted that the gendered patterns of school bonding are almost identical as those of academic performance previously discussed, suggesting that the gendered associations between children's schooling and caretaking arrangements are robust across different measures of schooling.

MULTIVARIATE REGRESSION MODELS. I conducted multivariate regression analyses (table 5.2) to investigate the associations between caretaking arrangements and school bonding. As in the last section, I used model 1 as the baseline model and model 2 as the full model. The regression models suggest that caretaking practices, measured by caretaker monitoring/supervision, caretaker hostility and conflict, and caretaker–child bonding, potentially mediated the effects of caretaking arrangements. The magnitude of the association between two-grandparenting and school bonding, for example, decreased from $b = -0.08$ in model 1 to $b = -0.01$ in model 2, and the effect of maternal migration decreased from $b = -0.06$ (model 1)

TABLE 5.2

Multivariate regression models predicting children's school bonding (unstandardized regression coefficients)

	Total (n = 1177)		Male (n = 616)		Female (n = 523)	
	Model 1	Model 2	Model 1	Model 2	Model 1	Model 2
Intercept	3.87**	3.25**	3.80**	3.17**	3.85**	3.41**
Two-grandparent caretaking[a]	0.01	−0.01	0.01	−0.02	0.01	0.02
One-grandparent caretaking	−0.08	−0.01	−0.23*	−0.11	0.06	0.09
Maternal migration	−0.06	−0.01	−0.13	−0.10	0.07	0.15
Paternal migration	−0.05	−0.02	0.01	0.01	−0.03	0.03
Caretaker monitoring/ supervision		0.19**		0.18**		0.18**
Caretaker hostility		−0.13**		−0.11**		−0.16**
Caretaker–child bonding		0.08**		0.09**		0.08**
Age	−0.10**	−0.04	−0.06	0.00	−0.16**	−0.10**
Male[b]	−0.09*	−0.01				
Living in a school dorm[c]	0.08	0.07	0.19*	0.18*	−0.09	−0.10
Parental education	0.02	0.00	0.02	0.01	0.02	0.00
Household property	0.00	−0.01	0.01	−0.01	0.00	−0.01
Perceived family economic status	0.08*	0.05	0.05	0.04	0.11*	0.06
Marital status of biological parents[d]	0.07	0.03	−0.02	−0.03	0.19	0.13
Number of siblings	0.02	0.01	−0.01	0.00	0.03	0.01
R^2	0.04	0.21	0.02	0.17	0.07	0.27

Note: *p < 0.05; **p < 0.01.

[a] Children of nonmigrant parents as the reference group.

[b] Female as the reference category.

[c] Living at home as the reference group.

[d] Divorced or separated as the reference group.

to $b = -0.01$ (model 2). Such a drastic change in the magnitude of the regression coefficients suggests that the three measures of caretaking practices—all of which were statistically significant in model 2—potentially mediated the effects of caretaking arrangements on children's bonding with schools and classmates.

GENDERED ANALYSES: DOES CHILDREN'S GENDER MAKE A DIFFERENCE? Whether gender moderated the association between caretaking arrangements and children's school bonding was investigated by using subgroup analyses in multivariate regression models. Table 5.2 (model 1) shows that for the male subsample, one-grandparent caretaking was negatively and significantly associated with boys' school bonding ($b = -0.23$, $p < 0.05$). Maternal migration was also negatively associated with children's school bonding, but this association was not statistically significant ($b = -0.13$, $p > 0.05$). The other two types of caretaking arrangement—two-grandparent caretaking ($b = 0.01$, $p > 0.05$) and paternal migration ($b = 0.01$, $p > 0.05$)—did not exhibit significant differences in levels of school bonding compared with the reference group. When caretaking practices were introduced into the model (model 2), the effect of one-grandparent caretaking decreased noticeably, from $b = -0.23$ ($p < 0.05$) to nonsignificance ($b = -0.11$, $p > 0.05$), suggesting that the quality of caretaking practices potentially mediated the relationship between caretaking arrangement and children's school bonding.

The mediating effects of caretaking practices appeared to be less prominent for girls (table 5.2, female subsample). A comparison of the regression coefficients between model 1 and model 2 indicates that the effects of each type of alternative caretaking increased and became positive, suggesting that parental migration universally increased girls' bonding with schools when caretaking practices were controlled. Importantly, as shown in previous analyses, all three mediators—caretaking monitoring and supervision ($b = 0.18$, $p < 0.05$), caretaker hostility ($b = -0.16$, $p < 0.05$), and caretaker-child bonding ($b = 0.08$, $p < 0.05$)—were statistically significant in the posited directions. Coupled with the finding that regression coefficients of caretaking arrangements changed substantially from model 1 to model 2, these results suggested that like the male subgroup, caretaking practices potentially mediated the relationship between caretaking arrangement and school bonding for the female subgroup.

Alternative Caretaking and Children's Education: Analyses of Qualitative Data

Grandparenting and Schooling: We Can Only Ask, "Have You Finished Your Homework?"

The quantitative data provide remarkably consistent findings across varying measures of educational outcome, suggesting that children of maternal migration and one-grandparent caretaking achieved the lowest academic performance and exhibited the most tenuous bonding with peers and schools. Interestingly, these results are not fully supported by the qualitative data. In particular, the finding that those cared for by two-grandparent caretakers reported a similar level of school performance as those of nonmigrant parents is not supported. In fact, nearly every interviewee in the qualitative data—including migrant parents, grandparent caretakers, and children left behind—claimed that grandparenting in rural China would inevitably lead to poorer academic performance for children left behind. Grandparents, while expressing pride for their enormous contribution to childrearing and personal sacrifices for their multilocal families, also unreservedly admitted that their own disadvantaged education backgrounds hindered their ability to effectively monitor and supervise children's schoolwork, thus potentially offsetting the material benefits of parental migration. When discussing the likely undesirable effects of grandparenting on children's schooling, grandpa Xiao commented:

> [When] grandparents are raising children, it is totally up to the children themselves. Yeye and Nainai cannot help. How can Yeye and Nainai help? Nowadays those in the village, they (grandparents) do not even know how to write their names. Most of them don't know how to write their names. How can they help? What can they do to help?

Grandpa Xiao's observation is supported by previous research, which reveals that the majority (about 80%) of grandparent caretakers do not have formal education beyond elementary schools, with a small percentage being illiterate (Pan et al., 2013). Indeed, many grandparents concurred with grandpa Xiao regarding their lack of education and inability to assist with children's schoolwork. Grandma Zhang, who was living with her grandson Chuanqi (a seventh grader), said that she "did not recognize even one word, and his grandpa was illiterate too." When I asked Chuanqi where he could get tutoring, he said nobody at home could help, and he had to depend on himself most of the time. Sometimes he asked people living in the village, such as classmates or older children. Similarly, when asked about the studies of his granddaughter Wen, grandpa Zhou said that "both of us are illiterate. She counts on herself, she studies by herself.... The kid can only count on herself. Neither parent stays at home."

Indeed, one of the major concerns among migrant parents is that grandparents are incapable of supervising schoolwork of children left behind. When asked whether grandparents took good care of grandchildren, migrant mother Yan commented that they did a good job in monitoring children's daily activities and feeding them. She added:

> The only thing is, sometimes ... grandma is illiterate. That's the problem with old folks. Their grandpa sometimes needs to work outside and comes back very late. The little one stays at home. When he studies, he sometimes needs someone [to tutor him]. That's the problem here. We are rest assured that children will eat well and live well, but education is the biggest issue.

Migrant mother Chen provided an almost identical picture regarding grandparenting. When asked to evaluate the quality of grandparenting in her family, she responded:

> It's okay. Anyway, they will make sure they [children] eat well, dress well. Schooling, they definitely don't understand, right? No education. Their grandpa has some education. Grandma definitely has no education, never entered a school gate before. Grandpa has a little bit of education, probably finished primary school. Like now, they don't understand children's homework, they cannot tutor either. [Children] can only count on themselves.

In sum, the qualitative data reveal a consensus among migrant parents, children, and grandparents themselves regarding the inability of grandparent caretakers to assist with children's schoolwork. Interestingly, at-home parents of the student sample (seventh and eighth graders) encountered the same difficulties, but this problem received much less public attention. The student survey data found that the average education of parents was at a level lower than junior high school graduation, suggesting that whereas the average education of parents was substantially higher than that of grandparents, parents at home were also ill-equipped to tutor their seventh and eighth graders. Indeed, parents at home freely admitted that they were not capable of assisting with their children's schoolwork when they reached middle school. For example, mother Dasheng—who raised two daughters primarily by herself—commented on her inability to tutor two daughters:

> We cannot teach them. We don't know how to solve the problems ourselves. What can we do? In primary school, they did not need us. They knew how to do it. Middle school and high school, they did not [know]. They did not know, and their grades could only be at the average level. . . . You had no one to seek help. Only their teachers would talk with them. We never got any [extra] help. Who can you look for? You cannot find anyone. She did relatively well in the last exam. She ranked number five in her class. In the whole liberal arts class, she ranked around thirty to forty.

Student interviewees made similar comments. Chuangqi, the seventh grader mentioned previously, said his migrant parents could not help even if they were at home. "They do not come back, and they are illiterate too. My dad did not finish primary school. Neither did my mom." The intriguing question is, if neither grandparents nor at-home parents can provide tutoring for students who desperately need it, why there is such a loud outcry about grandparents but not about at-home parents? Delving further into the qualitative data, I speculate that children's age may moderate the influence of caretaking arrangements on children's academic performance, which may not be captured by the relatively homogeneous quantitative data. That is, while caretaking arrangements have little effect on children's schooling when children are in middle school or high school—during this life stage, household financial resources become more critical—caretaking arrangements can play a pivotal role in children's academic performance in primary school. Specifically, most parents are capable of tutoring primary-school-aged children, while most grandparents cannot successfully perform this role. Grandma Ming, a rare graduate of high school, told a story that exemplified grandparents' difficulties in helping children's schooling.

> I went to Nanchang [for a few days], and his aunt-grandma picked him [my grandson] up a few times. He did not know how to do his homework and asked the aunt-grandma. She did not know how to do it either. She said, "What could I do?" She said, "Don't tell your daughter-in-law Jihong. What can we do when we cannot even figure out homework of a first grader?" Now it is real that you need to really work on first-grade homework.

In this story, the aunt-grandma was embarrassed that she could not even tutor a first-grader. While none of the at-home parents mentioned this problem when tutoring children in elementary school, many grandparents expressed the same frustration. Grandma Ren, who was living with her first-grade granddaughter at the time of our interview in 2018, said, "We had very little education when we were young. My granddaughter asked for my help, and there were so many words I did not know." In particular, grandparents revealed that when they were in school, they never learned Pinyin—currently a standard method to learn Chinese pronunciation. Even grandma Ming said that she had to learn Pinyin by herself when she was tutoring her grandson. For other less-educated grandparents such as grandpa Jingpin, the challenge became nearly insurmountable to overcome. Grandpa Jingpin commented:

> Talking about tutoring, we only have three, four years of school, and school is more difficult now than before. Ask us to teach and we don't even know the answers ourselves. Now even primary school is quite difficult. When we were in school, teachers did not teach Pinyin. We did not know many of the Pinyin. Not to mention others, you cannot even tutor a first grader, you cannot even handle Pinyin . . .

Children quickly observed their grandparents' lower levels of education and their inability to tutor, which substantially eroded grandparents' authority on school-related issues. When grandma Ming's grandson—a first grader—found that she did not know Pinyin, he was pleasantly surprised. He said, "Grandma, you don't know them, and you need to read the book!" For many other grandparents, this led children to challenge their authority on school-related issues and ignore their demand to study hard and to finish homework. Grandpa Xiao described his grandsons' contempt when asked to do homework:

> They think they are better than us. Sometimes when we criticize them, they would say, "you don't know it yourself." It drives us crazy. . . . The grandchildren say, "You don't know it yourself "or "What do you know about this?"

When I say, "Go finish your homework, go review your schoolwork. [They then say] you only talk about study, only study, you don't talk about any other things."

As the preceding case demonstrates, the authority of grandparents on school-related issues deteriorates significantly when "they think they are better than us." Indeed, when grandparents pressured children to study or do homework, children sometimes took advantage of the lack of education of grandparents and pretended that they had already finished all the work, clearly knowing that grandparents could not check the quality or even know whether the homework was completed. Grandpa Jingpin complained when discussing his grandson's lack of study effort:

> My grandson is so naughty. He is so disobedient. You close your eyes for one second, and he is gone. Except when you stay with him all the time. You don't look at him, he is gone in a second. My grandson is like this, what can you do? He does not do his homework. That's basically it. Anyway, he cannot pass the teachers. He just scribbles and doodles. Just to finish the task.

Grandpa and grandma Xiao believed that the practice of "scribbling and doodling" was highly prevalent based on their observations and their own personal experience. They commented:

> They [grandparents] come back [from work] and ask, "Have you finished your homework?" They do not know if children have worked on their homework or not, they do not know whether they have finished it or not. They (children) say they have finished the homework; they have already been done. Yeye and Nainai do not have any way to check it. Whether they have finished them or not, how could I tell? It's just one superfluous question. [Grandma Xiao] We are not sure either. We can only ask, "Have you finished your homework?"

In summary, the qualitative data reveal that the effect of caretaking arrangements on children's academic performance is potentially moderated by children's age, which is both directly and indirectly supported by previous research. The study by Lu (2012), for example, provides direct support, showing that parental migration did not exhibit a desired positive effect and was particularly disruptive for younger children in primary schools. Most studies, although not directly investigating the moderating role of age and grade level, provide indirect support. Studies using data collected from primary school students (or a majority of primary school students) generally found that parental migration negatively impacted children's academic performance (Bai et al., 2020; B. Y. Hu et al., 2020; W. Liang et al., 2008; M. Zhou et al., 2014), whereas studies using samples of older children (middle school or high school students) found a positive or nonsignificant association (Dong et al., 2021; S. Hu, 2019; C. Zhou et al., 2015). A recent longitudinal study using panel data of more than 5,000 students from seventy-two primary schools in rural China (Bai et al., 2020), for example, reported that parental migration, particularly dual-parent migration, had a significant and negative impact on children's academic performance. By contrast, S. Hu (2019), using ninth graders as her sample, found that caretaking arrangements had no significant impact on children's educational aspirations as well as academic performance, measured by using Chinese, mathematics, and English test scores.

The Role of Positive Caretaking on Children's Schooling

The second theme emerging from the in-depth interviews is that positive caretaking—particularly active participation in children's lives, strict monitoring, and consistent discipline—plays a significant role in shaping children's school bonding and academic performance. While most grandparent caretakers, when facing the challenges of effectively monitoring children's behavior or assisting with their schoolwork, felt frustrated and sometimes helpless, a small number of grandparents appeared to find the magic recipe.

The first case is grandma Ming, the primary caretaker of her first-grader grandson—a seven-year-old. Working in a city in Jiangxi province, her son, Yun, visited the family about once a month. Her daughter-in-law, Jihong, although working in a nearby town, came back only on weekends. As the primary caretaker, grandma Ming was proud of her caretaking skills and her grandson's academic performance. She discussed in detail how she was actively involved in her grandson's schooling and set up strict rules:

> Before, he often played on his cell phone by himself. Now, [he] cannot play cell phone from Monday to Friday. You don't give children some rules, that is not going to work, you know? He cannot play on his cell phone from Monday to Friday. On Saturdays and Sundays there is little homework, he says teachers give him very little homework. You parents can give him some extra work to do. I let him practice Pinyin. He is not good at it. I let him practice a little more, there is no harm there. In addition, practice Chinese character writing. I read and he writes. This is what he needs to do every week. Sometimes teachers don't give much homework, and he finishes everything in a short time. . . . Like Uncle's two grandsons, they do not finish their homework. This is absolutely not allowed. You are a student and you do not even finish homework? How could this work? . . . His math teacher said, "You taught the child well." He said, "Some parents did not teach as well as you did. You raised the child well." He said, "You helped him develop a good life habit."

Besides establishing strict rules, grandma Ming also emphasized the importance of teaching children based on their personality strengths. She compared her caretaking style and philosophy with that of her brother, who had two grandsons who failed to go to academic-track senior high schools. She commented:

At that time, my brother said to me, "Boys need to be raised outside, and girls need to be raised inside." His two boys were raised outside from being little. I know regardless of whether it is raised outside or inside, first you need to know who your child is, and what kind of methods you can use to deal with him. Some children are already troublemakers, and you still raise them outside? You cannot raise them outside. Some children are simple-minded, these children need to be raised outside. You cannot say that boys need to be raised outside, and girls need to be raised inside. My grandson cannot be raised outside either, to be honest. You need to have strict control. He is now seven years old, when he was a six-year-old, he already had many [fictive kin] brothers and sisters. I asked him why he needed so many people, he said that older brothers can protect him. [He] knows he needs to find someone to protect him, [knows] he is only one person and does not have others [siblings]. My grandson is quite smart. The only concern is whether I can monitor his behavior. If I cannot, he will walk astray. That will be troubling. He is smart, to be honest.

The second case is grandpa Pan, living with his wife and three grandchildren at the time of our interview in 2018. Grandpa Pan had one son and one daughter—both were married and had their own children. Grandpa Pan's son, who was working in a nearby town with his wife, only visited home occasionally due to a busy work schedule. As the primary caretaker to three grandchildren, grandpa Pan was delighted with their outstanding school performance, proudly showing me a wall in the living room decorated with certificates of achievement. He explained why his grandchildren fared better in school than other children:

> Another thing is, I do better in management than others [grandparents]. Better management, and their grades are all good. Now what you see is only a small fraction of the certificates of awards. Last time, the electronic wire was broken, and the wall needed to be repaired. Otherwise, the certificates of awards can start from this side to the other side [of the wall].

Like grandma Ming, grandpa Pan attributed the academic success of his grandchildren to strict monitoring and discipline, or his "management." All three children followed a rigorously enforced daily schedule: getting up at 5:30 A.M., reading from 5:30 A.M. to 6:30 A.M., and eating breakfast from 6:30 A.M. to 7:15 A.M. before going to school. After the children returned from school at around 5:30 P.M., they worked on their homework first before playing outside. After dinner, the two younger children (who were in elementary school) went to bed at 8:00 P.M., and the eldest child—an eighth-grader—went to bed based on the workload of homework. Even during summer break, the three children created their own daily schedule, outlining the major activities (homework, reading time, etc.) during each time block, and posted these schedules on the wall of their living room. Grandpa Pan highlighted the importance of the "system" and the self-governance developed over time:

You need to decide on the system first. As long as the system is set, they can govern themselves. Sometimes the three are at home, we need to go out, and we can go out. They know what and when to do certain things. Sometimes we go out and cannot return before lunchtime. They cook for themselves. Although they cannot cook anything complicated, some simple ones, like making eggs, cooking noodle, they can do it (laughing).... So rules need to be established first, and they need to be strictly followed. You need to follow them strictly, otherwise ...

The development of self-governance was extended to other areas of daily life for children. For example, while other grandparents "spoil" their children by buying all kinds of snacks for them, grandpa Pan said when he bought snacks, he spent fifty yuan every time and then put all the snacks in one paper box. Each child was allowed to eat (at most) one piece in the morning, one in the afternoon, and one while at school. Another aspect of the "system" was an award given to children for small or large academic achievements. As grandpa Pan explained:

Everyone has a piggy bank. If they do well during regular tests, like they get the first place, the second place, or the third place, they are awarded a small prize. The first, second, and third place, that is three yuan, two yuan, and one yuan. If the tests are middle-term or final-term exams, then it is ten yuan, eight yuan, and seven yuan for the first three places. Merit student (san hao xue sheng), that is fifty yuan. But the money is not immediately spent, they put the money into their piggy bank. Then if they want to buy something, such as school-related items, books, or a bicycle, they can buy those things.

Consistent with our quantitative data, these case studies demonstrate the positive influence of consistent discipline and active involvement of caretakers on children's educational performance. Coupled with findings in previous chapters (i.e., caretaking practices differ across types of caretaking arrangements), these results provide solid support for the mediation arguments—the effects of caretaking arrangements are conveyed through caretakers' voluntary or involuntary adoption of certain caretaking practices. For example, although dual parental migration negatively influences children's academic performance during early ages (i.e., elementary school), close monitoring and unconditional support provided by dual-grandparent caretakers offer children an opportunity to even the playing field and compete academically with children of nonmigrant parents in high school. In contrast, sole-grandparent caretakers, as discussed in chapter 3, are often physically and emotionally overwhelmed, leading to an inconsistent and nonresponsive caretaking style and, hence, poor academic performance of left-behind children.

The same logic can be applied to understanding the deleterious effect of maternal migration on children's academic performance—one of the major findings in the quantitative data. As discussed in chapter 3, fathers left behind are often reluctant to cross gender boundaries and perform sufficient mothering, leading to children being poorly monitored and inconsistently disciplined and ultimately achieving poor academic performance. Compared with at-home mothers who are sometimes considered to be "nagging" by their children, at-home fathers are often busy with their own business and neglect children's difficulties encountered in school or other fields. The lack of involvement was exemplified in my interview with father Lu, who returned home when his father passed away. Father Lu commented on his daughter's schooling:

> Her grade is not good. What can you do when she can only get [a grade of] seventy-something? She never talks with me [about school and grades]. I [tried to] teach her the methods to study. I said school was not something so difficult. You are not testing for graduate school, only for a middle-level university, that should still be hopeful, right? Whatever you say, she does not listen. In the morning, you cannot hear her reading aloud. It's not like when we were young. Children nowadays, what do they mainly do? One is, they only want to have fun. The methods you teach them, they don't listen to you. Asking her to write and she does not listen either, eyes opening widely. . . . To improve her grade, I feel that [she needs to use] my method. You pay attention to the class. If you don't understand, ask questions. You need to understand the problems after teachers explain them. You have to understand the problems first, then you can remember them. You cannot just go through rote learning, that's not going to work . . .

Regardless of whether father Lu's study methods were effective, of particular note in this conversation was his lack of acknowledgment of the role of parents as agents of monitoring, supervising, and tutoring; that is, father Lu attributed his daughter's academic standing solely to her own efforts. When his presumptively effective study methods were not fully embraced by his seventh grader, father Lu made little effort to use more concrete methods (e.g., tutoring) to assist with his daughter's study. Rather, he blamed the attitude and presumed laziness of his daughter as the critical factors. The lack of involvement among at-home fathers was also evident in my interview with another left-behind father, Laojiu, whose wife migrated to Nanchang—the capital city of Jiangxi province. When his son asked for tutoring assistance, Laojiu responded, "I said, 'You study every day, and I work every day, and I never ask you for help.'"

Long-Distance Parenting and Children's School Performance

As discussed in chapter 4, long-distance parenting—precipitated by the widespread use of smartphones and "polymedia" in rural China—has become increasingly prevalent. While strongly endorsed by local governments and telecommunication corporations as an effective method to alleviate temporal and spatial separation among family members in multilocal families, the effects of long-distance parenting on education have not been fully investigated. In this final section, I study whether long-distance parenting has any noticeable effect on two dimensions of schooling—academic performance and school bonding. Because I focus on children left behind in this section, data used here are limited to those who were spatially separated from at least one parent during the past twelve months.

I used three variables to measure the various dimensions of long-distance parenting, including children's visits to the host cities of migrant parents, parent–child communication, and the degree to which migrant parents express concern about children's school performance. The first measure, *children's visits to the host cities* of migrant parents, asked whether children visited the host cities of their migrant parents, with response categories ranging from 1 = never to 5 = at least two times a year. The second measure, *parent–child communication*, asked how often migrant fathers and mothers communicated with children left behind through phone calls, audio chat, or video chat through smartphones or other electronic devices (e.g., iPad or computer). The response categories for this variable ranged from 1 = no communication or less than once every half a year to 6 = communicate every one or two days. Finally, the last measure, *caring about school*, asked children how much their migrant parents cared about their schooling, with response categories ranging from 1 = do not care at all to 4 = care about it very much.

Table 5.3 reveals the findings of multivariate regression models studying the associations between long-distance parenting and school involvement among children left behind, controlling for a host of variables such as characteristics of children (i.e., age, sex, and whether living in boarding schools), characteristics of

TABLE 5.3
Distant parenting and children's school involvement (standardized regression coefficients)

	Academic performance	School bonding
Children's visit	−0.06	−0.06
Parent–child communication	−0.03	0.08*
Parents care about children's school performance	0.18**	0.24**
R^2	0.22	0.29

Note: *$p < 0.05$; **$p < 0.01$; $n = 560$. Characteristics of children and parents, household social economic status, and at-home caretaking practices were controlled in the models.

parents and households (i.e., parental education, number of household properties, family economic status, number of siblings, and marital status of biological parents), and caretaking practices. In other words, these models investigated whether long-distance parenting explained further variations in children's schooling beyond the influences of caretaking quality at home. To simplify the presentation, I only reported the net associations between each of the three measures of distance parenting and the dependent variables.

Regarding children's academic performance, the standardized regression coefficients of two measures of long-distance parenting—children's visits to host cities of migrant parents and the frequency of parent–child communication—were not statistically significant; however, the degree to which parents cared about children's academic performance was highly significant (β = 0.18, p < 0.01). When regressed on school bonding, the frequency of children's visits to migrant parents was not statistically significant, while parent–child communication (β = 0.88, p < 0.05) and parents' concern about children's education were significant (β = 0.24, p < 0.01). The two multivariate regression models explained a moderate amount of variance, accounting for 22 percent of the variance of academic performance and 29 percent of the variance of school bonding.

As indicated in table 5.3, children's visits to migrant parents had virtually no effect on the two measures of schooling, perhaps because children's visits during summer breaks or holidays act as an indirect measure of long-distance parenting. Although this measure reflects an intention of and a potential opportunity for migrant parents to emotionally connect with children, the number of children's visits and the duration of each stay are more reliant on the spatial distance between migrant-sending communities and host cities and the cost of urban living. Understandably, children of intra-province migrant parents visit their parents more frequently than those of inter-province migrant parents, who often spend more than ten hours on the road and transfer from long-distance buses to trains multiple times for each trip. More importantly, when children do visit, they often find that they are trapped in one small apartment most of the time due to the busy working schedules of parents and safety concerns. Indeed, I was told multiple times that children pleaded for parents to send them back earlier than scheduled. In other words, the good intention of bonding with children during summer visits rarely materializes.

In contrast, parent–child communication—in the form of phone calls or audio and video chats through the popular WeChat platform—significantly increased children's bonding with school and classmates. As discussed in chapter 4, a major topic of long-distance conversation is schooling. Migrant parents often use their own humbling experiences in urban areas to underline the importance of education, attributing much of their hardship to a lack of education or "low quality." The sacrifices they have made for children and the translocal family—perceived or actual—in turn, are conveyed to children through direct conversations or indirectly through family members at home. Migrant mother Guo characterized her typical conversation with her elder daughter as such:

> I just asked her to study hard. I said she can only get somewhere when she has a good education. It will benefit her a lot. Like every day we work overtime until eleven or twelve am, and we only make such a meager amount of money. I told her things like this, letting her know that *dagong* is very toiling, and she needs to study well. Every time I told her this. And every time I send her money for living expenses, I tell her that this money, it is my half a month's salary, and that she needs to spend it carefully and study well, like this (laughing).

Migrant mother Chen made similar comments when she discussed her conversation with her daughters:

> When I talk with them, I just ask them to study well. I said you need to study hard. If you can continue [to study well], even if I don't have money, I can get a loan. I said as long as you can study well, as long as you can go to college, no money, I will get a loan to support your study.

As seen in these conversations, the humbling sacrifices of migrant parents in urban areas, including working overtime until 11 or 12 P.M. or "getting a loan" when necessary, are often either formally or casually communicated to children, motivating them to study hard and to fulfill their obligations as part of the "striving team" (Murphy, 2020). Indeed, as demonstrated in table 5.3, the degree to which migrant parents cared about children's school performance not only increased children's attachment to school and classmates but also directly improved children's academic performance. While caretaking at home is a more proximal factor and imposes a substantial influence on children's educational performance, parenting through long distance in rural China also matters.

Conclusion

In this chapter, I investigated the associations between parental migration and children's school involvement, focusing on two dimensions of children's schooling—academic performance and school bonding. Guided by the overarching theoretical model, I assessed the direct effects of caretaking arrangements on children's schooling as well as the mediation through caretaking practices. Moreover, I explored whether the oft-discussed long-distance parenting improved children's academic performance.

First, the results from the quantitative data reveal that two types of caretaking arrangement—maternal migration and one-grandparent caretaking—exhibited the most deleterious effects on children's school involvement in middle school. Compared to children living with nonmigrant parents, children cared for by a left-behind father or one grandparent reported the lowest levels of academic performance and school bonding. By comparison, children of other alternative caretaking arrangements (i.e., paternal migration and two-grandparent caretaking) did not exhibit significantly poorer school outcomes. Complementing the quantitative findings, the interview data suggest that grandparenting—regardless of one-grandparent or two-grandparent caretaking arrangements—hindered the academic success of children left behind; this relationship, however, appeared to be stronger during the elementary school years and substantially weaker when children attended junior high schools, when household resources (e.g., socioeconomic status) played a more prominent role in shaping children's school involvement.

Second, the data consistently suggest that the effect of parental migration on children's schooling was largely indirect, mediated by the form and content of caretaking practices. As expected, the three measures of caretaking practices were significant predictors of at least one of the two school outcome variables. The level of caretaker monitoring and supervision was a consistent predictor of academic performance and school bonding, while caretaker hostility and a low level of caretaker–child bonding decreased children's bonding with school. These caretaking practices explained much of the associations between caretaking arrangements and children's schooling.

Third, the results demonstrate that gender moderated the associations between caretaking arrangements and children's school involvement. The direct effects of caretaking arrangements were generally similar across gender; however, the mediation processes observed in the full sample were highly gendered. For example, the effect of one-grandparent caretaking through poor caretaking practices appeared to be salient for boys but not significant for girls. By contrast, the effect of maternal migration through caretaking practices was more pronounced for girls than for boys. These results reveal a complex interplay between the gender of caretakers, caretakers' generational status, and the gender of children. These factors collectively shape how children are monitored, supervised, and nurtured and how they respond to varying caretaking practices, ultimately influencing the academic development and future life trajectories of children left behind.

Finally, this chapter extends previous research by showing that long-distance parenting imposed noticeable effects on children's schooling beyond proximate familial characteristics and individual traits. Children left behind were constantly reminded, either directly through audio or video conversations by migrants themselves or indirectly by family members left behind, that migrant parents sacrificed tremendously for their education by working "outside." The experience of living and working in urban areas, including the observation of "education fever" among the urban middle class, marginalized socioeconomic status, and immense life hardship, precipitated migrant parents to instill in children the belief that education was the only plausible path for their future economic success and family intergenerational mobility.

6

Are Left-Behind Children More Deviance- and Delinquency-Prone?

When he was little, the school was very close. He did not have much contact (with other children), and he did not have the guts to go far away. Now he is a little bit older and has become a little bit braver. He walks further and further away, and he knows more people, right? . . . He is now in middle school, and he knows all the boys in the township. The whole township is so big, right? So it is so difficult to supervise him.

—grandpa Xiao

We don't have much pocket money for him. He just took it himself. Sometimes we put money somewhere, he would take it, twenty to thirty yuan, and he spent all of it in one day. . . . If you took some money, then use it for a few more days. (He) uses up whatever amount he takes. . . . He is still a child; it will be much more difficult when he is older.

—grandpa Jingpin

Now children surfing cell phone and the Internet, it is atrocious! In his class, many kids sneaked out at night, playing for a whole night (at Internet bars). My two grandchildren were living in a teacher's house, they were less bold, and they did not have the guts to go out at night. Four kids living in a teacher's house, sometimes they sneaked out at night and came back until early morning, and the teacher had no idea! They were all asleep, how did they know? Another kid in the same class, living with his aunt. His aunt suspected that he sneaked out at night. She then put a flowerpot on the window. He tried to climb out of the window, and BANG, the flowerpot fell. His aunt did not want him to live there again. She said, "Your parents put you here, and I am responsible for you. If you don't stay here, I have no responsibility."

—grandparent Xiao

One of the most documented research findings in criminology is the age–crime curve, which indicates that delinquency and the crime rate increase dramatically from ten to twelve years old, peak around the age of eighteen to twenty, and then decrease and level off around the age of thirty (Farrington, 1986; Matthews & Minton, 2018). While there is some debate about whether the age–crime curve is universal or culturally specific (Steffensmeier et al., 2017, 2019), there is no doubt that adolescence is a critical period, entailing rapid physical and mental growth, the expansion of friendship networks and social activities, and the formation of self-identities—all critical correlates of children's involvement in delinquency and deviant behavior.

Do parental migration and alternative caretaking arrangements influence a child's development during this critical life stage? More specifically, do they increase a child's chances of becoming involved in deviant or delinquent behavior? Media stories and criminal justice data provide some anecdotal evidence that left-behind children and young rural-to-urban migrant workers (most of whom are former left-behind children) are disproportionally trapped in the criminal justice system—arrested, detained, or incarcerated by authorities (X. Chen, 2021; A. Shen, 2018; L. Zhang, 2017). Yet empirical studies have found little evidence that this group has a higher level of criminality than other youth groups. Whereas some studies find that left-behind children have a higher risk of deviance and delinquency than their counterparts living with nonmigrant parents (X. Chen, 2017; X. Chen & Jiang, 2019), others report no significant differences between the two groups (H. Hu et al., 2014; Luo et al., 2018). Given the joint influence of poverty, marginal socioeconomic status, and institutional discrimination against children who are left behind, it remains unclear whether the connections made between this group and criminal behavior are accurate or simply rooted in bias.

In this chapter, I attempt to understand whether children's deviant and/or delinquent behaviors are associated with parental migration and alternative caretaking arrangements and whether these associations are exacerbated or lessened by the influence of other protective and risk factors. During my interviews with migrant parents and grandparents, behaviors considered problematic—particularly deviant behaviors such as playing video games at Internet bars (a place where children and young people pay a small amount of money to play video games or surf the Internet) during school days, association with "bad" companions, and minor acts of delinquency such as small theft—were most frequently mentioned. Migrant parents and grandparent caretakers were concerned that these activities would derail children's academic trajectories and even get them entangled in the criminal justice system. Based on these accounts, I focus on three dimensions of children's problematic behaviors in this chapter: association with deviant peers, deviant behavior, and minor delinquency. I first explore whether left-behind status and alternative caretaking arrangements increase children's involvement in these behaviors and whether these associations are mediated by more proximate factors such as caretaking practices and school bonding. Following this discussion, I turn to long-distance parenting and examine whether intensive long-distance parenting (e.g., long-distance communication and children's summer visits) can effectively reduce children's involvement in deviant and delinquent behaviors.

Parental Migration and Involvement in Problematic Behaviors: The Theoretical Model

The overarching theoretical model presented in chapter 1 (fig. 1.1) guides the analyses in this chapter. Informed by family process theory (Broderick, 1993) and the integrated theory of crime and delinquency (Elliott et al., 1979, 1985; Menard & Johnson, 2015), this theoretical model attempts to identify the social mechanism underlying the association between parental migration and problematic behaviors. As discussed in chapter 1, an essential component of this theoretical model is derived from the family process theory, which proposes that a family is a system in which each member has specific roles and obligations prescribed by deeply embedded social and cultural norms. In Peace County, for example, a married man is often perceived as the main provider and is responsible for the family's survival, growth, and prosperity. A man who fails to provide for the household is perceived as "lazy" and "incapable" and is looked down on by family members, neighbors, and friends. As a result, certain types of parental migration and caretaking practice (e.g., maternal migration)—which prompt a reconfiguration of a family's division of labor—may severely disrupt the balance of the family system, creating chronic stress and dysfunction within the family.

This model also draws from mainstream criminological theories (e.g., strain, social learning, and social bonding theories (Agnew, 1992; Burt, 2020), proposing that chronic parental absence (i.e., parental migration) results in an accumulation of stress and weakened bonding with parents, which then directly lead to problematic behaviors. Furthermore, this model asserts that the effect of parental migration can be exacerbated or mitigated depending on the presence and strength of proximate factors such as caretaking practices and school bonding. Strict but not harsh monitoring and discipline, for example, could lead to strong bonding between children and conventional institutions, thus reducing the detrimental effect of parental absence. By contrast, harsh and punitive caretaking can push children away from the family sphere, increasing their unsupervised and unstructured time with peers, weakening their bonding with school and classmates, and ultimately resulting in elevated involvement in delinquent and deviant behaviors.

Association with Deviant Peers

I first investigate whether parental migration and caretaking practices are associated with children's association with deviant peers. The measure *association with deviant peers* is a scale adapted from the National Youth Survey (Elliott et al., 1985), which asked participants how many of their current friends participated in thirteen types of delinquent and deviant behavior in the past twelve months. These behaviors include friends' substance abuse such as drinking and smoking and involvement in minor delinquent behaviors (e.g., damaging property, stealing, carrying weapons to school, fighting, cheating on tests, and burglary). For each item, response categories ranged from 1 = none of them to 5 = all of them. I used the average of the thirteen items to create a composite score for this scale (α = .094), with a high score indicating a higher level of association with deviant friends.

Caretaking Arrangements and Children's Affiliation with Deviant Peers

The bivariate analyses also indicate that caretaking arrangements were differentially associated with deviant peer affiliation (fig. 6.1). Specifically, the peer affiliations of children cared for by the mother (i.e., paternal migration) and those cared for by both grandparents did not differ significantly from those living with both nonmigrant parents. Yet children primarily cared for by a father (i.e., maternal migration) and those cared for by one grandparent reported a higher number of friends entangled with deviant or delinquent activities. Further analysis reveals that this pattern was largely driven by the boys rather than the girls. An almost identical pattern was observed among boys, with children living with a father reporting the highest number of deviant friends (mean = 1.81) and those cared for by one grandparent the second highest (mean = 1.69). This pattern was not replicated among the girls; rather, girls cared for by one grandparent reported the highest level of associating with deviant peers (mean = 1.42), while those living with both grandparents reported the lowest level (mean = 1.28).

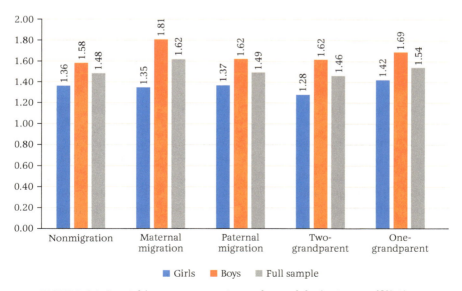

FIGURE 6.1 Caretaking arrangements, gender, and deviant peer affiliation.

TABLE 6.1
Multivariate regression models predicting children's association with deviant peers (unstandardized regression coefficients)

	Total (n = 1,177) Model 1	Total Model 2	Male (n = 616) Model 1	Male Model 2	Female (n = 523) Model 1	Female Model 2
Intercept	2.28	1.93	2.63	2.28	2.25	1.89
Two-grandparent caretaking[a]	−0.03	−0.02	0.01	0.02	−0.11**	−0.10**
One-grandparent caretaking	0.03	0.05	0.04	0.06	0.01	0.02
Maternal migration	0.08	0.08	0.16*	0.17*	−0.06	−0.08
Paternal migration	0.01	0.00	0.04	0.04	−0.03	−0.04
Caretaker monitoring/ supervision		0.00		0.01		−0.03
Caretaker hostility		0.10**		0.12**		0.09**
Caretaker–child bonding		−0.01		−0.02		0.00
School bond		−0.08**		−0.12**		−0.04
School performance		0.06*		0.07*		0.04
R^2	0.20	0.24	0.16	0.21	0.14	0.19

Note: *$p < 0.05$; **$p < 0.01$. Demographic and family background variables such as age, sex, living in a school dorm, parental education and economic status, marital status of biological parents, and number of siblings were controlled in the model.

[a] Children living with nonmigrant parents as the reference group.

I then investigated whether these bivariate associations remained robust in multivariate analysis when a series of individual and household-level characteristics were controlled (table 6.1, model 1). These control variables, including a child's age and sex, whether living in a school dorm, parental education, family economic status, the marital status of biological parents, and the number of siblings were described in detail in chapter 3. In addition, I controlled for children's self-control, a predictor strongly and consistently associated with deviant and delinquent activities in the literature (Burt, 2020). Adapting from Grasmick, Tittle, Bursik, and Arneklev (1993), I used a twenty-one-item scale to capture the six dimensions of children's self-control: impulsivity, preference for simple tasks, risk-seeking, physical activity preference, being self-centered, and bad temper. The response categories for each item range from 1 "completely disagree" to 4 "completely agree." I computed the final composite score by reverse-coding and then averaging these twenty-one items (α = 0.95). A higher score indicates a greater level of self-control.

Using the full sample, model 1 reveals that the pattern observed in the bivariate analyses is largely replicated when children's individual and household characteristics are considered. In the full sample, children with a migrant mother reported the highest level of affiliation with deviant peers (b = 0.08), children with one grandparent caretaking were second (b = 0.03), and children cared for by the mother or two grandparents reported the lowest levels of associating with deviant peers (b = 0.01 and b = –0.03, respectively). These regression coefficients were not statistically significant, suggesting that the observed differences in deviant peer affiliation across types of caretaking arrangement were not significant. Additionally, this model explained a moderate amount of variance (R_2 = 0.20), with sex (b = 0.25, p < 0.01) and family economic status (b = 0.06, p < 0.05) significantly predicting deviant peer association. Finally, consistent with much of the previous research (Burt, 2020), children's self-control had a large and significant effect (b = –0.34, p < 0.01) and emerged as the primary contributor to the predictive efficacy of this model (results not shown in the table).

Further analysis reveals that the lack of significant differences in the full sample was due to the opposite effects of caretaking arrangements across gender groups. Left-behind girls generally (except the one-grandparent caretaking) had *lower* levels of association with deviant friends, with those cared for by two grandparents reporting a significantly lower level of association (b = –0.11, p < 0.01) than those living with both parents (table 6.1, female model 1). In sharp contrast— regardless of caretaking arrangements—left-behind boys reported *higher* levels of association with deviant peers, particularly those living with a left-behind father (i.e., maternal migration, b = 0.16, p < 0.05).

Risk and Protective Factors: Caretaking Practices and School

Guided by the theoretical model in chapter 1 (fig. 1.1), I investigated whether caretaking practices (e.g., monitoring and supervision, hostility, and caretaker–child bonding) and children's school performance (e.g., school bonding and academic performance) increased or lessened children's risk of affiliation with deviant peers (table 6.1). Model 2 examined whether caretaking practices (e.g., caretaking monitoring and supervision, caretaker–child bonding, and children's perceived hostility toward caretakers) and children's school bonding (i.e., bonding with school and peers, academic performance) were significantly associated with children's affiliation with deviant peers. Out of the three caretaking practice measures, children's perception of caretaker hostility was the only significant factor, which consistently predicted the outcome variable in the full sample (b = 0.10, p < 0.01) and across gender groups (b = 0.12, p < 0.01 for boys and b = 0.09, p < 0.01 for girls, respectively). When children were verbally or emotionally rejected (or perceived to be rejected) by primary caretakers, they were more likely to seek companionship and emotional support from same-aged peers.

Model 2 also examined the effects of school bonding and academic performance on children's association with deviant peers. Interestingly, while children's strong bonding with school decreased deviant peer affiliation ($b = -0.08$, $p < 0.01$), academic performance had the opposing effect ($b = 0.06$, $p < 0.05$). These associations were more salient among boys than among girls, with both regression coefficients being statistically significant for boys ($b = -0.12$, $p < 0.01$ and $b = 0.07$, $p < 0.05$, respectively) but none for girls. While the protective effect of school bonding on children's association with deviant peers has been extensively documented in the literature, the risk effect of high academic performance has been less discussed. I suspect that, given the importance of academic performance in Chinese society, academically strong children may be more popular in school and thus have more expanded and diverse friendship networks. Finally, the regression coefficient of each type of caretaking arrangement barely changed from model 1 to model 2, indicating that caretaking practices and school bonding played a nonsignificant role in mediating these associations.

Engagement in Deviant Behaviors

In this section, I turn to children's engagement in deviant behaviors. The scale *deviant behavior* consisted of three items: drinking, smoking, and playing games at Internet bars during school days in the past twelve months. Children were asked how many times they had drunk alcohol, smoked cigarettes, or visited an Internet bar during school days in the past twelve months. While these behaviors are not considered illegal in China, they are the most prevalent activities considered deviant among adolescents and largely frowned upon by parents and schoolteachers. About one-quarter of these seventh and eighth graders reported that they drank alcohol (25.9%), one-tenth (11.2%) smoked a cigarette, and a similar percentage (10.5%) visited Internet bars to play games or hang out with friends during school days. I dichotomized each of the three items (1 = yes and 0 = no) and summed them up to create a variety score for children's *engagement in deviant behaviors*, with the score of this index ranging from 0 to 3. In total, about half of these children (47.1%) reported that they were engaged in at least one of the three types of deviant behavior.

Caretaking Arrangements and Children's Engagement in Deviant Behaviors

I further investigated differences in involvement in deviant activities across caretaking arrangement types. The results indicate that two types of caretaking arrangement noticeably differed from other groups, with children living with a stay-at-home father reporting the highest percentage of engaging in one of the three types of activities (63%) and those living with one grandparent the second highest (59%). The remaining three groups, children living with both parents (47%), children living with an at-home mother (43%), and children living with two grandparents (42%), exhibited similar rates.

TABLE 6.2
Ordinal regression models predicting children's participation in deviant activities (unstandardized regression coefficients)

	Total (n = 1,177)		Male (n = 616)		Female (n = 523)	
	Model 1	Model 2	Model 1	Model 2	Model 1	Model 2
Threshold #1	0.23	0.30	−0.48	−0.73	−1.16*	−0.39
Threshold #2	0.91	0.97	0.15	−0.09	−0.32	0.45
Threshold #3	1.52	1.58	0.79*	0.55	0.23	1.00
Two-grandparent caretaking[a]	−0.09	−0.09	0.04	0.05	−0.38*	−0.38*
One-grandparent caretaking	0.18	0.18	0.41*	0.41*	0.06	0.06
Maternal migration	0.22*	0.23*	0.31*	0.31*	0.07	0.07
Paternal migration	−0.06	−0.06	−0.10	−0.10	0.09	0.09
Caretaker monitoring/supervision		0.00		−0.10		0.01
Caretaker hostility		0.17**		0.13**		0.28**
Caretaker–child bonding		0.00		0.02		0.00
School bond		−0.29**		−0.29**		−0.37**
School performance		0.06		0.03		0.07
Pseudo R^2	0.37	0.40	0.24	0.30	0.19	0.28

Note: *$p < 0.05$; **$p < 0.01$. Demographic and family background variables such as age, sex, living in a school dorm, parental education and economic status, marital status of biological parents, and number of siblings were controlled in the models.

[a] Children of nonmigrant parents as the reference group.

Because of the ordinal nature of the dependent variable, I used an ordinal regression model to assess whether the differences found in the bivariate analyses remained intact when individual and household characteristics were controlled (table 6.2, model 1). Consistent with the bivariate analysis, model 1 shows that children with a migrant mother (i.e., maternal migration) reported the highest level of engagement in deviant behavior ($b = 0.22$, $p < 0.05$), statistically higher than those living with both parents, children cared for by two grandparents, and those cared for by the at-home mother (i.e., paternal migration). Likewise, children cared for by one grandparent reported a higher level of participation in deviant activities than children living with both nonmigrant parents; this difference, however, was not statistically significant ($b = 0.18$, $p > 0.05$).

The gender subgroup analyses (table 6.2) revealed that the associations between caretaking arrangements and involvement in deviant activities were moderated by children's gender. For the male subsample, one-grandparent caretaking had the most deleterious effect ($b = 0.41$, $p < 0.05$), and maternal migration ranked the second ($b = 0.31$, $p < 0.05$). The other two caretaking arrangements, paternal migration, and two-grandparenting, by contrast, differed little from the reference group—caretaking by two nonmigrant parents. Interestingly, a vastly different pattern was observed within the female subsample. Compared with the reference group, being left behind but living with two grandparents showed a tremendous protective effect, significantly reducing girls' participation in deviant activities ($b = -0.38$, $p < 0.05$). Other types of caretaking arrangement, including one-grandparent caretaking, maternal migration, and paternal migration, had no significant detrimental effects.

Risk and Protective Factors: Caretaking Practices and School

I proceeded to explore whether caretaking practices, school bonding, and academic performance further explained children's involvement in deviant activities. Like our findings of deviant peer association, caretaker hostility—measured by asking how often a caretaker criticized, yelled at, or argued with the respondent—was significantly associated with the participation in deviant activities ($b = 0.17$, $p < 0.01$). Caretaker hostility had statistically significant effect on the boys ($b = 0.13$, $p < 0.01$) but appeared to have larger effect on the girls ($b = 0.28$, $p < 0.01$). Moreover, strong bonding with school, teachers, and students served as a protective factor overall ($b = -0.29$, $p < 0.01$), and these effects were statistically significant for both gender groups ($b = -0.29$, $p < 0.01$ for the boys, and $b = -0.37$, $p < 0.01$ for the girls, respectively).

Finally, table 6.2 shows that although caretaking practices and school bonding influenced children's participation in deviant activities in different ways, these variables did not explain away the effects of caretaking arrangements. Because the comparison of unstandardized regression coefficients across nested models—a common method to determine potential mediating effect—is not appropriate in generalized regression analysis, I adopted the approach proposed by MacKinnon and Dwyer (1993) and examined the change in standardized regression coefficients. The comparison of model 1 to model 2 revealed little evidence for a potential mediating effect (results not shown). The standardized regression coefficients of caretaking arrangements remained largely unchanged between model 1 and model 2—within the full sample and across gender groups.

Involvement in Minor Delinquency

The final scale tapping children's problematic behaviors was their participation in *minor delinquency*, which was measured by using thirteen items representing the self-reported frequency of involvement in minor delinquent activities in the past twelve months (Elliott & Ageton, 1980). Children were asked whether they engaged in delinquent activities such as stealing, graffiti, group fighting, truancy, damaging school property, and taking money from others without permission. For each item, response categories were 1 = never, 2 = one time, 3 = two times, 4 = three or four times, and 5 = five or more times (α = 0.77). The final scale *minor delinquency* was a dichotomized measure, with the score = 0 when a child did not participate in any of the thirteen delinquent activities and the score = 1 when the child participated in at least one of the activities in the past twelve months.

Descriptive analyses show that the percentage of engagement in minor delinquency differed significantly across gender groups. Close to half of the children (47%) participated in at least one of the thirteen delinquent activities in the past twelve months. Compared with the girls (36%), the rate was significantly higher for the boys (57%), and the gender difference was highly significant ($p < 0.01$).

Caretaking Arrangements and Children's Engagement in Minor Delinquency

In comparison with deviant peer affiliation and involvement in deviant behaviors, delinquency participation across different types of caretaking arrangement exhibited a slightly different pattern. Overall, children cared for by one grandparent reported the highest level of participation (57%), those cared for by one at-home-parent next (50% for either paternal or maternal migration), and children living with two grandparents (46%) or both nonmigrant parents (45%) reporting the lowest rates.

Logistic regression models in table 6.3 (model 1) demonstrate that, after accounting for demographic and household characteristics, the pattern observed in the preceding descriptive analysis remains robust. Compared with the reference group (living with both nonmigrant parents), the odds of participating in delinquent acts was 59 percent higher for those cared for by one grandparent ($\exp(b)$ = 1.59, $p < 0.05$), while the differences between other groups of left-behind children and the reference group were nonsignificant. The gendered analyses indicate that the deleterious effect of one-grandparent caretaking was similar across both gender groups, although the coefficient in neither subgroup reached statistical significance, probably due to smaller sample sizes.

Risk and Protective Factors: Caretaking Practices and School

Consistent with previous analyses in this chapter, caretaker hostility was a strong and consistent predictor of children's involvement in minor delinquency. This association was statistically significant in the full sample; with each unit increase of caretaker hostility, the odds of participation in minor delinquency increased by 54% ($\exp(b)$ = 1.54, $p < 0.01$). Interestingly, although this risk factor was statistically significant for both gender groups, it had more severe detrimental effect on the girls than on the boys ($\exp(b)$ = 1.36, $p < 0.01$ for the boys, and $\exp(b)$ = 1.76, $p < 0.01$ for the girls). As expected, school bonding was a protective factor again minor

TABLE 6.3
Logistic regression model predicting children's participation in minor delinquency (odds ratio)

	Total (n = 1,177)		Male (n = 616)		Female (n = 523)	
	Model 1 exp(b)	Model 2 exp(b)	Model 1 exp(b)	Model 2 exp(b)	Model 1 exp(b)	Model 2 exp(b)
Two-grandparent caretaking[a]	1.02	1.09	1.36	1.37	0.79	0.90
One-grandparent caretaking	1.59*	1.72*	1.51	1.46	1.76	1.99*
Maternal migration	1.01	1.01	1.38	1.35	0.64	0.60
Paternal migration	1.31	1.25	1.20	1.16	1.43	1.38
Caretaker monitoring/ supervision		0.99		0.94		1.01
Caretaker hostility		1.54**		1.36*		1.76**
Caretaker–child bonding		0.94		1.04		0.92
School bond		0.81*		0.85		0.72
School performance		0.99		0.97		1.11
Pseudo R^2	0.18	0.19	0.15	0.18	0.14	0.17

Note: *$p < 0.05$; **$p < 0.01$. Demographic and family background variables such as age, sex, living in a school dorm, parental education and economic status, marital status of biological parents, and number of siblings were controlled in the models.

[a] Children of nonmigrant parents as the reference group.

delinquency. With every one unit increase in school bonding, the odds of participating in minor delinquency decreased by 19% (exp(b) = 0.81, $p < 0.01$). Although the effect of school bonding did not reach statistical significance in gender subgroup analyses, the effect size remained similar in both male (exp(b) = 0.85) and female groups (exp(b) = 0.72), suggesting that the lack of statistical significance were due to smaller sample sizes.

Finally, it bears mention that the comparison between model 1 and model 2 revealed that the standardized regression coefficients of caretaking arrangements did not change, suggesting that—contrary to the expectation—measures of caretaking practice and social bonding did not mediate the effects of caretaking arrangements on minor delinquency (MacKinnon & Dwyer, 1993).

Summary: Caretaking Arrangements and Children's Involvement in Problematic Behaviors

In this section, I summarize the major findings from the preceding quantitative data and discuss whether interview and field observation data provide additional support for these findings. In particular, I focus on four main aspects: (1) the associations between caretaking arrangements and children's involvement in problematic behaviors, (2) whether a child's gender serves as a moderator, and (3) the mediating effect of caretaking practices and school bonding.

Do Alternative Caretaking Arrangements Increase Children's Involvement in Problematic Behaviors?

I investigated this question by exploring the effects of caretaking arrangements on three related dimensions of children's problematic behaviors: deviant peer affiliation, deviant behavior, and minor delinquency. The results unequivocally demonstrate that alternative caretaking arrangements had significant but differential effects on children's problematic behaviors. While the results varied more or less across the three outcomes, the pattern was fairly clear. Being left behind influenced children's participation in problematic behaviors; the extent of this influence, however, depended on the specific type of caretaking arrangement. Two types of arrangement—father-only caretaking (i.e., maternal migration) and one-grandparent caretaking—were consistently associated with increased problematic behaviors, while the other two—mother-only caretaking (i.e., paternal migration) and two-grandparent caretaking—did not differ noticeably from the conventional two-parent caretaking arrangement.

These findings have important empirical and policy implications. Left-behind children, particularly left-behind boys, have faced increasing scrutiny in the past two decades, as media reports and criminal justice data show that those left behind (or formerly left behind) are disproportionally arrested, detained, or incarcerated (A. Shen, 2018; L. Zhang, 2017). Yet empirical studies on this subpopulation have been less conclusive. Many studies find that LBC exhibit a higher risk of engaging in delinquency, substance use, and problematic behaviors (X. Chen, 2017, 2021; Gao et al., 2010). At the same time, others contradict these findings and reveal that outcomes for left-behind children do not differ significantly from those cared for by two at-home parents (Graham & Jordan, 2011; Guo et al., 2012; H. Hu et al., 2014; Luo et al., 2018). The finding of the differential effect of caretaking arrangements provides further insight into this controversy, demonstrating that it is the type of caretaking arrangement—not the left-behind status of children—that matters the most.

First, for solo-parent migration, paternal migration appears to have a less detrimental effect on children's development when compared with maternal migration. A large body of domestic and transnational migration research sheds light on this difference, revealing that maternal migration drastically violates traditional social norms in patriarchal societies—in this case, the normatively gendered division of labor in rural China (Oliveira, 2018; Parreñas, 2005b, 2008). While a woman in Peace County actively participates in agricultural labor as much as a man does, she is often perceived as the *main* homemaker and her husband as the *main* provider. As such, the migration of a mother and her subsequent role reversal (i.e., now as the main provider) often lead to a series of chain reactions, pushing the remaining father—and many times others in the extended household—to fill the large space vacated by the migrant mother. The at-home father, as discussed in chapter 3, often struggles to fulfill homemaking roles such as cooking, cleaning, laundry, and providing emotional support for children. By contrast, the migration of a father, who maintains the prescribed main provider role when migrating, imposes little disruption in labor allocation and other relationship dynamics in the household; therefore, this migration is often seen as a continuation of the father's normative provider role and is thus accepted and appreciated by other household members.

This differential attitude toward maternal and paternal migration is vividly documented in studies of transnational migration in many developing countries (Oliveira, 2018; Parreñas, 2005a). In the Philippines, for example, children struggle to accept the reconstitution of a mother as a main economic provider and also lament the lack of emotional intimacy when the mother migrates. Yet they accept paternal migration without much protest. Interestingly, children in Peace County rarely complained about the absence of a mother, probably reflecting a lack of local employment opportunities and the prevalence of dual-parent migration at the research site. On the contrary, almost every grandparent interviewed implied that their daughters-in-law migrated too soon, leaving them to shoulder the heavy responsibility of caring for babies or toddlers. The following interviews demonstrate this general theme:

> Then the mother left and went out to *dagong*. (The baby was) one year and four months old . . . he was one year old in April, and she (the mother) left in August. This is the older daughter-in-law. The little one was one year old in February. She (the mother) left sometime in January. He was born on February 23, (the mother) left in January. Not even one year old, not even able to walk . . . two children, one could walk a little bit, another did not know how to walk.
>
> —grandpa Xiao

> We raised her from (when she was) three years old. (Actually) before she was three. Her mother went to *dagong* when she was one year old. She did it for one year and came back (and stayed) for another year, and then went to *dagong* again. After that, she has been out for a few years now.
>
> —grandpa Yubao

My daughter-in-law only stayed at home for nine months. After that, we were the ones to raise the children.

—grandpa Jingpin

Note that the fathers of these children were conspicuously absent in these conversations. It is clear that in the eyes of the grandparents, migrant mothers—who had to *dagong* to support their families and newly arrived children—were the ones to be blamed and criticized. The absence of the fathers did not generate any dissatisfaction or other negative emotions among the grandparents interviewed. Although traditional social norms regarding gender and gendered labor divisions have been increasingly challenged, they appear to be firmly held by older generations and are likely to be transmitted intergenerationally.

Another key finding of this study is that the effect of grandparent caretaking on children's problematic behaviors is not homogeneous. The findings reveal two-grandparent caretaking as an equivalent, if not better, substitution for normative two-parent caretaking, whereas one-grandparent caretaking appears to increase a child's likelihood of behavioral problems. Indeed, compared with two-parent caretaking, one-grandparent caretaking was consistently associated with increased participation in the three dimensions of problematic behaviors.

Although the findings on two-grandparent caretaking may appear counterintuitive, a small body of literature suggests that grandparenting is not worse than the traditional nuclear family arrangement and has advantages over some other arrangements (e.g., maternal migration; X. Chen, 2021; X. Chen & Jiang, 2019; X. Chen et al., 2017; Wen & Lin, 2012). It is possible that the prevalence of grandparent caregiving in rural China—regardless of parental migration status—makes this arrangement more socially acceptable for children left behind (Hu & Scott, 2016; Logan & Bian, 1999). Indeed, even among nonmigrant households in Peace County, it is quite common that grandparents—even when officially counted as members of a different household—live under the same roof with one married son (most often the youngest one) and provide needed childcare services.

In terms of the disparate effects of two-grandparent versus one-grandparent caretaking, I suspect that the differences are due to three factors. First, the responsibility of caretaking shared by two grandparents may be too physically and mentally challenging when shouldered by a single caretaker, particularly when simultaneously tasked with labor-intensive farming obligations (for details, please see chapter 3). In addition, as chapter 2 reveals, one-grandparent caretaking is often the direct product of an interaction between extreme household poverty, poor physical and mental health of family members, and marital dissolution—characteristics that exacerbate the challenges faced by left-behind children and caretakers. Furthermore, I suspect that the average age of one-grandparent caretakers is older, and as such, they may be more physically and mentally vulnerable than the two-grandparent group. Given that the divorce or separation rate is extremely low for this demographic group in rural China (Q. Wang & Zhou, 2010), the most likely reason a child would be living with one grandparent is when the other grandparent is already deceased, a situation that is often health- or age-related.

Do the Effects of Caretaking Arrangements Differ by a Child's Gender?

Gender is possibly one of the strongest correlates of deviant and delinquent behaviors in most societies due to the influence of sociocultural factors such as the internalization of gendered ideology and social roles and gender-structured differential opportunities conducive to deviance and delinquency (Kruttschnitt, 2013; R. X. Liu, 2019). My analyses uncover two major gender-related findings. First, consistent with much of the literature, there were substantial differences in deviance and delinquency across gender groups; boys in Peace County were at substantially higher risk of associating with deviant peers, engaging in minor delinquency, and participating in deviant activities than girls.

Second, the preceding analyses extend previous literature on left-behind children and demonstrate that the effects of caretaking arrangements are conditional on children's gender. For boys, those under alternative caretaking arrangements either *increased* or had the same level of problematic behaviors as children cared for by both parents. By contrast—and with the exception of one-grandparent caretaking—girls under alternative caretaking arrangements either *reduced* deviance/delinquency involvement or did not differ significantly from the reference group. In particular, maternal migration significantly increased boys' participation in deviant activities and affiliation with deviant peers. Conversely, maternal migration had a negligible effect on girls' involvement in problematic behaviors. Moreover, two-grandparent caretaking served as a protective factor against problematic behaviors for girls but had a much less protective effect on boys. Even when compared with their counterparts under normative two-parent caretaking arrangements, girls cared for by two-grandparent caretakers reported significantly *lower* participation in deviant activities, weaker association with deviant peers, and a similar level of involvement in minor crimes.

These gendered effects are likely the direct product of the interplay between traditional norms regarding childrearing and gender-structured opportunities conducive to deviance and delinquency—further exacerbated by parental migration and alternative caretaking. In Peace County, a common childrearing philosophy is that boys should be raised "outside" and girls raised "inside." As such, boys tend to spend more time in unsupervised and unstructured activities outside the home, while girls stay at home studying, watching TV, or playing with their cell phones. Consequently, these gendered lifestyle patterns generate more opportunities for boys to engage in deviant and delinquent behaviors.

These gender-structured opportunities conducive to delinquency and deviance are further exacerbated by parental migration and alternative caretaking arrangements. Girls—when one or both parents migrated—were under even stricter supervision and monitoring compared with their pre-migration level. This was observed particularly when grandparents were the primary caretakers. Like migrant parents, grandparents were concerned that their teenage granddaughters might associate with "bad" companions, develop a premature romantic relationship with boys, or become victims of sex or other types of crimes. Particularly, a girl's engagement in delinquency, deviance, or exposure to victimization could put into play a series of lifelong adverse physical and emotional consequences—potentially jeopardizing the family's honor. As such, grandparents often became overprotective and imposed more stringent rules on girls, restricting their association with friends and their involvement in unsupervised and unstructured activities. This quote from MiaoMiao, a fourteen-year-old girl living with her younger brother and grandparents when interviewed (also quoted in chapter 3), highlighted these strict rules:

INTERVIEWER: Are your grandparents strict with you?

MIAOMIAO: Well, it's okay. It depends . . . they are strict in some areas, but not in others. . . . For example, school, because they don't really know, they cannot be very strict with it.

INTERVIEWER: How about your social life?

MIAOMIAO: They control *everything*! For example, I need to tell them every time when I go out; I cannot go out when there are only two girls; (they need to know) whom I go with; I cannot be too far away.

INTERVIEWER: That means you need to go out with boys?

MIAOMIAO: No, they don't allow me to go out with boys. It means there should be at least three girls together. I feel, er, they just don't like me to go out. . . . We rarely go out to play.

What surprised me most in this interview was how strict and specific the rules were. MiaoMiao was not allowed to go out with boys and could only go out when there was a group of *three* girls, which substantially reduced her time spent outside with friends. In fact, she (correctly) sensed that her grandparents probably did not like her to go out at all! Other girls echoed MiaoMiao's comments. Xiaomei, another fourteen-year-old, said that since she did not have many friends in her village, she mostly stayed at home during weekends, studying or watching TV by herself. On the other hand, while boys in this sample also complained about strict supervision by grandparents, they freely admitted that they played with other boys or that they snuck out to play video games or sports during weekends. Several grandparents complained that they had no idea where their boys were during many weekends.

Do Caretaking Practices and School Bonding Play a Role?

I originally hypothesized that the differential effects of caretaking arrangements would be explained by strengthened or weakened bonding with conventional institutions such as school and family. In other words, parental migration and alternative caretaking arrangements may indirectly influence children's deviance and delinquency because left-behind children are more likely to experience weakened bonding with parents/caretakers, school, teachers, and student peers. To test these hypotheses, I first investigated whether the hypothesized mediators (i.e., caretaking practices and school bonding) were significantly associated with the three dimensions of problematic behaviors.

Granted, caretaking practices and school bonding were statistically associated with children's engagement in problematic behaviors. But interestingly, out of all three measures of caretaking practices, only the measure of hostile and punitive caretaking practices (e.g., yelling at, criticizing, and arguing with children) was significant, consistently predicting all three measures of problematic behaviors. Moreover, these associations were robust in the full sample and across both gender groups. The other two measures, caretaker–child bonding and caretaker monitoring and supervision, surprisingly, had no significant effect on any of the three dimensions—in the full sample or across the two gender groups. These findings suggest that the exposure to harsh discipline had the strongest effect on children's delinquency, most likely because it led to negative emotions (e.g., anger and resentment) requiring the use of corrective actions (e.g., rebellious or illegal activities; R. X. Liu, 2015, 2019).

Likewise, strong bonding with school, teachers, and peer students was a robust but slightly less consistent protective factor against problematic behaviors. While the strength of these associations varied to some extent, the overall protective effects of school bonding were similar across the two gender groups. Interestingly, school performance had no significant effect on children's involvement in minor delinquency and deviant behavior; however, it did slightly increase children's—particularly boys'—association with deviant peers. I suspect that this unexpected finding may be due to the higher social status accorded to academically gifted students in their schools. As we have seen in chapter 5, in China, academic success is often the only criteria used to evaluate a student's potential success. In contrast with American high schools, which grant more prestige to athletes, academically successful students in China are highly respected by their student peers and thus more likely to have diverse friendship networks. This claim is also supported by the finding that academic performance is not associated with deviant behavior or engagement in minor delinquency, suggesting that academic performance—rather than deviant or delinquent behaviors—may simply lead to an expanded and diverse social network.

I further explored whether caretaking practices and bonding to school mediated the relationship between parental migration/caretaking arrangements and children's engagement in deviance and delinquency. Surprisingly, I did not find a mediating effect in any of the models predicting the three dimensions of problematic behaviors. I suspect that this lack of mediating effect—in the full sample and for both gender groups—is due to two reasons. First, these measures, adapted from scales developed in the Western culture, may not be sensitive enough to fully capture the dynamic relationships between children and primary caretakers in Peace County. The caretaker monitor/supervision scale, for example, consisted of items such as whether caretakers knew where children were and whether children reported their whereabouts to caretakers. Although informative, this measure failed to capture the high intensity of caretaker control (e.g., the case of MiaoMiao discussed previously) prevalent among many rural families, potentially leading to weakened statistical power explaining the associations between caretaking arrangements and problematic behaviors (S. Li et al., 2022). Second, some unspecified social mechanisms may be at work and play a more critical role in explaining these associations. For example, the attitude of primary caretakers toward gender roles may influence children's behaviors more profoundly than daily monitoring and supervision practices. These attitudes can be manifested in diverse ways, including verbal and nonverbal gestures and emotions. Children, as many studies have demonstrated, are keen on observing and absorbing the trivial cues and readily use them to assess whether their behaviors are approved by caregivers (Giordano, 2010).

Long-Distance Parenting and Children's Involvement in Problematic Behaviors

In chapter 5, I established that long-distance parenting was associated with children's academic success, with many parents using their humble experience in urban areas and the "striving" ethos (Murphy, 2020) to motivate children to study hard and to "get ahead." This finding is expected, given the pivotal role academic performance plays in rural families' and individuals' aspirations for intergenerational mobility. Do migrant parents provide the same level of attention to other aspects of children's life, specifically their association with deviant peers and engagement in deviant and delinquent behaviors? I explore these topics in this section.

In the student survey, I asked children when they communicated with migrant parents and to what extent parents were concerned about their health, moral character, academic performance, food, mental issues, personal safety, and friends. The response categories for each item ranged from 1 = very concerned to 4 = not concerned at all. I investigated three items—moral character, personal safety, and association with friends—since these items have been documented to be either correlates or outcomes of children's involvement in deviance and delinquency.

Among the three items, children's personal safety ranked first, with 88 percent of the students reporting that their parents were very or somewhat concerned. The percentage of children reporting that migrant parents cared about their moral character was slightly lower, with 78 percent being very or somewhat concerned. Finally, migrant parents did not appear to be too worried about children's friendship networks, with less than two-thirds (64%) reporting that parents cared very much or somewhat about the association with friends. These numbers—albeit relatively high—paled in comparison with parents' concerns about other items such as children's academic performance and physical health. For example, 93 percent of parents were very or somewhat concerned about children's test scores, and 90 percent were very or somewhat concerned about children's physical health.

My interviews with migrant parents reveal similar findings. Among a dozen migrant parents interviewed, only one expressed concerns about his son's problematic behaviors, claiming that he had "lost" his son because of the child's truancy, running away, association with deviant peers, and other deviant or delinquent behaviors. Most parents did not even mention the possibility of children getting into any legal trouble. I suspect that this is due to the relatively low rate of deviance and delinquency in rural China as well as the strong presence and social control conventional institutions such as schools and families exert in these small rural communities. In Peace County, deviant role models and opportunities to engage in delinquency and deviance were extremely limited, as older children either were enrolled in high schools located in county seats or had already migrated to urban areas for employment. The relatively high concern about children's personal safety likely originated from local news regarding traffic accidents and drownings—reports often circulated among residents or exaggerated by local and national media. These concerns became relevant because an increasing number of children in Peace County, particularly middle school students, ride electronic motorcycles to and from schools. Migrant mother Xu, for example, gave us an example of a drowning in a nearby village that occurred when a student was riding a motorcycle and distracted by his cell phone:

> Around Spring Festival, a kid in Xing village, he was crossing a bridge. He was crossing the bridge while also checking his cell phone. Such a big kid, fell into the river and drowned! This is the problem, they don't even check the road, so addicted to their cell phone!

Migrant mother Guo mentioned a traffic accident involving several middle school students in the small town near her village:

> Just a few weeks ago, there occurred this huge accident. Three middle school children on an electronic motorcycle, one rider carrying two others, ran straight into a bus! All three kids died, three kids riding recklessly and killed themselves!

While parents were concerned about children's exposure to victimization and accidents, parental concerns regarding left-behind children's delinquency and deviance remained relatively low. Nevertheless, I investigated whether long-distance parenting influenced the three dimensions of children's problematic behaviors. Like my analyses in chapter 5, my purpose here was to explore whether long-distance parenting (e.g., frequency of communication, children's visits to host cities) was associated with children's problematic behaviors and whether these

TABLE 6.4
Multivariate regression model predicting long-distance parenting and problematic behaviors

	Deviant peers (nonstandardized coefficient)		Minor delinquency (odds ratio)		Deviant behaviors (odds ratio)	
	Model 1	Model 2	Model 1	Model 2	Model 1	Model 2
Number of children visiting	−0.00	−0.00	1.06	1.08	1.04	1.05
Frequency of parental call	0.02	0.03	0.99	0.99	0.96	0.97
Parental concerns	0.06*	0.04	1.02	0.87	1.02	0.91
Caretaker monitoring		−0.02		1.08		0.85
Caretaker hostility		0.04		1.63**		1.54**
Caretaker–child bonding		−0.00		0.89		1.06
R^2/Pseudo R^2	0.25	0.26	0.23	0.26	0.30	0.33

Note: *$p < 0.05$; **$p < 0.01$. Demographic and family background variables such as age, sex, living in a school dorm, parental education and economic status, marital status of biological parents, number of siblings, and self-control were controlled in the models.

effects were independent and beyond the influence of caretaking practices (e.g., monitoring and discipline) performed by at-home primary caretakers. Like chapter 5, I conducted this analysis among the subpopulation of currently left-behind children.

Table 6.4 shows the multivariate regression results predicting children's association with deviant peers, involvement in minor delinquency, and participation in deviant behaviors. I used model 1 to explore whether long-distance parenting—measured by the number of children's visits to migrant parents, the frequency of long-distance communication, and parental concerns about children's behaviors—was associated with children's engagement in problematic behaviors. In model 2, I added the caretaking practice factors to investigate whether long-distance parenting had an independent effect on children's behaviors beyond caretaking from primary caretakers at home. The demographic and family background variables used in previous regression models in this chapter (e.g., age, sex, self-control) were also controlled in these models.

Table 6.4 indicates that, overall, long-distance parenting had little effect on children's involvement in problematic behaviors. The only exception is parental concerns—an additive measure of concerns about children's moral character, personal safety, and association with friends. Parental concern was significantly associated with children's affiliation with deviant peers, but not significantly associated with involvement in minor delinquency or deviant behavior. Interestingly, the association between parental concerns and deviant peer association was positive, suggesting that this association may be a reflection of parental responses to children's problematic behaviors rather than an effective social control mechanism preventing deviant peer affiliation. Moreover, the three measures of long-distance parenting failed to predict minor delinquency and deviant behaviors. We suspect that this is probably due to the covert nature of these behaviors. Compared with deviant peer association—more outwardly visible to primary caretakers and local village residents—engagement in minor delinquency and deviant behaviors is more secretive and thus less likely to be observed by at-home caretakers, let alone by geographically distant parents.

Another important finding is that the effect of long-distance parenting, already weak, pales in comparison with the effects of caretaking practices at home. Consistent with results from previous analyses in this chapter, caretaker hostility toward left-behind children was a significant factor in predicting deviant behaviors and minor delinquency. One unit increase in caretakers' hostile attitude toward children increased the odds of children engaging in minor delinquency by 63 percent and in deviant behaviors by 54 percent. Moreover, the addition of measures of caretaking practices rendered the association between parental concerns and deviant peer association nonsignificant. Taken together, these results suggest that the effect of long-distance parenting on children's problematic behaviors was weak and much less significant when compared with caretaking practices at home.

Conclusion

Criminal and delinquent behaviors among left-behind children and young rural-to-urban migrants (who are also likely to be former left-behind children) have gained much public attention in recent years. There is anecdotal evidence suggesting that this group is more crime and delinquency prone when compared with other youth groups. Empirical research on this topic, however, is inconclusive. In this chapter, I addressed this research gap by investigating the influence of parental migration on three dimensions of problematic behaviors: deviant peer affiliation, deviant behaviors, and involvement in minor delinquency. Moreover, I explored whether these effects are exaggerated or mitigated by at-home caretaking, children's school success, and long-distance parenting.

I have reached several major conclusions. First, a child's left-behind status does influence problematic behaviors. The effects of being left behind, however, are far from being homogenous; rather, the extent and direction of these effects depend on the type of alternative caretaking arrangements. Overall, children living in mother-away families (i.e., maternal migration) or children cared for by one-grandparent caretakers have the highest risk of participation in deviant or delinquent activities, while children in father-away families (i.e., paternal migration) or those cared for by two-grandparent caretakers exhibit a similar or even lower likelihood of engaging in problematic behaviors. These associations, additionally, are conditioned by a child's gender. Particularly, maternal migration generally increases boys' problematic behaviors but has little influence on girls, while two-grandparent caretaking decreases girls' engagement in deviance or association with deviant peers but has a less noticeable protective effect on boys. It should also be noted that the detrimental effect of one-grandparent caretaking appears to be universal across gender groups.

I hypothesize that these associations would be explained by proximate social factors such as caretaking practices and school bonding; however, these hypotheses are not supported by our empirical data. While caretaking practices (e.g., caretaker hostility) and bonding with school and classmates have a direct effect on children's problematic behaviors, they do not explain away the effects of caretaking arrangements. I suspect that this is due to the cultural insensitivity of these measures—derived from and established in the Western literature. Prior research, for example, has documented that parenting measures such as caretaker warmth and support and monitoring/harsh discipline cannot fully capture the dynamic relationships at play in Chinese families, and utilizing these measures often fails to replicate findings commonly produced using data collected from European and American countries (Braithwaite, 2015; J. Liu, 2009). The development and refinement of culturally rooted theories and measures are thus urgently needed in local Chinese studies (J. Liu, 2018; Messner, 2015).

Finally, long-distance parenting does not have a noticeable effect on preventing children's involvement in problematic behaviors. Children's visits to host cities and more frequent parent–child long-distance communications, for example, do not lessen children's odds of participation in deviance or delinquency. Migrant parents do appear to be aware of their children's association with deviant friends and frequently use long-distance communication tools to remind children of its potential detrimental consequences. These strategies, however, are more of a response to children's problematic behaviors rather than an effective social control mechanism. While the influence of long-distance parenting is less observed in this chapter, I expect that it has a more visible effect on a child's appreciation and affection toward migrant parents and on a child's psychological well-being—the topics of chapter 7.

7

Children's Psychological Well-Being

Caretaking Practices, Long-Distance Parenting, and Ambiguous Loss

In a lovely sunny morning, Lulu, a five-year-old boy, was playing by himself in a cotton field where his aunt was there busy weeding. Lulu seemed to be a little bit unhappy, and his aunt asked why. Lulu said sadly, "My father went outside, my mother went outside, and now my older sister is going outside too. Now I am the only one left."

At the time of this interview, Lulu and his sister—about ten years his senior—were living with their maternal grandparents. His father had gone to *dagong* long before he was born, while his mother returned and stayed with him until he was three years old. Contrary to Lulu's expectations, his sister was not going out to *dagong*; rather, she had just been accepted by a senior high school in the county seat and would return home every two weeks. However, five-year-old Lulu could not possibly understand this distinction—he was simply upset that his sister would leave him too, just like his migrant parents.

Stories like Lulu's were quite common among children left behind in Peace County. Grandparents, for instance, recounted stories of children hysterically chasing parents as they left or refusing to speak for days or even weeks following a parent's fresh departure after a brief return visit. The relationship between parental absence and poor psychological outcomes appears intuitive, as it inevitably involves prolonged disruptions to family relationships, transitions in parenting and caretaking roles, and reliance on the functioning of the at-home parent or family members—all chronic and additional stressors for children (Dittman, 2018). Previous research has long established that parental absence such as parental divorce or separation results in a myriad of negative psychological outcomes, including psychological and physical anxiety, suicidal ideation, depression, and loneliness (Dittman, 2018; Zhang, 2020). The effect of parental migration, however, is more ambiguous. Previous studies on transnational migration have provided mixed findings, with some showing children of migrant parents exhibiting negative emotional outcomes while others provide null or even positive findings (Antia et al., 2020; Asis, 2006; Graham & Jordan, 2011; Mazzucato et al., 2015; Oliveira, 2018). For example, in their investigation of the effects of international parental migration in Ghana, Nigeria, and Angola, Mazzucato and colleagues (2015) found that parental migration was not associated with decreased levels of well-being per se, but rather, broader characteristics in the population such as transnational family arrangement and cultural context played a significant role.

The impact of China's internal parental migration on children's emotional well-being is likewise inconclusive. Numerous studies have found that parental migration engenders negative psychological outcomes—these studies suggest that children of migrant parents suffer poor psychological well-being in general and develop depression, anxiety, loneliness, and suicidal ideation (Fu & Law, 2018; H. Hu et al., 2014; Y. Liang et al., 2017; Tang, 2017; W. Wu et al., 2019; C. Zhao et al., 2018; X. Zhao et al., 2014). In a large-scale study with more than 4,500 students surveyed, M. Fu and colleagues (2017) found that children left behind were more likely to develop symptoms of depression, social anxiety, physical anxiety, and suicidal ideation. Likewise, X. Zhao et al. (2014) found a relatively higher level of social anxiety among LBC as well as substantial differences in causes and consequences associated with the LBC status. Finally, in their meta-analysis of recent publications, Y. Liang and colleagues (2017) concluded that left-behind children's depression level was significantly higher when compared with non-left-behind children.

On the other hand, several recent studies employing national data or more rigorous research designs (e.g., fixed effect methods) appear to provide contradictory evidence (Murphy et al., 2016; Ren & Treiman, 2016; W. Wu et al., 2019; H. Xu & Xie, 2015). Using data from the 2010 wave of the China Family Panel Studies, Ren and Treiman (2016) documented weak and inconsistent findings regarding the deleterious effects of parental migration, concluding that parental migration had negligible impact on the emotional well-being of children in the Chinese context. Similar findings were reported by H. Xu and Xie (2015), who used the same data but employed different methods and reported somewhat different outcomes. Summarizing recent studies, a meta-analysis conducted by W. Wu and colleagues (2019) revealed that the impact of parental migration appeared to be age sensitive and varied across children's developmental stages. Whereas the incidence of serious mental health status was nearly 2.7 times higher among LBC, there was no significant difference between LBC and those living with nonmigrant parents during their primary and junior high school years.

The inconsistent findings may be due to differences in research design, measurement, and sample characteristics. Moreover, many studies focus almost exclusively on the impacts of parental migration and caretaking arrangements, neglecting the mediating role of individual characteristics and familial dynamics in shaping these effects. For example, children who develop intimate relationships with migrant parents through long-distance communication or those who strongly bond with teachers and school may be less vulnerable to the detrimental effect of parental absence.

My goal in this chapter is to disentangle the complex associations between parental migration, caretaking arrangements, and children's psychological well-being, focusing on the intervening role of children's attitudes toward parental migration, parent–child long-distance communication, and caretaker–child interactional patterns. My investigation begins with analyses of the associations between parental migration/caretaking arrangements and multiple indicators of children's psychological well-being, including children's social anxiety, self-injurious behavior, social withdrawal, and physiological symptoms. Next, I explore whether the immediate environment, particularly at-home caretaking practices and children's bonding with school, influences children's psychological well-being beyond the impact of caretaking arrangements. Then I explore whether remote parenting, in the form of long-distance communication, parental return, and children's visits to parents, improves children's psychological well-being. Finally, using the ambiguous loss lens proposed by Pauline Boss (2002, 2016), I discuss children's ambivalent feelings toward parental migration and migrant parents themselves, studying the intricate associations between caretaking arrangements, ambiguous loss, and children's psychological well-being.

Children's Psychological Well-Being and Caretaking Arrangements

My first goal in this chapter is to explore whether the LBC status and caretaking arrangements are associated with elevated psychological problems among children in rural China. I began by using a series of statements adapted from measures in prior research to capture children's psychological well-being (F. Chang et al., 2019; R. Chen & Zhou, 2021). Students were asked to what extent these statements described what they had experienced in the past six months, with response categories of 0 = it did not match at all, 1 = it matched sometimes, and 2 = it matched very well. Based on each item's face validity and the findings of exploratory factor analyses, these statements were then grouped into four interrelated measures of psychological well-being: *self-injury*, *social anxiety*, *social withdrawal*, and *physiological symptoms*.

First, *self-injury* was measured by two items, asking children whether they had intentionally injured themselves or attempted suicide and whether they thought about committing suicide in the past six months. Thirteen percent of the respondents reported that they had intentionally injured themselves or attempted suicide, and an alarming one-quarter of students (24%) reported that they thought of committing suicide. The two items were then combined to create a dichotomized measure of *self-injury*, with 1 = ever thought or attempted to commit suicide or hurt themselves and 0 = otherwise. Overall, more than one-quarter of children (27.9%) attempted self-injurious behavior or attempted/thought about committing suicide.

TABLE 7.1
Sex, caretaking arrangements, and children's negative emotions

	Self-injury	Social anxiety	Social withdrawal	Physiological symptoms
Total	27.9%	0.70	0.38	1.33
Sex	**	**		**
Male	23.3%	0.64	0.37	1.21
Female	32.7%	0.78	0.40	1.47
Caretaking arrangements				
Living with both parents	25.9%	0.69	0.36	1.30
Maternal migration	34.6%	0.70	0.42	1.43
Paternal migration	29.0%	0.75	0.43	1.42
Living with both grandparents	27.8%	0.72	0.37	1.35
Living with one grandparent	30.8%	0.70	0.46	1.41

Note: **$p < 0.01$.

Social anxiety was measured with five items including whether children felt constantly nervous, were afraid/anxious, felt guilty, were easily embarrassed, and felt very shy over the past six months. I averaged the scores of the five items to create the final scale of *social anxiety*, which exhibited acceptable reliability, with a Cronbach's alpha score of 0.74. The third scale, *social withdrawal*, included four items inquiring to what degree children agreed with the four following statements: (1) I prefer staying by myself and do not want to be with others, (2) I don't like to speak to others, (3) I always try to hide myself, and (4) I try not to interact with other people. Similarly, I averaged the scores of these four items to create the final scale of *social withdrawal*, with a Cronbach's alpha score of 0.73. Finally, the scale of *physiological symptoms* consisted of just two items: whether children always felt dizzy or tired in the past six months. The two items were summed to compute the composite scale of *physiological symptoms*, with a Cronbach's alpha score of 0.70.

Table 7.1 investigates whether parental migration and caretaking arrangements are associated with these four measures. Overall, children living with two nonmigrant parents (non-LBC) consistently reported the lowest level of psychological problems, including self-injury, social anxiety, social withdrawal, and physiological symptoms. Within the LBC group, children of migrant mothers reported the highest rate of self-injury and physiological symptoms, children of migrant fathers reported the highest level of social anxiety, and children of one-grandparent caretakers reported the highest level of social withdrawal. Nevertheless, the differences between LBC and non-LBC and differences within the LBC subpopulation were not statistically significant, suggesting that the status of LBC or types of caretaking arrangements does not explain these variations.

Given that gender is one of the primary factors shaping children's development, correlates, and consequences of mental health problems (Rosenfield & Mouzon, 2013), table 7.1 also investigates the association between children's gender and psychological problems. Consistent with a large body of previous research (Anand, 2020; Rosenfield & Mouzon, 2013), girls in Peace County were significantly more likely to experience psychological problems than boys. Specifically, girls were more likely to engage in self-injurious behaviors, experienced more anxiety, and reported a significantly higher level of physiological symptoms. Moreover, although the association between gender and symptoms of withdrawal was not statistically significant, girls nevertheless reported more withdrawal symptoms than boys.

Do Left-Behind Children Have Poor Psychological Well-Being?

My bivariate analyses (table 7.1) suggest that LBC experienced a similar level of psychological problems as non-LBC and that caretaking arrangements had an insignificant effect on children's development of psychological problems. While these findings contest much of the previous research on international migration and studies of domestic rural-to-urban migration in China, they are consistent with some recent studies (Biao, 2007; Ren & Treiman, 2016; L. Wang et al., 2019; H. Xu & Xie, 2015). H. Xu and Xie (2015), for example, used the propensity score matching methods to estimate the effect of parental migration on children's subjective well-being, finding little difference between LBC and non-LBC across multiple life domains. Using the same data set, Ren and Treiman (2016) found that children left behind were not at risk of increased emotional difficulties compared with children living with both nonmigrant parents, ultimately concluding that in the Chinese context, migrant families remained "socially intact even when physically separated" (Ren & Treiman, 2016, p. 46). Biao (2007), in his review of the left-behind children literature, concludes that "left-behind children face various problems, but they are not evidently worse off than those who live with their parents" (p. 186).

I reason that the lack of significant differences is due to the complex interplay between two factors: the normalization of parental migration and alternative caretaking arrangements in rural China and the material and nonmaterial benefits of remittance. First, parental migration is so prevalent in Peace County and many other areas in rural China that children and adult caretakers have already normalized the practices of parental migration and alternative caretaking arrangements, thus lessening the development of psychological problems among LBC. Indeed, in the two villages where I conducted my field observation, rural-to-urban migration was such a widespread practice that children sometimes encouraged parents to work "outside," understanding that *dagong* was a viable and sometimes inevitable option for most parents and young adults. In addition, children in the same village often share their experiences of alternative caretaking after being left behind with each other, thus providing mutual support and creating a new "normal," ultimately reducing the emotional costs of parental migration and absence. Indeed, left-behind children in Peace County did not consider themselves a marginalized and vulnerable group, as most of their peers were in the same position with at least one parent or older sibling working "outside." As Rachel Murphy (2020) observed in her study, some non-LBC children were even envious of their LBC peers because they were cared for by more affectionate, more forgiving, and less strict grandparents and thus were often relieved of many housework chores or agricultural obligations.

The second factor contributing to this null finding is that parental migration generally improves a household's financial status and provides children with better access to nutritious food, spacious housing, quality education, and other basic needs, potentially enhancing their overall emotional well-being (R. Chen & Zhou, 2021). Although the positive effect of remittance on children's psychological well-being is not well documented, some studies suggest that this effect can also be transmitted intergenerationally (F. Chen & Liu, 2012; Choi & Zhang, 2021). Choi and Zhang (2021), for example, found that grandparents providing care to grandchildren exhibited better mental health than those providing no care. My field observations in Peace County offer additional sociocultural nuances for this finding. First, I observed that this association was particularly strong when migrant parents had stable and decent financial sources, potentially assuring grandparents of eldercare and support for when they become physically or mentally unable to support themselves. As discussed previously (chapter 3), although many grandparents did not regularly receive financial compensation for childcare services, there was a mutual understanding that financial or emotional support would be made available in the future when needs arise. As grandfather Longer succinctly commented, "When I cannot move, cannot do anything, you can give me money." Second, many grandparent caretakers expressed feelings of pride and fulfillment when adult children were financially successful, acknowledging that they were part of the "striving team" and that their childcare and other sacrifices greatly contributed to their adult children's financial success. Many grandparents, for example, humbly stated that although they could not do much, at least they helped raise grandchildren so migrant parents did not need to worry about them much. These cross-generational feelings likely contribute to the development of intimacy and emotional bonding between grandparents and children and positively influence children's overall psychological well-being.

Given that I find no significant difference in psychological well-being between LBC and non-LBC, in the remaining section, I focus on the subpopulation of children left behind, exploring the salient influences of their immediate surroundings (e.g., caretaking practices and school bonding), long-distance parenting, and the role of children's ambivalent feelings toward both migration and their migrant parents.

Caretaking Practices, School Bonding, and Psychological Well-Being among Left-Behind Children

Left-behind children's psychological well-being is associated with a myriad of individual and environmental factors, but of critical importance is their interaction with the immediate environment—namely, the interaction with at-home caretakers, school, and student peers (Bryan et al., 2012; R. Chen & Zhou, 2021; Cheng & Sun, 2015; C. Zhao et al., 2017). R. Chen and Zou (2021) reported that parental migration increased children's depression via the reduction of parental involvement. Likewise, in their study of a random sample of children recruited from schools in migrant-sending rural areas in the Zhejiang and Guizhou provinces, C. Zhao and colleagues (2017) highlighted the prominent roles that both children's relationship bonds with nuclear family members and school performance play in shaping children's psychological health status. Employing multivariate regression models, table 7.2 illustrates the associations between children's psychological well-being, caretaking practices, and school bonding when caretaking arrangements, children's individual traits, and household characteristics were controlled in the analyses.

Among the three indicators of at-home caretaking (i.e., caretaker monitoring/supervision, caretaker hostility toward children, and caretaker–child bonding), children's perception of caretakers' hostility and rejection was the only variable significantly associated with children's emotional well-being. When children believed that they were disliked or rejected by caretakers, they were more likely to experience self-injurious behaviors, social anxiety, and physiological symptoms. Caretaker hostility, however, was not significantly associated with withdrawal symptoms among children left behind. Interestingly, caretaker monitoring and supervision and child–caretaker bonding did not exhibit a protective effect, suggesting that conflictual and negative family dynamics were the main forces influencing children's emotional well-being.

Regarding child–school dynamics, school bonding—rather than academic performance—emerged as a protective factor against heightened psychological problems and was consistently and significantly associated with all four outcome variables. It is worth noting that bonding with school and classmates—among all the measures of the immediate environment—was the only significant factor associated with children's social withdrawal symptoms. Children strongly bonded with classmates and school may be predisposed to be more socially active; however, it is also possible that children actively interacting with teachers and student peers learn necessary interpersonal skills that can be applied to other social settings, thus allowing them to become more socially competent. It is also interesting to note that when children's bonding with school, teachers, and classmates was controlled, school performance was not significantly associated with any of the four indicators of psychological well-being, suggesting that in the era of education fever (Y. Chen et al., 2021; Yu & Suen, 2005), children may face ambient and never-ending

TABLE 7.2
Multivariate regression models predicting the associations between caretaking practices, school bonding, and children's psychological well-being

	Self-injury	Social anxiety	Social withdrawal	Physiological symptoms
Intercept	0.62**	1.27**	0.96**	2.17**
Caretaker monitoring/supervision	0.04	−0.01	0.02	0.03
Caretaker hostility	0.14**	0.10**	0.01	0.19**
Caretaker–child bonding	−0.03	0.03	−0.03	−0.09
School bond	−0.17**	−0.08*	−0.19**	−0.21*
School performance	0.02	0.01	0.02	0.02
One-grandparent caretaking	0.02	−0.03	0.07	0.00
Maternal migration	0.03	−0.03	0.02	0.03
Paternal migration	−0.01	0.01	0.06	0.04
Male	−0.12**	−0.15**	−0.09*	−0.36**
Age	0.02	−0.01	0.03	0.10
Boarding school	−0.08	−0.02	−0.01	−0.04
Parental education	0.00	−0.02	0.02	−0.01
Household property	0.01	0.05	0.01	0.08
Perceived economic status	−0.01	−0.12*	0.01	−0.08
Parents divorced	−0.11*	−0.11*	−0.10*	−0.28*
Number of siblings	−0.03	0.00	−0.01	−0.02
R^2/Pseudo R^2	0.12	0.13	0.11	0.10

Note: *$p < 0.05$; **$p < 0.01$. $N = 560$.

[a] Children whose parents both migrated and are living with two grandparents as the reference group.

pressure to achieve better academic performance—a goal nearly impossible to satisfy for parents, caretakers, teachers, and even children themselves.

Consistent with the bivariate analysis, none of the four measures of children's psychological well-being was associated with types of caretaking arrangement. Among control variables, two variables stood out. First, a child's gender was a statistically significant correlate, with girls consistently scoring higher in self-injurious behaviors, social anxiety, social withdrawal, and physiological symptoms. Second, the marital status of biological parents was consistently and significantly associated with children's emotional well-being. Specifically, when children's biological parents were divorced or separated, children exhibited more psychological problems, including higher levels of self-injury and suicidal ideation, social anxiety, social withdrawal, and more physiological symptoms. Finally, perceived family economic status—measured by asking the children to rank their families' economic conditions in their villages—was significantly associated with children's social anxiety, suggesting that left-behind children—at an early age—were aware of family economic status and its relevant implications (e.g., educational investment).

What Are the Immediate Protective and Risk Factors Associated with Left-Behind Children's Psychological Well-Being?

Although much research has investigated differences in psychological well-being between LBC and non-LBC, relatively few studies have explored the variations within the population of left-behind children and investigated contributing immediate environmental factors. The analyses produce two noteworthy findings.

First, the multivariate analyses indicate that types of caretaking arrangements did not significantly influence left-behind children's psychological well-being. While previous research has demonstrated that certain types of parental migration and caretaking arrangements—particularly dual-parent or maternal migration—negatively influence children's emotional well-being, these studies also show that proximate factors (e.g., caretaker–child interactions and school bonding) play a more direct and salient role in shaping children's psychological well-being (R. Chen & Zhou, 2021; Lu et al., 2019b; Ren & Treiman, 2016). My analyses provide further support for this line of research, demonstrating that children's perception of caretaker hostility was the deciding factor in dampening children's psychological well-being. It is possible that children left behind, with one or both parents working "outside," have no other adults from whom to seek material or emotional assistance when the primary caretakers ignore or are indifferent to their needs. The fact that many children are cared for by those culturally deemed "unnatural" caretakers (e.g., at-home fathers or extended family members such as uncles and aunts) may exacerbate such negative feelings, pushing children to internalize them and thus develop social anxiety, physiological problems, and self-injurious behaviors.

The key protective factor against the development of psychological problems among LBC was children's connection with the school, teachers, and student peers. The protective effect of school bonding appeared to be universal, reducing children's self-injurious behavior, levels of social anxiety, symptoms of social withdrawal, and the development of negative physiological symptoms. Consistent with the few studies examining the effect of school bonding among left-behind children (Bryan et al., 2012; L. Wang et al., 2019), left-behind children's desire and effort to perform well in school as well as their strong connection with peer students and teachers effectively shielded them from the development of psychological and emotional problems. This association is particularly strong for high school students in rural China, given that school is the primary social setting in which these students spend all weekdays from around 7 A.M. to at least 5 P.M. Yunhao, a seventh grader, for example, explained that on weekdays, he arrived at school at 7 A.M. (and he left home at 6:20 A.M.) to participate in the morning self-study section and left once formal classes ended at 5:05 P.M. In addition, students who lived close to schools or attended boarding schools were required to participate in the night self-study section, which generally ended around 10:00 to 10:30 P.M. Finally, as many students in Peace County commented, because of a lack of extracurricular activities, friends and teachers in school were often the only social connections they had besides family members and relatives. In other words, strong bonding with the school and student peers might be the only way these children can be connected to others, particularly for those who are the only children in the household.

It should also be noted that although children's academic performance did not have a pronounced positive effect on children's psychological well-being, academic performance and school bonding are inextricably linked and should be understood as a package (Bryan et al., 2012). Students with excellent academic performance, for example, are typically well respected by student peers and adored by schoolteachers, thus enjoying a better social status among their peers. Indeed, parents and grandparents in Peace County encouraged their children to befriend academically gifted students while discouraging association with students with poor grades, concerned that the latter would lead their children down wayward paths. The lack of academic performance's direct positive effect may reflect that in the era of education fever (Y. Chen et al., 2021; Yu & Suen, 2005), students at this stage (i.e., junior high school) face enormous and never-ending pressure to achieve the best grades possible so that they can excel in entrance exams and be accepted by key senior high schools with the hopes of ultimately enrolling in prestigious universities and achieving intergenerational mobility. Stress resulting from this pressure may offset any potential positive effects on children's overall psychological well-being.

Long-Distance Parenting and Left-Behind Children's Psychological Well-Being

The impact of long-distance parenting—in the form of long-distance communication, parental return during holidays, and children's visits to parents—on left-behind children's psychological well-being has not yet been systematically studied. While descriptive studies demonstrate that long-distance communication facilitates the development of intimacy between geographically separated children and parents (P. L. Liu & Leung, 2017; Pan et al., 2013; Parreñas, 2005a), so far, I have not located a prior study that empirically quantifies such a relationship. I propose, in addition to the ubiquitous influence of immediate surroundings (i.e., at-home caretaking and school bonding), that long-distance parenting is a critical way to build emotional intimacy between migrant parents and left-behind children, potentially elevating children's psychological well-being. Using multivariate regression models, table 7.3 illustrates the relationships between indicators of long-distance parenting and children's negative emotions when the duration of parental migration, individual traits, and household characteristics were considered.

I used five indicators to measure long-distance parenting, including the number of times that children visited migrant parents in host cities (1 = never, 5 = at least two times a year), the frequency of long-distance communication such as phone calls or video calls (1 = not applied, 7 = every one or two days), the extent to which migrant parents were concerned about children's mental and psychological issues (1 = not at all, 4 = very much), and the frequency of father's and mother's visits home (1 = never came back, 4 = once every three to six months). In addition, I controlled the father's and mother's cumulative time of working "outside" in the model. For each item, I asked the children how long their fathers and mothers worked outside over time (1 = not migrated, 4 = nine years or more).

In the regression models, two measures of long-distance parenting—the frequency of long-distance communication and parental concerns about children's psychological and mental issues—stood out. The frequency of long-distance communication played a significant role in shaping children's emotional well-being, with more frequent communication significantly reducing children's self-injurious behaviors ($b = -0.04$, $p < 0.05$) and social withdrawal symptoms ($b = -0.05$, $p < 0.01$). Frequent migrant parent–child communication, however, did not significantly decrease children's feelings of anxiety or the development of physiological symptoms. Moreover, parental awareness of and open discussion with children regarding their mental and psychological issues played a prominent role in improving children's psychological well-being. When migrant parents were able to acknowledge, identify, and openly discuss these issues with children, children were less likely to exhibit self-injurious behavior ($b = -0.08$, $p < 0.01$), social anxiety ($b = -0.05$, $p < 0.05$), social withdrawal ($b = -0.06$, $p < 0.01$), and physiological symptoms ($b = -0.17$, $p < 0.01$). Interestingly, children's visits to the host cities of migrant parents and parents' yearly visits to their hometown were not significantly associated with any of the four outcome variables, suggesting that continuous and positive parent–child communication—albeit mediated through long-distance tools—may have a more profound influence on children's mental and psychological development than these intensive but short-duration interactions.

Consistent with the findings illustrated in table 7.2, gender and marital status of biological parents were both significant predictors of children's psychological problems, with girls and those whose biological parents divorced or separated exhibiting greater vulnerability to emotional problems. In addition, the multivariate regression analyses show that age—despite the small range in our sample—was a statistically significant correlate of social withdrawal and the development of physiological symptoms, with older children exhibiting more of these symptoms. Given that psychological problems increase when children are exposed to a higher level of stress, I expect that children left behind may be more vulnerable to

TABLE 7.3

Multivariate regression models predicting long-distance parenting and negative emotions (unstandardized regression coefficients)

	Self-injury	Social anxiety	Social withdrawal	Physiological symptoms
Intercept	0.73	1.38	0.60	2.21
Children's visits to parents	−0.01	0.02	0.00	−0.03
Frequency of parental call	−0.04*	−0.01	−0.05**	−0.05
Conversation about mental issues	−0.08**	−0.05*	−0.06**	−0.17**
Frequency of father visiting home	0.04	−0.01	0.00	0.04
Frequency of mother visiting home	0.00	0.02	0.01	−0.04
Accumulative time of paternal migration	−0.03	0.03	0.02	0.11
Accumulative time of maternal migration	−0.01	−0.03	−0.03	−0.06
One-grandparent caretaking	0.03	−0.04	0.08	0.01
Maternal migration	0.10	0.00	0.07	0.20
Paternal migration	0.04	0.04	0.08	0.01
Male	−0.11**	−0.14**	−0.07	−0.32**
Age	0.04	0.00	0.05*	0.14*
Boarding school	−0.04	0.01	−0.01	−0.02
Parental education	0.01	−0.02	0.02	−0.01
Household property	0.03	0.05	0.02	0.10
Perceived economic status	−0.02	−0.13*	0.00	−0.10
Marital status of biological parents	−0.13*	−0.14*	−0.08	−0.32*
Number of siblings	−0.03	0.00	−0.01	−0.02
R^2/Pseudo R^2	0.11	0.10	0.09	0.10

Note: *$p < 0.05$; **$p < 0.01$; $N = 560$.

[a] Children living with two grandparents as the reference group.

psychological and emotional problems when they are in ninth grade or senior high school—a critical period for Chinese children as they face enormous pressure and increasing scrutiny to succeed academically.

Does Long-Distance Parenting Improve Children's Psychological Well-Being?

Although long-distance parenting—particularly mobile parenting—has become an increasingly popular topic in domestic and transnational migration research (Alinejad, 2019; Pan et al., 2013; R. Zhou et al., 2017), the influence of long-distance parenting on children's psychological well-being is surprisingly scarce. My results demonstrate that long-distance parenting improves children's psychological well-being, with intensive long-distance communication negatively associated with specific types of psychological well-being such as children's self-injurious behavior and symptoms of social withdrawal and open and honest conversation about mental and psychological issues decreasing children's psychological and emotional problems in general. The protective effect of long-distance communication can potentially be explained by two factors. First, frequent, constant, and timely information flow (e.g., education performance, children's health, the health of parents and caretakers) among members of the translocal family creates a "virtual presence" of parents, thus increasing parent-child intimacy and lessening feelings of strangeness or abandonment. The frequent information exchange—particularly information regarding undesirable living conditions, demanding work schedules, and discrimination and prejudice migrant parents experience in everyday life—may help children further understand and appreciate parents' sacrifices, motivating them to study hard in school and contribute as a member of the "striving team." One story told by Laojui, a forty-year-old man when interviewed, exemplifies the hardship of migrant parents' everyday life and the prejudice and discrimination against them:

> I was in Guangzhou, I worked in Guangzhou for a short period in 2012. I had a whole day of hard work and took a bus to go back to my apartment at night. I was so tired. My clothes were wrinkled, dirty, and smelled bad. My whole body smelled bad, I guess. The bus was very crowded. I stood there, and no one was sitting or standing close to me like I was a pile of dog shit in a crowded bus. . . . I was embarrassed, but I was angry too! I worked my tails off every day and all the city people looked down and despised me . . .

In my interviews, migrant parents recounted numerous such stories. These stories were often intentionally or unintentionally conveyed to children left behind by at-home parents or grandparents, instilling and reinforcing the idea that migrant parents were paying huge emotional and physical costs for the benefit of the family and children. The authenticity of these stories was often validated by children's firsthand experiences or observations when they visited their parents.

These stories and firsthand observations, in turn, motivated children to study hard and perform well in school, thus potentially steering them away from self-pity or other injurious behaviors. At the same time, this may also explain why long-distance communication failed to ease children's symptoms of physical or social anxiety, as children also felt the enormous pressure to join the "striving team" by achieving academic excellence in school or behaving well at home (e.g., being obedient and helping household chores).

The finding regarding the protective effect of conversation about psychological and mental issues is somewhat surprising. As discussed in chapter 4, parent–child long-distance conversation mostly focused on children's school performance, the physical health of children and caretakers, and daily routines. Whereas only slightly more than half of the migrant parents (52%) had conversations with their children about mental and psychological issues, their beneficial effects were strongly supported by the empirical data. Given that psychological and mental health issues are rarely taught and discussed in China's middle school classrooms, communication with parents regarding these topics helps children better understand their nature, identify potential social and individual causes, and develop appropriate and effective coping strategies. More importantly, long-distance communication with parents provides children a good opportunity to express their frustration, anger, and other inner feelings, thus decreasing their stress level while simultaneously improving bonding with the geographically separated parents.

Children's Ambiguous Loss and Psychological Well-Being

In recent years, the ambiguous loss framework as described by Pauline Boss has been promoted to examine the family experiences of transnational migration (Boss, 2009, 2016; Falicov, 2012; Perez & Arnold-Berkovits, 2018; Suárez-Orozco et al., 2002). Boss argues that unlike a loss such as a natural death—which is clear-cut and often concludes with a formal grieving ceremony (e.g., a funeral)—losses such as missing family members or elderly with dementia do not have a predetermined or definite closure, making the grieving incomplete, postponed, or ambiguous. Boss identifies two types of ambiguous loss: (1) loss among families with members who are physically absent but psychologically present, such as children missing or members lost during a war, and (2) loss among families with members who are physically present but psychologically absent, including those who suffer severe mental illness and are thus cognitively and emotionally unavailable to those around them. Migration is considered a "cross-over" (Boss, 2016), as it contains elements of both types of ambiguous loss—those who migrate are not physically present but remain keenly present in the psyche of those left behind (and vice versa); at the same time, the stresses of adaptation may make it difficult for some family members to meet the emotional and mental well-being needs of others. For example, a left-behind father may be reluctant to cross gender boundaries and fail to provide "emotional work" for children.

This discrepancy—being psychologically connected but physically absent—may create confusion, anger, and other negative emotions for those left behind, particularly when the affected family cannot successfully reconfigure itself and effectively allocate limited resources to those with pressing physical and emotional needs. An emerging literature in transnational migration research reveals that ambiguous loss can manifest in multiple forms, including persistent doubts about the benefits of migration, repeated attempts to reinterpret the benefits and costs, and negative emotions such as confusion, depression, anger, and resentment (Carranza, 2022; Perez & Arnold-Berkovits, 2018; Pottinger, 2005; Solheim et al., 2016; Suárez-Orozco et al., 2002). A key concept in the ambiguous loss framework is "boundary ambiguity," defined as family members not knowing who is in and who is out of the system after a certain period (Boss, 2016; Falicov, 2012; Perez & Arnold-Berkovits, 2018). When parents migrate during children's early childhood or are absent for a long duration, they may miss the opportunity to develop emotional ties with geographically separated children, or children may gradually establish a new caregiver–child dyad, transferring their emotional connections to current adult caregivers. As a result, the lasting psychological presence of parents may remain underdeveloped, leading children to question the membership of migrant parents within the family system.

Children's Ambivalent Feelings toward Migrant Parents and Boundary Ambiguity

The in-depth interview and observations reveal four major themes: (1) the prevalence of children's ambivalent feelings toward parental migration, (2) weakened emotional connection between children and migrant parents, (3) feelings of strangeness and awkwardness when parents return, and (4) children's reluctance to accord the insider status to migrant parents in the family system.

The first major theme emerging from the data is that children left behind in Peace County had ambivalent feelings toward their parents' migration. While most children—particularly older ones—understood the necessity to work "outside" and appreciated parents' sacrifices and efforts, many were concerned about the loss of living together as a family. Jingwen—a seventh grader—did not hesitate to say that her parents' migration was good because "my daddy said he went outside to *dagong* and make money for us to go to school." Lu, another seventh grader, was a little more reserved, contending that "it is good and bad. The good thing is that it improves the family (financially), not that poor anymore. The bad part is there is no time together." MiaoMiao, another seventh grader, had similarly ambivalent feelings toward parental migration. She said, "I don't know. If they stay at home, then the family's financial sources will be lost. But when they work outside, grandparents have a tough job . . . emotionally, definitely want to stay together."

The second major theme is that many left-behind children in Peace County felt an "empty space" in their emotional relationships with their parents and felt frustrated, depressed, lonely, and sometimes angry. When children were asked to rate their relationship with migrant parents, they provided at most lukewarm responses, ranging from "feeling like strangers" to "it's fine." Most of the students readily acknowledged that these relationships were not strong. Ping, a seventh grader, said her relationship with her parents was "very, very faint." Jiahui, an eighth grader, said, "It's okay. After all, we don't communicate often." Indeed, among all the children interviewed, only one student said that she had a good relationship with her migrant parents. Wei, an eighth grader, declined to answer this question, saying that he "did not know"—understanding that an honest answer would be considered socially undesirable or "unfilial." In sharp contrast, children almost unanimously contended that they had a "good" relationship with grandparent caretakers. When pressed to compare his relationship with migrant parents versus with grandparents, Wei simply said that "it is incomparable."

Most children in Peace County who contended that they had "weak" or "it's fine" emotional connections with migrant parents understood the economic justification and more or less accepted the prolonged parental absence. Junhao, whose parents were divorced and who was cared for by his maternal grandparents, revealed that he had a better relationship with his grandparents than with his mother or biological father. Nevertheless, he reported that he had a decent relationship with his mother, characterizing the relationship as being "fine." In addition, while preferring to live with his grandparents, Junhao was not opposed to living with his mother. After all, he felt that his mother had done her best to support him financially and emotionally. She had tried to compensate for her sparse yearly visits (i.e., during Spring Festivals) by calling him every week and bringing him to Chongqing, where she worked, during summer breaks over the previous few years.

At the other side of the continuum of emotional ambivalence was Chuangqi, an eighth grader, who was much blunter and more critical of his parents. The following interview quotes provide details about the evolving relationship between him and his parents:

INTERVIEWER: How is your relationship with your parents?

CHUANGQI: It's so-so . . .

INTERVIEWER: What do you mean so-so?

CHUANGQI: It's not as good as my relationship with my grandparents.

INTERVIEWER: When your parents were in Fujian province, did you miss them?

CHUANGQI: Not really . . . because when I was little, I did not remember much about them. I was raised by my grandparents from I was little. In total, my mother raised me for less than two years . . . we did not have a connection . . .

INTERVIEWER: Does this affect you?

CHUANGQI: Yeah, it does. When they came back to visit, they would ask me, sometimes, not to do this or not to do that. I felt like, you did not raise me, why did you want to supervise my behavior now? I feel that there is a generational gap between me and those two. For example, when they come back, I feel that I am not very excited, because they, I feel that they are like strangers, not even as intimate as those in the village. Friends in the village, grandpa, grandma. Feel like every year, they come to visit just one time, come back one time, and go back one time . . . it's like they are strangers.

INTERVIEWER: Now they are back and living in DeAn, are you going to go there and live with them?

CHUANGQI: No, I am not willing to go. I will not go.

INTERVIEWER: I suppose you still need to go in the future.

CHUANGQI: No, I don't think so.

In this conversation, Chuangqi characterized his relationship with migrant parents as "so-so," "like they are strangers," and "not even as intimate as those in the village." In fact, Chuangqi was quite defiant when his parents attempted to supervise him during their visits, claiming that since "you did not raise me, why did you want to supervise my behavior now?" Moreover, he made it clear that he would not live with his parents even after they had already returned and lived just one hour away. By contrast, Chuangqi had developed a strong emotional connection with his grandmother, grandma Zhang, and appreciated her care and love. During our interview, grandma Zhang revealed a conversation between her and Chuangqi. She recalled:

> My grandson is so lovely. He said, "Grandma, I will study hard, and I will bring honor to you." I said, "I don't need any honor, (studying hard) is for your own benefit." He said, "That's not true. Others will say that my grandma is so awesome, and she raised a grandson to college" [laughing]. My grandson said it himself, he will bring honor to me.

Chuangqi's feelings of estrangement and anger were direct results of a lack of time spent with his parents ("in total, my mother raised me for less than two years") and the resulting emotional transfer to his grandparents. From the interview, I found that Chuangqi had never visited his parents' host city—which was locally deemed as a lack of responsible parenting—during their more than ten years' *dagong* in Fujian province. Moreover, due to their poor physical health and meager income, Chuangqi's parents provided little financial support for him and his nine-year-old sister. In fact, over the previous few years, his father's health status had further deteriorated—a deciding factor for the couple's return—and he was recently granted *dibao*, a form of governmental assistance for low-income families in rural areas. In our caretaker interview, grandma Zhang mentioned multiple times that the parents did not send remittances or pay even the children's basic living costs (i.e., food and school). Apparently, Chuangqi felt abandoned and was angry, contending that his parents did not have the right to monitor or supervise him, since "you did not raise me"—which can be construed from physical, emotional, and financial perspectives.

The third theme is that due to prolonged absence, children often felt uneasy and awkward about or unsure of what to do when parents returned during holidays or other events. Chuangqi, for example, remarked that "When they come back, I feel that I am not very excited." MiaoMiao said during the first few days of her parents' visits, they "did not have much conversation, and felt a little bit of strangeness." Some children coped with this additional stress by pretending that they "did not care." In an informal gathering, migrant father Ping lamented the lack of interaction during these visits:

> When I was at home, he (the son) did not stay with me either. My daughter was a little bit better . . . neither talked with me much . . . my oldest daughter (who also went outside to *dagong*) came back about one or two times a year. They then become so talkative and clingy to the older sister! When the older sister comes back, all three hug and play together! They are happy as hell! (Grandma Ping) They do not talk with their dad or their mom. Their mom even said, she said, "When I came back, my daughter behaved like she was adopted, not my own." She does not care. She sees them but behaves like she does not see them. That's it. Two kids are all like that.

The phrases "not care" or "feel like they are strangers" were frequently referenced in these interviews, reflecting children's confusion about or reluctance to accord insider status to migrant parents. Falicov (2012) contends that short- and long-term effects of chronic migration separation and reunification among family members may become unbearable and lead to boundary ambiguity. Our interview data support this contention, suggesting that prolonged separation creates confusion among children about the insider/outsider status of migrant parents and thus elicits children's reluctance to accord migrant parents status at the same level as the grandparent caretakers. Indeed, while most children in Peace County recognized migrant parents' membership in the family, they also intentionally or unintentionally relegated parents to a more marginal status. As the eighth grader Wei succinctly commented (quoted previously): "It's incomparable."

The issue of boundary ambiguity is particularly salient for the sampled youth as well as those of the same or younger cohorts. Parents of these children, compared with those who migrated in previous years (roughly before the beginning of the 2000s), migrated at an earlier age and stayed outside for a longer duration (Chan & Ren, 2018), thus substantially increasing the time of absence and reducing parent–child interaction opportunities. Indeed, as the interview with Chuangqi (also see chapter 3) indicates, many parents spent a total of less than one or two years with children and became physically and emotionally unavailable during children's critical developmental stages (e.g., infancy and early childhood). Grandpa Xiao described how the prolonged separation, particularly a lack of maternal presence, dramatically changed the mental construct of mothering among infants, potentially engendering a long-lasting impact on children's emotional and mental development. He said:

One thing about children raised by grandparents, when they cry, they never ask for their mom. Anytime a child cries, she does not ask for the mom, no matter what you do. A child (who is) raised by parents, she will ask for her mom when she cries. They (children left behind) never ask for the mother, never ask . . . they do not ask for the mother, just crying. Not asking for the mother, not asking for anything. These are children raised by grandparents, the word "mom" is strange to them . . . the number of times she (the mom) comes back, just one to two times a year, mostly just one time. Just returning before Spring Festivals. . . . Parents coming back, there was not so much about whether children being clingy, they did not even want them.

The Scale of Ambiguous Loss: Indicators and Dimensions

Although previous research has documented symptoms of ambiguous loss among children left behind (Carranza, 2021; Solheim et al., 2016), this concept has not been quantitatively measured and validated. Drawing from the ambiguous loss theory and relevant transnational migration literature (Boss, 2016; Falicov, 2012; Solheim et al., 2022), I created a scale to measure children's *ambiguous loss* using eight items, intending to tap into children's understanding and appreciation of parents working "outside" as well as their feelings of estrangement and abandonment. Table 7.4 presents the eight indicators of children's *ambiguous loss* and their respective frequencies. For the first item, "I appreciate my parents going out to *dagong*, and I know they do that for my benefit," about 80 percent (79.08%) agreed or very much agreed with this statement, and the rest (20.92%) disagreed or very much disagreed. A similar distribution was found for the statement "I have a good relationship with my migrant parents," with 23.74 percent disagreeing or very much disagreeing with it and 76.26 percent agreeing or agreeing very much with it. Moreover, more than 90 percent of the middle school students (90.53%) understood why their parents went out to *dagong* (the statement "I understand why my parents go out to *dagong*"); however, only three-quarters (74.6%) believed their parents sacrificed themselves for children's benefits.

The remaining four items asked about children's feelings of estrangement and abandonment. While only about 10 percent of the left-behind children (12.39%) agreed that sometimes they felt that they were abandoned by parents (the statement "Sometimes I feel I am being abandoned by my parents"), more than 20 percent said that they sometimes felt that their migrant parents were like strangers (20.9%, the statement "Sometimes I feel that my parents are strangers"), close to 40 percent said they sometimes felt awkward when parents came back to visit (37.88%, the statement "I sometimes feel awkward when parents come back to see me during festivals"), and almost half (46.03%) said that compared with migrant parents, caretakers such as grandparents were more like their parents.

Combined, these findings suggest that children left behind felt emotionally ambivalent toward their geographically separated parents. Only a small percentage of children felt that they were abandoned by migrant parents and most—

TABLE 7.4
Frequency of indicators of ambiguous loss (%)

Items	Very much disagree	Disagree	Agree	Very much agree
I appreciate my parents going out to *dagong*, and I know they do that for my benefit.	7.24	13.68	46.48	32.60
Sometimes I feel that my migrant parents are strangers.	50.41	28.69	13.93	6.97
I have a good relationship with my parents.	8.32	15.42	45.44	30.83
I understand why my parents go out to *dagong*.	4.14	5.33	45.56	44.97
Parents going out to *dagong* is making a sacrifice for me.	11.29	14.11	43.35	31.25
Sometimes I feel I am being abandoned by my parents.	59.50	28.10	7.64	4.75
I sometimes feel awkward when parents come back to see me during festivals.	35.64	26.48	26.07	11.81
Compared with migrant parents, my caretakers (e.g., grandparents) are more like my parents.	23.42	30.55	28.11	17.92

Note: N = 560.

approximately three-quarters to 80 percent—understood and appreciated parents working outside and making efforts to provide for the family. At the same time, about 40 percent to half of the respondents reported being emotionally distant from parents, feeling uncomfortable when migrant parents visited during festivals or holidays, and acknowledging that they had closer relationships with grandparent caretakers than with their geographically distant parents. Note that the percentage of children agreeing with the statement "Compared with migrant parents, my caretakers (e.g., grandparents) are more like my parents" (46.03%) was similar to the percentage of grandparent caretaking (49%, as reported in chapter 2), suggesting that almost all children cared for by grandparents had established stronger emotional connections with grandparents than with migrant parents.

The second step was to conduct an exploratory factor analysis to assess the dimensionality and reliability of this newly developed scale. The results indicated that this concept was multidimensional, with two factors emerging after using

TABLE 7.5
Exploratory factor analysis of ambiguous loss

Items	Feelings of understanding and appreciation	Feelings of strangeness and abandonment
I appreciate my parents going out to *dagong*, and I know they do that for my benefit.	**0.70**	0.03
Sometimes I feel that my migrant parents are strangers.	0.16	**0.72**
I have good relationship with my parents.	**0.67**	0.23
I understand why my parents go out to *dagong*.	**0.82**	0.09
Parents going out to *dagong* is making a sacrifice for me.	**0.77**	−0.04
Sometimes I feel I am being abandoned by my parents.	0.20	**0.70**
I sometimes feel awkward when parents come back to see me during festivals.	0.07	**0.76**
Compared with migrant parents, my caretakers (e.g., grandparents) are more like my parents.	−0.14	**0.69**

Note: N = 560.

the Principal Component Analysis (PCA) and varimax rotation method (table 7.5). The first factor—labeled as *feelings of understanding and appreciation*—consisted of four items: appreciating parents going out to *dagong*, having a good relationship with parents, understanding why parents go out to *dagong*, and believing that parents sacrificed themselves when going out to *dagong*. These four items loaded highly on this factor, with factor loadings ranging from 0.67 to 0.82, substantially higher than 0.4—a cutoff point commonly used in exploratory factor analysis. The second factor—labeled as *feelings of strangeness and abandonment*—consisted of the four remaining indicators: sometimes feeling that migrant parents are strangers, feeling abandoned by parents, feeling awkward when parents come back during festivals, and feeling that caretakers are more like parents. Similarly, these four items were highly loaded on the factor *feelings of strangeness and abandonment*, with factor loadings ranging from 0.69 to 0.76. Based on these results, I averaged the scores of the respective items and computed a composite score for each subscale. For the scale of *feelings of strangeness and abandonment*, the higher the score, the higher the level of emotional distance. For the scale of *feelings of appreciation*

TABLE 7.6
Multivariate regression models predicting associations between ambiguous loss and psychological well-being

	Self-injury	Social anxiety	Social withdrawal	Physiological symptoms
Intercept	−0.09	0.94**	−0.19	0.76
Lack of appreciation/ understanding	0.06*	0.01	0.07*	0.12
Feeling of strangeness/ abandonment	0.14**	0.12**	0.13**	0.26**
One-grandparent caretaking	0.03	−0.02	0.09	0.03
Maternal migration	0.08	0.00	0.06	0.11
Paternal migration	0.05	0.05	0.09	0.13
Male	−0.10*	−0.14**	−0.07	−0.31**
Age	0.04	0.00	0.05	0.13*
Boarding school	−0.03	0.02	0.00	0.03
Parental education	0.00	−0.02	0.02	−0.01
Household property	0.02	0.04	0.01	0.07
Perceived economic status	−0.01	−0.11*	0.01	−0.07
Parental marital status	−0.13*	−0.12*	−0.07	−0.28*
Number of siblings	−0.02	0.00	0.00	−0.01
R^2/Pseudo R^2	0.11	0.11	0.09	0.09

Note: *$p < 0.05$; **$p < 0.01$; $N = 560$.

[a] Children whose both parents migrated and living with two grandparents as the reference group.

and understanding, the higher the score, the lower level of understanding of and appreciation of parental migration. Both subscales had acceptable reliability, with the former having the Cronbach's alpha of 0.74 and the latter 0.70.

Children's Ambiguous Loss and Psychological Well-Being

After examining the distribution of each item and the scale's overall reliability, I proceed to investigate the associations between the two dimensions of ambiguous loss and children's psychological well-being. Table 7.6 illustrates the effect of children's ambivalent loss on the four indicators of psychological well-being when caretaking arrangements, individual characteristics, and household traits were controlled. Both dimensions, *a lack of appreciation/understanding* (b = 0.06, p < 0.05) and *feelings of strangeness/abandonment* (b = 0.14, p < 0.01), were significantly associated with children's self-injury and suicidal ideation, suggesting that when children experienced a higher level of ambiguous loss, they were more like to engage in self-harm behaviors. The regression analyses provide similar findings for children's reports of social withdrawal, with both dimensions of ambiguous loss, *a lack of appreciation/understanding* (b = 0.07, p < 0.05) and *feelings of strangeness* (b = 0.13, p < 0.01), showing statistical significance. Interestingly, none of the control variables was associated with children's social withdrawal symptoms, further highlighting the impact of children's ambiguous loss on their interpersonal relationships.

For the outcome variable social anxiety, the subscale *children's feelings of strangeness/abandonment* was statistically significant (b = 0.12, p < 0.01), while the *lack of appreciation/understanding* was not, suggesting that the fear of being abandoned—relationally or financially—had a significant impact on children's anxiety levels. Nearly identical findings resulted from our regression analyses regarding children's physiological symptoms, in which the subscale of *feelings of strangeness/abandonment* was also statistically significant (b = 0.26, p < 0.01).

Conclusion

Numerous studies have investigated the impact of internal parental migration on children's psychological well-being in rural China. While seemingly intuitive, this body of research has so far produced mixed findings, with many demonstrating a deleterious effect and others showing a null or even positive impact. In this chapter, I disentangled this oft-debated relationship by investigating the role of immediate environmental factors, long-distance parenting, and children's attitudes and behaviors. Specifically, I explored whether at-home caretaking and children's bonding to school, long-distance communication and parent–child interactions during short visits, and children's feelings of ambiguous loss shape and modify these associations.

First, I concluded that parental migration and caretaking arrangements are not associated with variations in children's emotional well-being, consistent with some recent studies using national data or more rigorous research designs (Ren & Treiman, 2016; H. Xu & Xie, 2015). I suspect that the local culture of migration coupled with material and social support from extended family members (i.e., grandparents) plays a determining role in shaping such an association. Researchers have reached similar conclusions when data are collected from migration-concentrated areas (Murphy et al., 2016), suggesting that the normalization of migration as well as material and nonmaterial benefits of remittance can protect children from or at least minimize these negative emotions.

Second, the analyses reveal both universal and migration-specific risk and protective factors associated with emotional health within the LBC subpopulation.

The results show that caretakers' hostile attitudes toward children and undue criticism increase children's self-injurious behaviors, social anxiety, and physiological symptoms. Conversely, strong bonding with both the school and student peers serves as a protective factor against social withdrawal, social anxiety, physical anxiety, and self-harm or suicidal ideation. I have also identified risk and protective factors specifically associated with parental migration, with intensive mobile parenting—measured by the frequency of child–parent long-distance communication and parent–child conversations regarding psychological and mental issues—significantly reducing children's emotional problems. By quantitatively demonstrating the effects of long-distance parenting on children's psychological well-being, I provided evidence that the use of advanced long-distance communication tools may create a "virtual presence" and potentially reduce the spatial and psychological gaps between children and migrant parents.

I then adopted the ambiguous loss lens to understand the impact of parental migration on children's emotional and psychological well-being. Previous research using qualitative data has shown that ambiguous loss due to parental migration is associated with children's negative emotions (e.g., anger and resentment) and diminished psychological well-being; these findings, however, have not been empirically validated by quantitative data. Employing a mixed methods approach, I found that left-behind children exhibit prevalent ambivalent feelings toward parental migration—while they understand its economic justification, they are simultaneously burdened by the loss of family life and a lack of intimacy with parents. Children left behind are particularly troubled by their loose emotional connections with migrant parents but strong bonding with grandparent caretakers, a contradiction ostensibly violating the nuclear family social norms valued in rural China. Consequently, many children cope with this additional stress by presenting a front of "don't care" attitude or relegating migrant parents to a marginal status within the family system.

Our analyses of the quantitative measure of ambiguous loss corroborate findings from in-depth interviews and field observations, revealing that children's ambiguous loss consists of two associated dimensions: feelings of understanding and appreciation of parental migration and feelings of strangeness and abandonment. Moreover, while inextricably associated, the impact of ambiguous loss goes beyond caretaking arrangements, as the two dimensions of ambiguous loss are consistent and significant predictors of children's psychological well-being. Combined, these results demonstrate the predictive and construct validity of our quantitative measure of children's ambiguous loss as well as the importance of applying and extending this ambiguous loss lens to the field of internal and transnational migration and the examination of psychological and emotional implications related to left-behind children, migrant parents, and adult caretakers.

8

Conclusion

In this conclusion, I summarize the major findings derived from the data and then address two emerging areas of importance: the resilience of children left behind and the future of these children going forward. First, the summary section highlights my major findings, illuminating the complex and dynamic interplays between reconfigured family structures, alternative caretaking arrangements, parenting and caretaking practices, and children's behavioral, psychological, and emotional development. Attention to these social mechanisms, particularly the nuanced analyses of grandparenting and long-distance parenting, sets this study apart from most prior studies. Following the summary section, I revisit the theoretical model adopted in this book and turn my attention to children's resiliency, identifying potential contributing individual, family, and cultural factors. Finally, I discuss the future of left-behind children in rural China, highlighting the urgency of institutional reform (e.g., *hukou* and educational policy reform) as well as the development of evidence-based programs tailored specifically for left-behind children in China.

Summary of Previous Chapters

Guided by the overarching theoretical model (chapter 1, fig. 1.1), I first identified external factors—at macro, meso, and micro levels—shaping rural parents' decisions regarding migration and child caretaking arrangements (chapter 2). The study identifies four types of alternative caretaking arrangement among translocal households: (1) maternal migration where the father is the main caretaker, (2) paternal migration where the mother is the main caretaker, (3) two-grandparent caretaking after both parents have migrated, and (4) one-grandparent caretaking after both parents have migrated. As documented by prior research, institutional constraints, particularly the *hukou* system and ever-increasing rural–urban and coast–inland income disparities, are the primary contributors to the alarming number of children left behind in rural China (X. Ma et al., 2018; Mallee, 1995). In particular, China's local and national educational policies make it difficult—if not impossible—for children to migrate to urban areas with their parents. Almost all migrant-destination cities have enacted discriminatory educational policies against migrant children, severely restricting their access to public schools and driving them to either costly private schools (which rural-to-urban migrants cannot typically afford) or low-quality migrant schools. Even when children do migrate with their parents and attend schools in host cities, most provinces only allow students with a local *hukou* to take the National College Entrance Examination. Given that most provinces have unique curriculums and exam questions, cross-province migrant children are placed at a severe disadvantage if they finish their high school education in the destination province but return to their registered place of residence for these life-altering exams. As a result, we saw many migrant parents at the research sites send their children back to rural areas before junior high school, thus providing children plenty of time to familiarize themselves with the local educational curriculum.

At the micro level, the availability of physically and mentally capable grandparents was a robust predictor of caretaking arrangements, reflecting the importance of intergenerational support for domestic migration in rural China. Indeed, grandparenting was the most prevalent type of childcare arrangement at the research sites, with some grandparents serving as surrogate parents for more than a decade. Unfortunately, this type of arrangement—often necessitated by household poverty—greatly increased the physical and mental burden of some grandparents. In particular, I found that the one-grandparent-caretaking arrangement inflicted much hardship and suffering on aged grandparent caretakers, who often struggled physically and emotionally to provide caregiving.

In chapter 3, I investigated to what extent caretaking practices in translocal households differ from nonmigrant households. The results reveal that children's perceptions of caretaking practices were conditional on their caretakers' gender and hierarchical positions in the household. Maternal migration overall was perceived to have a more detrimental impact than paternal migration. This perception reflects children's gender-based expectations but also the suboptimal performance provided by stay-at-home fathers, who were often reluctant to cross gender boundaries to perform sufficient "mothering." Chapter 3 also finds that grandparenting's impacts on caretaking practices were complicated and multidimensional. Contrary to the negative picture generated by public discourse, the outcomes of the two-grandparent caretaking did not differ significantly from nonmigrant households in conventional caregiving practices (e.g., monitoring, supervision, and caretaker–child bonding). In fact, children of the two-grandparent-caretaking arrangement reported a lower level of caretaker–child conflict compared with those living with nonmigrant parents. In sharp contrast, children cared for by one-grandparent caretakers exhibited the lowest level of monitoring and supervision and the weakest caretaker–child bonding, providing further support for the previous finding regarding the vulnerability of caretakers and children in one-grandparent-caretaking households.

Long-distance parenting (chapter 4) is another critical dimension of caretaking, composed of three types of practice employed by migrant parents at the research sites: (1) mobile parenting via modern information and communication technology (ICT), (2) migrant parents' short visits, and (3) children's visits to parents in host cities during summer breaks or other holidays. Not surprisingly, migrant parents frequently employed these three methods to perform "responsible parenting." Like their transnational counterparts, Chinese parents used mobile parenting to develop intimacies with children from afar. The rapid development of advanced ICT and the prevalence of mobile devices (e.g., smartphones) make mobile parenting appealing; however, I found that numerous barriers, particularly migrant parents' long working hours, time zone differences, and children's conflicting schedules, rendered mobile parenting largely ineffective. Long-distance parent–child communication was infrequent (i.e., about one or two times a week), most conversations were perceived by children as superficial and routine, and conversations were often initiated and motivated by migrant parents rather than by children.

Traditional strategies such as parental visits to children and children's visits to migrant parents in host cities also provided limited opportunities for children and parents to interact with one another. Many migrant parents, particularly those who migrated across provincial boundaries, visited children and family members only during Spring Festivals and remained at home for less than two weeks. Occupied by intensive social activities (e.g., visiting relatives and friends) during the yearly visit, migrant parents barely had time to connect with children to develop intimacies. Moreover, in contrast with their transnational counterparts, many left-behind children in rural China visited their parents in host cities during summer breaks or other holidays, sometimes spending about one to two months with them. While this strategy was frequently employed by migrant parents to demonstrate their devotion to children and family members and to perform "responsible parenting," this study revealed that both poor living conditions in host cities (e.g., extremely limited living space) and parents' irregular and overextended work hours undermined these efforts—resulting in frustration for children or/and accompanying caretakers (e.g., grandparents) and reluctance to embark on subsequent visits.

I further studied whether parental migration and caretaking arrangements are associated with children's behavioral, psychological, and emotional development and whether these associations are mediated by caretaking practices—whether at home or from afar. One robust finding highlighted in chapters 5 to 7 is that the impact of a child's left-behind status was far from being homogenous. That is, the extent and the direction of the influence of being left behind were conditional on who remained at home as the primary caretaker and the developmental outcome studied. This study identifies two distinctive caretaking arrangements that are consistently linked to adverse developmental outcomes: maternal migration (i.e., the father is the primary caretaker) and one-grandparent caretaking after both parents have migrated. Children living with an at-home father (after the mother has migrated) or children cared for by one grandparent performed poorly in school and bonded tenuously with the school and other students. Conversely, children's school outcomes within the other two arrangements—paternal migration (with the mother staying at home to be the primary caretaker) and two-grandparent caretaking—did not differ significantly from those of traditional two-parent-caretaking. A nearly identical pattern was found when considering children's participation in delinquency. Children living in families where a father (i.e., maternal migration) or one grandparent caretaker was the primary caretaker exhibited the highest risk of participation in delinquency and deviance. Interestingly, whereas numerous studies have found that parental migration adversely influences children's psychological well-being (e.g., Fu & Law, 2018; W. Wu et al., 2019; C. Zhao et al., 2018), the study, echoing recent research using more rigorous sampling designs (Biao, 2007; Ren & Treiman, 2016; L. Wang et al., 2019; H. Xu & Xie, 2015), found that parental migration or type of caretaking arrangement was not associated with variations in children's emotional well-being.

This study also works to identify the underlying social mechanisms linking parental migration, caretaking arrangements, and children's behavioral and emotional development. The overarching theoretical model highlights the critical role of caretaking practices at home and in long-distance parenting. The results provide partial support for this theoretical model. In particular, children's schooling outcomes (i.e., academic performance and school bonding) were largely explained by caretaking practices at home. The degree to which at-home parents or grandparent caregivers were able to consistently supervise their children's activities, discipline them for any wrongdoing, and build harmonious and close-knit relationships explained much of this effect. Interestingly, caretaking practices at home—although directly contributing to children's delinquent and deviant behaviors—failed to serve as a mediator linking caretaking arrangements to children's deviant behaviors. Similarly, caretaking practices—particularly caretakers' hostile attitudes toward children—were found to increase children's psychological and emotional problems, including self-injurious behaviors, social anxiety, and other physiological symptoms. Nevertheless, at-home caretaking practices did not serve as the mediating social mechanism underlying the associations between parental migration and children's psychological problems.

I found that parenting from afar (i.e., mobile parenting, parental visits to children and family members, and children's visits to parents in host cities) had complicated and multidimensional effects on children's behavioral and emotional development. Mobile parenting—in the form of migrant parents constantly reminding children of the value of education—had a noticeable effect on children's educational outcomes. Children's visits to parents in host cities had some unintended consequences, providing children opportunities to observe firsthand their parents' marginalized socioeconomic statuses in host cities. These visits subsequently deepened children's appreciation of their parents' sacrifices and reinforced their understanding of the value of education to their future life opportunities. In the same vein, intensive mobile parenting, including frequent parent–child communication and open discussion of psychological and mental issues, reduced children's psychological and emotional problems. By contrast, long-distance parenting did not have any protective effect on children's engagement in delinquent behaviors, reflecting the importance of the immediate environment (e.g., caretaking and peers) in preventing or encouraging children's delinquency involvement.

The linkage between caretaking arrangements, caretaking practices, and children's development is further complicated by salient individual and family characteristics. In particular, children's gender, age, and parental marital status were found to be the most influential. The dominant patriarchal system in rural China, coupled with gendered practices of socialization, influenced how resources were allocated and how children were raised and socialized across genders. The age effect, which overlapped with the cohort effect in this study, also merits research attention. Particularly, it is interesting to see how younger children—many of whom had been separated from their migrant parents since one or two years old—fared in the long term. Finally, whereas the effect of parental divorce on children's behavioral and psychological development has been widely recognized (e.g., Lan & Sun, 2022; C. Zhang, 2020), its effect on left-behind children has been far less investigated. The effects of parental divorce can be exacerbated among children left behind, as they have to cope with this adverse event without much parental support, are regularly exposed to familial tension and drama, and are under constantly changing caretaking arrangements.

Children's Development of Resilience

The preceding summary reveals that parental migration and caretaking arrangements, directly or indirectly, influence children's developmental outcomes in both the short and long term. Yet many children appear to do reasonably well or even thrive despite prolonged parental separation and exposure to many enduring adversities. Pan, a fourteen-year-old girl who was living with her grandparents and two younger brothers when interviewed, exhibited such resilience. Pan's parents had been "outside" for many years, working in Zhejiang and Fujian provinces during the first few years and then later in Xi'an City in western China. They had finally moved back five years before our interview because of a work-related injury. Pan's parents had since opened a small business in a nearby town, living there by themselves and only visiting Pan and her siblings (two boys) during ceremonies and festivals. Despite this adversity, Pan had grown to become an independent, mature, outgoing, and confident child. She excelled in school and ranked academically in fifth place in eighth grade. In addition, she reported an "excellent" relationship with her migrant parents and enjoyed generally "normal" and "relaxing" communications with her grandparent caretakers. She proudly explained how she achieved this feat:

> I thought about this a long time ago, and I helped other people [classmates] to deal with this issue. [We] need to obey their wishes. If they say happy things, we stand aside, listening to them and complimenting them on [what they have achieved]. Then they will be happy. And take the initiative to help with household chores, helping them share some difficulties. . . . Not any great difficulties, just listen to their small complaints and then echo their views. And achieve good grades. Always be positive and motivated. This is how you make them happy. Like, [if] Grandma cut her hands today, and we little ones would say that we would help you wash clothes. Like, if parents say they are too tired today, I would then help them do something, washing dishes or other stuff.

The preceding narrative demonstrates Pan's agency in navigating dynamic and evolving relationships with her grandparent caretakers and migrant parents. Rather than sitting idly and complaining about life challenges, Pan skillfully dissected various scenarios and developed responses guided by traditional Chinese family values (e.g., filial piety) and thus built "super good" relationships with her grandparent caretakers and migrant parents. The critical question here is, who are these resilient children like Pan, and under what structural, cultural, and situational conditions do left-behind children in rural China develop such resilience?

Researchers have defined resilience in different ways, but the concept is commonly used to denote "patterns of positive development in the context of adversity" (Masten & Barnes, 2018, p. 2), including "the process of, capacity for, or outcomes of successful adaptation" (Masten et al., 1990, p. 426) in suboptimal conditions. Early research mostly defines resilience from an individualistic perspective, contending that those who are disadvantaged can "beat the odds" by exercising personal agency. Individual characteristics such as self-efficacy, prosociality, a sense of coherence, and high IQ are identified as protective factors rendering a person less susceptible to adversity and more amenable to change. However, since the 1970s, this body of research has shifted toward a more holistic understanding of resilience, emphasizing the intricate interactions between people and the environment in which they are embedded. In his groundbreaking work, Rutter (1987) argued that social processes operating at family, community, and cultural levels played a more significant role than personal attributes, proposing that continuous and reciprocal person–environment interactions would hinder or improve an individual's successful adaptation in suboptimal conditions. In other words, this new perspective adopted a more contextualized and dynamic approach, highlighting the congruence between changing individual needs and environments in which a person is embedded. For example, previous research on left-behind children found that caring and strict grandparents could provide sufficient care, affection, and guidance for children, adequately making up for the chronic absence of migrant parents (X. Chen & Jiang, 2019).

A small number of studies has recently emerged investigating resilience among children left behind in rural China and other developing countries (Ba Nguyen & Van Nguyen, 2022; B. Dong et al., 2019; S. Hu, 2019; Mu, 2018). Overall, these studies have identified a series of protective factors contributing to children's resilience, including individual characteristics (e.g., high IQ, even temperament, and positive attitude); features of external environments (e.g., caring at-home parents and grandparents, migrant parents' use of telecommunication such as video chatting); or positive development reflecting the reciprocal person–environment interactions (e.g., academic success, involvement in extracurricular activities). These relatively universal protective factors can also be found within the data and are important to the understanding of left-behind children's development of resilience. For example, I have repeatedly found that exceptional school performance improves children's self-esteem and helps develop close relationships between children, migrant parents, and adult caretakers.

Importantly, in the discussion of resilience in this chapter, I focus on varying factors largely determined by the unique cultural, structural, and situational characteristics associated with Chinese culture in general and rural China in particular. This focus is particularly important since parental migration in rural China is deeply shaped by rural–urban inequality, local economic development, and cultural values associated with migration, gender, family, and intergenerational relationships. My in-depth interview and survey data have identified three major contributing factors to children's positive development: (1) the critical role of education, (2) the pervasiveness of family-oriented social values manifested by translocal family members accepting their unique responsibilities and obligations, and (3) children's participation in household chores and farming.

Resilience Development: The Role of Education

Education plays a pivotal role in children's lives in rural China, in part because children spend almost all their time and energy in school or on schoolwork (see chapter 5) and also because pursuing higher education is one of the few, if not the only, practical avenues for rural children and their families to detach themselves from the lowly rural status and achieve employment security. The prominent status of education in contemporary China has deep cultural and historical roots, primarily because national institutional exams (e.g., the Civil Service or *keju* exam) implemented in the last several thousand years provided selected scholars access to high-level, high-power government positions, bringing themselves and their entire families enormous wealth, power, legal privileges, and social status. While the value of education was drastically reduced during Chairman Mao's Cultural Revolution era, it has been reinstated since China's Opening Up and Reform era in the late 1970s. For rural children in particular, obtaining a college diploma provides them access to urban formal employment, higher wages, and opportunities to seek the sought-after local urban *hukou* (particularly in central cities) and permanent migration to the city. Indeed, the return on education is perceived to be so large that an "education fever"—originated within China's urban middle class and characterized by parents' unrealistically high expectations of children's academic performance and relentless investment in children's education—has now spread to rural areas. In a survey of more than 1,000 students in rural schools in Jiangxi and Anhui provinces, Murphy (2020) found that more than three-quarters of children wanted to get at least an undergraduate degree. Yet China's 2020 census revealed that only 7.4 percent of the general population were college-educated (National Bureau of Statistics of China, 2021), demonstrating a massive gap between aspiration and reality.

Past research has shown that strong commitment to and intensive involvement with educational and other school activities greatly contribute to the development of resilience for children left behind by migrant parents (Dreby, 2010; Mu, 2018; Oliveira, 2018). This is particularly the case for children in rural China. My data indicate that the value of education has been successfully transmitted to and embraced by most children in rural Jiangxi province, who acknowledged the significance of education and its potential life-changing impact. In the questionnaire, I asked the students whether they agreed with five statements about school and education: (1) It's very important for me to have good grades; (2) I always finish my homework on time; (3) Education is very important because knowledge is very important to me; (4) School education can change my life; and (5) Compared with life outside, studying in school is a waste of time. It appears that children fully understand the importance of education and its potential effects on their future job opportunities and careers. For example, regarding the statement "It's very important for me to have good grades," about three-quarters (75.1%) agreed or very much agreed, only a small fraction (7.7%) disagreed or very much disagreed, and 17.2 percent reported that they were not sure. Similar responses were recorded for the statement "Education is very important because knowledge is important to me," with three-quarters of children (74.9%) agreeing or very much agreeing with the statement, 8.4 percent disagreeing or very much disagreeing, and 16.7 percent of children being ambiguous about this statement. The other three items exhibited similar patterns.

In addition, children who excelled in school often received many compliments and admiration from external immediate environments (e.g., parents, schoolteachers, peers, and neighbors), gaining popularity and social status in these networks. In the rural schools I visited, children's academic performance was public knowledge, with teachers and neighbors knowing and openly commenting on students' grades and possibilities to be accepted by an academic-track high school and/or a first-tier tertiary institution. During my interviews, I counted six times parents and grandparents expressed their admiration toward a neighbor's child or their children's classmates for their superior academic performance. Parents and grandparents praised academically gifted children for being "smart," "aspiring," "capable," "striving," and "making the family proud." Grandma Xiao, for example, was amazed by the academic performance of her grandson's classmate, noticing that "her total points in the last midterm were twenty points higher than the second-ranked student in her class" and claiming that "she is truly capable." Oftentimes, this conversation was referenced in the context of parental migration, the child's chance to be accepted by a college, and a potential "good life" for the child and their parents. These admirations, compliments, and expectations help children build confidence and find meaning in their everyday lives, thereby developing resilience despite chronic parental absence and other adversity.

One unintentional function of children's superior school performance is that it provides a plausible justification for parents' out-migration. Worldwide, parents often cast their migration as a sacrifice to encourage children to study hard and achieve good grades (Dreby, 2010; Murphy, 2020). In the same vein, parents in rural China often claim that their out-migration is for their children's future educational investment. Jingwen, a seventh-grade girl, said that her dad went outside to *dagong* to "make money, paying for our school." Indeed, almost every child interviewed was constantly reminded by their parents or grandparent caregivers that their parents' migration was in support of their current or future education. This claim is justified when children do well in school and have a realistic chance of attending an academic-track high school and ultimately a decent college. As briefly discussed in chapter 5, the costs of attending high school and college are prohibitively high in China, making it difficult for rural parents to support their children's education with just local earnings. On the other hand, this motivator becomes less relevant if a child performs poorly in school and thus has no realistic chance of enrolling in an academic-track high school or college. In other words, children's superior school performance legitimates parents' out-migration and chronic absence, potentially diminishing or even eliminating children's feelings of abandonment and instead facilitating the development of an appreciation and stronger parent–child bonding across distance.

It should be noted that the overemphasis on academic performance is a double-edged sword, causing less academically gifted children to feel inferior, depressed, and anxious. While parents in rural China generally have less lofty expectations for their children than their urban counterparts, most do expect their children to achieve decent grades and go to college. Most rural children, unfortunately, realize that they are unlikely to meet such expectations when they reach eighth or ninth grade, sometimes leading to the development of mental and behavioral problems and ultimately dropping out of school. A review of the total number of students enrolled in rural middle schools in Peace County ($n = 19$) provided some empirical evidence for this speculation. In 2018, a total of 2,603 students attended seventh grade in these nineteen rural schools; this number dropped to 2,165 in eighth grade and 1,799 in ninth grade. In total, approximately one-third of the students enrolled in seventh grade either dropped out or transferred to other schools before they even graduated from junior high school. While some students transferred to urban schools to seek better education, it was highly likely that many children chose or were forced to drop out because of their diminished chance of enrolling in an academic-track high school. Indeed, in the two villages where I did my field observation, several students dropped out and attended technical/vocational schools or followed their parents' footsteps to *dagong*.

Resilience Development: Family Values and Striving

An equally important contributor to children's resilience development is the pervasiveness of traditional family values, which imbues each member of a household with specific roles, responsibilities, and obligations. Transnational migration literature is littered with examples of migrant parents gradually cutting ties with their children after migration and prolonged separation (e.g., Dreby, 2010). Interestingly, migrant parents in rural China, despite years of separation, maintain a strong commitment to family and children left behind. Indeed, I rarely heard stories of migrant parents intentionally abandoning their children, never returning, or completely revoking financial support. The one exception was when migrant parents were physically or mentally incapable and could not even provide for themselves.

The significance and pervasiveness of traditional family values are probably best encapsulated by migrant parents' visits during China's Spring Festivals, an annual mass movement of humanity that has become a perennial spectacle and captured much national and world media attention. During the Spring Festival break, migrants travel hundreds to thousands of miles on extremely overcrowded trains or long-distance buses to attend the Lunar New Year's Eve family dinner with parents, children, and other extended family members. In 2019—the last year before the global COVID-19 pandemic—nearly three billion people traveled during the forty days of the Spring Festival break. Needless to say, traveling during Spring Festivals is particularly challenging for rural-to-urban migrants, who face increased difficulties in purchasing train or bus tickets, long hours of travel, increased travel costs, and sometimes severe weather conditions. An epic example is that in 2008, around 400,000 passengers were stranded at Guangzhou railway station due to a weather crisis (i.e., heavy snow and rain), which is documented in creative works such as Li Xin Fan's acclaimed documentary *Last Train Home*.

Shaped mainly by Confucianism, traditional Chinese family values emphasize family unity and growth, filial piety, respect for elders, and marriage and childbirth. These traditional values and practices have gradually evolved—particularly in the past half-century—adapting to dramatic and continuing structural and cultural changes. In his influential book *Private Life under Socialism: Love, Intimacy, and Family Change in a Chinese Village, 1949–1999*, anthropologist Yunxiang Yan (2003) observed profound changes in family life and values in northern China during the second part of the twentieth century. In particular, Yan's research revealed a significant decline in the proportion of extended families, the waning of the patriarchal order, and a crisis of filial piety. In addition, he found that children gained more status in the family, with parents investing more resources in children's education and other expenses. The latter change has persisted and appears to be reinforced in the twenty-first century. Rongmei, a forty-year-old mother with two children, explained how consideration of children's development shaped their family's decisions regarding migration and caretaking arrangements:

> Right now, [our] children are still little, and we cannot help worrying about them [if both migrated]. We are thinking of waiting until they are a little bit older, and a little bit more independent, then we can both go outside to *dagong*. . . . Ultimately, whatever we do right now is for the children. Staying at home is for them and making money [outside] is for them. You cannot just focus on making money and ignore them. When they grow up, they will blame you, right? Everything is for them.

This "everything is for them" mentality has been one of the driving forces for migrant parents to endure extended hours of labor, adverse working conditions, and exposure to blatant stigmatization and discrimination. Like Rongmei, many parents claimed that they sacrificed their health, dignity, and leisure time for their children's education and overall well-being by working "outside." This mentality was even more pronounced among grandparent caretakers, whose "them" included not only left-behind grandchildren but also adult migrant children. Grandparents, for example, rarely refused to serve as the caretakers of children, even when they had been overwhelmed by long years of caretaking and were exposed to a great deal of hardship and suffering. Grandparents Nei—referenced in chapter 3—for example, had been primary caretakers of seven grandchildren in the past two decades. During my last visit, I observed that four grandchildren, ranging from a two-year-old toddler to a junior high school teenager, were watching TV or playing with each other in the house. Grandma Nei discussed the hardship they had endured during these years:

> I took care of a total of seven children. Seven grandchildren, they were all raised by me. First, two grandchildren of my older son. Both of them were in college now. . . . One went to Nanchang University; another was accepted by Chengdu University in Sichuan province. Then two kids of my older daughter; the older one is already in high school. She is now in the Elite class in the county's First High School. . . . Later my younger son brought two children here, and now the younger daughter brought one here. Now I have four in the house and one in high school. When she comes back during summer breaks, she will also be here. . . . We don't have other ways. As we said, if we can help, we will help. This is what you elders need to do. If it cannot be done, then that's it. Nowadays yeye nainai (paternal grandfathers and grandmothers) and waigong waipo (maternal grandfathers and grandmothers) are all like this. Isn't this how everyone lives?

The preceding narrative reveals a quite surprising fact about grandparenting rarely addressed in the previous literature. That is, grandparenting was not a discrete event nor a short-term endeavor; rather, it could occur across one or even two decades, with many grandparents providing full-time care for grandchildren of vastly different ages. This interview also reveals that these grandparent caretakers, due to aging, deteriorated physical health, and demanding farming labor, struggled tremendously to raise these children. For example, grandpa Nei broke his leg three months before our interview after bringing one of his granddaughters to school on a motorcycle. This injury made it impossible for him to work on the farm or participate in any other physical activities, adding emotional and financial stress to the family. Despite all the difficulties, grandparents Nei—like many other grandparent caretakers interviewed—insisted that it was their responsibility to help children, as "this is what you elders need to do," and that's "how everyone lives" nowadays.

While the preceding narrative reaffirms grandparents' commitment to the family and their children, it also reveals an interesting phenomenon contrary to what Yan observed in his study. As reported by Yan and many researchers, family division—an adult son establishing a financially independent nuclear family after marriage—became normative around the middle of the twentieth century in rural China. Indeed, Yan reported that starting from Mao's era, the percentage of stem families (i.e., a family consisting of three generations) declined while the percentage of nuclear families increased significantly. These changes led to other significant repercussions, particularly the decreased influence of the patriarchal order and the crisis of filial piety. This trend, however, appears to have been reversed or at least redefined after the 1990s. Grandparents, now tasked with primary childcare obligations, become critical resources and have thus gained more prominent status in translocal households. Indeed, compared with those in the 1980s and 1990s described in Yan's book, grandparents now have tighter and more intricate emotional and economic relationships with their migrant children and grandchildren.

Most of the skipped-generation families in the United States are due to parents having physical or mental problems (e.g., substance addiction problems, death) or being entangled with the criminal justice system (incarceration, child neglect, or abuse). The skipped-generation families in rural China, however, are essentially a by-product of parental migration. These families are not independent economic units or legal family units in the eyes of migrant parents or other villagers. Indeed, most of these families receive continuous financial support from migrant parents, with remittance as a primary income source for many. Some migrant parents even voluntarily relinquish their control of economic resources to grandparents, essentially transforming a nuclear family into a stem family (i.e., a family with grandparents, parents, and children in a household). Grandpa Pan—a former community (*minbang*) elementary schoolteacher—elaborated on his relationships with his son and daughter-in-law and the control of financial resources in this translocal household:

Many families, sons, and daughters-in-law, want to separate [from their parents]. We haven't had a family division yet. . . . In the past, they were outside to *dagong*, and we were the ones to take care of the children. Whatever the costs, they were all on us. . . . Our family grows our rice, now I have more than ten *mu* of rice. We sell them every year. If you [migrant children] need them, take them from the house. It's better than buying them from the street [store]. Oil too, right? Other folks asked me how much money my daughter-in-law gave me, I said it was not even a question that I asked them for money, nor a question that how much money they needed to give us. Our family is still like doing collectivization in Mao's era. Many people don't believe it, many say I took care of the children each year, how much money I received. I said that I didn't lie to them. We are yeye and nainai, and taking care of children is the rules and orderliness of heaven and earth (tian jin di yi). It does not exist that they owe me anything, that is like treating us as outsiders. It's the same for them [migrant children and daughter-in-law]. Every year they returned, they gave me money, like in the era of collectivization. My son gave what he made, and my daughter-in-law did the same. Many people don't believe me, but that's the truth.

The preceding narrative reveals that the relationships between grandparents and adult migrant children—emotionally and economically—are so complicated that the traditional classification of family structures (e.g., stem family or nuclear family) cannot be readily applied. While grandpa Pan's case may be an exception and most translocal households consist of at least two financially independent units, these units are often emotionally and financially entangled, with both grandparents and migrant parents intentionally or unintentionally obscuring the boundaries. When asked whether they sent remittance to the grandparents—who were primary caretakers of their two children—migrant mother Han said, "Sometimes we gave them money. And sometimes they don't want it even if you give it to them. Except that when they really don't have any left, they will ask you."

These tighter emotional relationships alongside more frequent but opaque economic transactions between grandparents, migrant parents, and children left behind reflect what Murphy (2020) termed as a "striving" team in rural China. The fundamentally restructured rural-to-urban migration policies and the massive rural-to-urban migration present both challenges and opportunities for people in rural China. Whereas migration is mostly a survival strategy, it also provides opportunities—regardless of how small they are—for migrants to achieve financial stability, freedom, and intergenerational mobility. However, their marginal socioeconomic status requires these translocal households to pool all resources—physical, financial, and emotional—together to achieve these lofty goals. As Murphy highlights in her book *The Children of China's Great Migration* (2020), to achieve intergenerational mobility, translocal family members need to be motivated and united, with parents working tirelessly in factories in economically

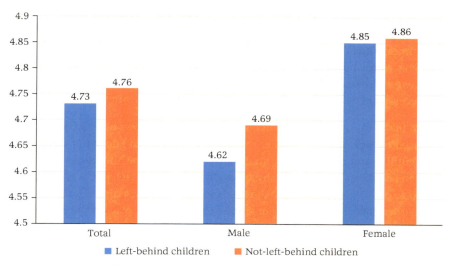

FIGURE 8.1 Status of left behind, gender, and children's participation in household chores.

developed areas, children studying hard in school, and grandparents staying at home, taking care of children, and farming the land. Collectively, this "striving" team provides children stability, affection, and motivation to transcend poverty and chronic parental absence and develop resilience over time.

Resilience Development: Household Chores and Farming

The third contributor to children's resilience development emerging from the data is children's participation in household chores and farming. Previous research reveals that children left behind are more heavily involved in household chores, farming, and other physical labor, greatly impacting their school success and healthy development (H. Chang et al., 2011; Jingzhong & Lu, 2011). My data, however, suggest otherwise. First, I found no significant difference in participation in housework and farming between children who were left behind and those living with both parents. Specifically, I asked students how often they participated in activities such as washing clothes, cooking, and agricultural work. Contrary to what was documented in prior literature (H. Chang et al., 2011; Jingzhong & Lu, 2011), the quantitative findings (fig. 8.1) indicate that children left behind were less likely to participate in household chores and farming than those living with both parents, although this difference was statistically insignificant. As discussed in previous chapters, I suspect that this is because the additional income generated by migrant parents eases the necessity of intensive farming, largely freeing adult caretakers from grueling agricultural activities and the necessity of children's participation in household chores.

Interestingly, while researchers do not consider children's participation in household chores and farming to be desirable or beneficial (H. Chang et al., 2011;

Jingzhong & Lu, 2011), a moderate level of involvement was welcomed by at-home caretakers. First, children's participation in these activities was necessary and sometimes critical in part because of the lost labor to migration. At-home mother Dasheng, whose husband and older daughter had migrated to a southern province to *dagong* and who was living with a teenage daughter when interviewed, described the necessity of her younger daughter's involvement in farming and housework:

> In the morning when I am busy, she will cook, she knows how to cook. If I need to cook and then ask her to eat, then what should I do? After I leave, shuffling and drying grain, things in the house like washing clothes, how can I do them? How can I wash clothes? In the morning I tell her, I say I need to go out to work, she knows she needs to cook rice, cook dishes, and wash clothes, that is her duty. . . . Sometimes I go out to play, playing Mahjong, if she does not have school, she will cook rice, she does not cook dishes, she will wait till I come back to cook dishes. If I work outside, she will cook dishes.

The preceding case illustrates the so-called "substitution effect" of parental migration, referring to left-behind adults' and children's reallocation of time to agricultural activities and housework to compensate for the lost labor. The substitution effect is often intertwined with the "income effect"—that is, remittances received by migrant households can potentially lessen family members' labor participation—rendering the total effect of parental migration on the adjustment for time allocation nonsignificant (H. Xu, 2017). In rural Jiangxi province, I observed substantial variation in the substitution effect across varying types of care arrangements. The effect was more pronounced for children cared for by a single adult caretaker (i.e., one-parent or one-grandparent caretaker households) but was rarely observed in two-grandparent-caretaker households.

While children's participation in farming and housework was sometimes out of necessity, this kind of practice had been long believed to be a training tool for children to develop self-confidence and work ethic. Enduring and overcoming hardship, commonly called "eating bitterness" in the Chinese culture, presumably makes children stronger physically, mentally, and emotionally. The comments from at-home father LaoJiu exemplify the prevalent attitude toward children's involvement in household chores and agricultural activities:

> Children, they like playing. You cannot let them get used to it. If something needs to be done, let them do it, you can sit there and take a break. Some heavy work, like carrying stuff, don't let them do it, that could hurt them [physically]. They need to develop good habits, so that in the future whatever they need to do, they know how to do it. [Now] after I pick up vegetables from my vegetable garden, he will immediately wash and cut them. Before, when his mom was here, he did not even look, sitting there watching TV. You need to even call him to eat. . . . Like this morning I finished washing

clothes, and I was building a pigpen for a neighbor. I didn't tell him, he didn't wake up at that time, [but] he knew it. Before I got home, he [already] hung all the clothes outside, already swept the floor.

LaoJiu believed that children's participation in household chores and farming, except for intensive manual labor such as "carrying stuff," provided sound training for the development of good work ethic and skills, "so in the future whatever they need to do, they know how to do it." Children left behind, although not necessarily in agreement with this philosophy, appear to benefit emotionally and psychologically when they can contribute to the growth of the translocal household. Indeed, when asked whether he helped his grandparents with household chores and farming, Junhao, a thirteen-year-old boy, proudly claimed: "Sometimes. When Yeye (grandpa) and Nainai (grandma) cannot do it, then I will do it. Sometimes they cannot carry bags of crops, then I will do it. Other things that they cannot do, only I can do them." His comments were echoed by his grandma:

Yes, he does help. Like we need to harvest grain and need to carry bags of grain back home. In the field, he needs to help pull [the bags to the roadside]. [We] cannot move them, he needs to help us move the bags. In addition, like drying the grain, or carrying the bags back home, [if] he is back, he will help do it. Last year, there was grain harvested from several *mu* of land drying on the road, grain of three *mu* of land, [they were] all carried in by him. Grain of three *mu* of land, he used a wheelbarrow to move all of them in. He knows grandparents don't have the strength to move them. He is such an attaboy!

Clearly, Junhao was proud of his physical strength and his modest contribution to the translocal household. Although he was not academically gifted and did not achieve a high academic ranking in his class, he found other unique ways to support and impress his grandparents, strengthening his position in the household as a critical and contributing member. It is also worth noting that Junhao's parents were divorced and he was in the custody of his mother and living with his maternal grandparents. As discussed in chapter 2, this living arrangement is relatively rare for children in rural China because of the deep influence of patriarchal values. Children under the care of maternal grandparents, particularly when cohabiting with cousins of the patriarchal line, may feel that they are "outsiders" and don't belong to the translocal household. Junhao's much-needed contribution ("Other things that they cannot do, only I can do them") alleviated some of these negative feelings and emotions.

Policy and Program Implications

The previous chapters demonstrate that the complex interplay between macro and micro factors shapes children's emotional, psychological, and behavioral outcomes.

The findings reveal that macrostructural factors (e.g., the *hukou* system and the rural–urban income gap) impose a profound influence on family members' decisions on migration and caretaking arrangements. At the micro level, caretaking arrangements, caregiving practices provided by at-home caregivers, and long-distance parenting impose more direct effects on children's well-being. In this section, I discuss policy and program implications derived from these empirical findings. In particular, I explore the direction of reforms and policies that can be enacted by central and local governments as well as the potential prevention and treatment programs at the community and state levels.

Reform at the Macro Level: Hukou *and Educational Policies*

This project highlights the prominent role of the *hukou* system and the national and local educational policies in marginalizing children of migrant parents as well as the urgent need to fully reform the *hukou* system. Unfortunately, despite China's dramatic social, economic, and cultural changes over the past half a century, the *hukou* system remains an enduring institution, serving the government's strategic needs of social control while reinforcing the vast rural–urban socioeconomic disparity. Nevertheless, as discussed in chapter 1, *hukou* has been under the scrutiny of researchers and public policy scholars from its first enactment and has since been through multiple amendments.

Incremental changes were enacted during the early years of China's "Reform and Opening Up" (K. Chan, 2019), and since the late 1980s, local governments have been granted more control over migration and the management of the *hukou* system. In 2002, small towns eased their *hukou* restriction, providing migrant workers with urban *hukou* and limited state-provided welfare. While more small or middle-sized cities have relaxed their *hukou* policies, these cities also typically have few employment opportunities and offer no significant social benefits. Some cities even dangled their urban *hukou* in exchange for rural residents' farming land while providing little or essentially no social benefits associated with the conversion. Moreover, during this period, the central government eliminated many benefits allocated by the planned system (e.g., food rationing), and the remaining *hukou*-related benefits such as pensions or children's access to public school were mostly location-based. In other words, whether a migrant can access entitled welfare and benefits depends not on whether they have an urban *hukou* but on whether they have a *local* urban *hukou*.

These reforms, coupled with the mounting pressure of rapidly increasing rural-to-urban migration in the twenty-first century, prompted the central government to enact policies to accelerate the urbanization process (K. Chan, 2019). In 2014, China's State Council announced its ambitious "National New-Type Urbanization Plan (2014–2020)," which proposed to provide urban *hukou* for 100 million rural-to-urban migrants. The steady flow of rural migrants, however, offsets some of these efforts, with the gap in access to location-based social benefits between migrants and local residents becoming even wider. In 2022, China's

National Development and Reform Commission (NDRC), a powerful government agency that plays a critical role in shaping China's economic development policies, called on cities with a population under three million to liberalize their *hukou* restriction (Jaramillo, 2022). Critics, however, pointed out that similar reforms were proposed in previous years without much success. More importantly, the regulations in megacities such as Beijing, Shanghai, Guangzhou, and Shenzhen as well as other main destination areas of migrants have become more rigid. For example, resident permits in megacities are reserved only for those who are financially privileged (e.g., those who buy luxury apartments in the area) or hold advanced degrees or professional qualifications.

Migrant children's lack of access to public schools in host cities—a critical *hukou*-based institutional implication—is another primary factor contributing to children being left behind in migrant-sending communities (Z. Liang et al., 2020; S. Zhou & Cheung, 2017). When children migrate with their parents to coastal areas or megacities, they face multiple barriers in the education system, leading to further social and economic disadvantages. Specifically, migrant children are marginalized by the educational system in host cities as they (1) encounter numerous difficulties accessing government-sponsored public schools and (2) are prohibited by most local governments to take the local high school entrance examination and the national university entrance examination.

The Compulsory Education Law requires all students to receive nine years of education, stipulating that "the state, community, schools, and families shall . . . safeguard the rights of compulsory education of school-aged children and adolescents." The reality, however, is more complicated. Migrant children often do not have equal access to government-funded public schools and are routinely blocked by a maze of barriers constructed by local governments and schools. In fact, in the 1990s when the problem of migrant children's education first emerged, the government's initial policy was to require children to attend schools in rural areas and to apply for urban schools only under unusual circumstances. These policy guidelines were modified at the beginning of the twenty-first century. The 2001 State Council Decision on Basic Education Reform and Development dictated that local governments and schools in migrant destination cities were responsible for providing compulsory education for migrant children. Nevertheless, since school funding was allocated based on the number of school-aged children with local *hukou*, local governments and schools were reluctant to provide funding for migrant children and often charged migrant children additional "educational endorsement fees." To address this issue, the Ministry of Finance issued a document in 2004 to protect migrant children's equal access to public schools, specifically prohibiting local governments and schools from charging these additional fees.

These policies were reiterated in the 2014 document "The Blueprint for New Type of Urbanization in China," which restated that migrant children's education should be part of local governments' education, school, and fiscal planning. Nevertheless, discriminatory practices against migrant children were prevalent. For example, migrant parents seeking to enroll their children in public schools in Beijing had to provide as many as "five certificates": temporary residence permits for both parents, a certificate of "no guardianship" in migrant-sending communities, household registration documents for children and parents, employment permits, and apartment leases in the district. These institutional regulations effectively discouraged migrant parents from bringing children with them and severely restricted migrant children's access to limited educational opportunities. A recent survey of migrant workers revealed that only 81.5 percent of migrant children in the compulsory school age range had access to public schools, and close to half (47.5%) reported that their children had experienced discriminatory school policies and practices (Z. Liang et al., 2020).

Another characteristic of the Chinese educational system—which is particularly detrimental for interprovincial migrant children—is how the transition to non-compulsory high school and college education is structured. Chinese children are required to take a test for senior high school and a test for university entrance, both of which are open for children with local *hukou* with few exceptions. In other words, migrant children are required to return to their home provinces to take these tests, an enormous disadvantage since each province has its unique curriculum and examinations. In 2012, the central government required each province and city to develop policies to relax these restrictions; however, most cities and provinces still exclude the majority of migrant children from taking these critical tests in their destination cities. The number of migrant children taking the university entrance exam in host cities was merely 4,400 in 2013 and 256,000 in 2020. While the increase appeared to be large, the latter number accounted for only 2.39 percent of the total number of students taking the exam. Moreover, migrant children, even those enrolled in local schools, were excluded from elite, academically oriented schools and were placed in low-quality public schools or migrant-dominant schools.

Overall, recent *hukou* reforms appear to be hardly relevant for the majority of the migrant workers, who do not have any "special talent" or financial resources to obtain a local urban *hukou*. As the Chinese saying "the thunder is loud, but the raindrops are tiny" indicates, the effects of many of the *hukou* reform initiatives are limited or simply nominal in nature. Unfortunately, while it is clear that the *hukou* system has become a major obstacle to the improvement of left-behind children's well-being, there is no clear evidence that the central government is ready to entirely abolish it. Reforms in the education system, while allowing many migrant children to attend schools in local cities, fail to address the root causes of the problem.

Local Programs Addressing Needs of Left-Behind Children
My empirical findings, particularly the identification of key intervening mechanisms, have great potential to inform the formulation and development of treatment and intervention programs at institutional and familial levels. Surprisingly,

while there is much research attention to left-behind children, intervention/ treatment programs and social services targeted specifically toward this subpopulation at the national level are almost nonexistent. Most programs are small in size and scope and are still at the research or experimental level. A scoping review conducted recently (L. Wang et al., 2019), for example, identified a total of only eighteen intervention studies focusing on health and related well-being outcomes of left-behind children. This number is disproportionally small given the large size of this vulnerable population and its sustained publicity.

These programs, ranging from education-based intervention to nursing services to sports intervention, produce largely positive results. An experimental study by X. Zhang and colleagues (2020), for example, found that programs focusing on family workshop interventions remarkably improved children's social adaptation, including improvement in emotional symptoms, peer problems, and attention span. Intervention programs adopting a holistic approach, in particular, are documented to produce positive outcomes. Jiang and colleagues (2019) found that community-based intervention, which consists of a children's center managed by a local Women's Federation representative and assisted by volunteers, significantly improved children's psychosocial well-being. These studies demonstrate that programs targeting children left behind in rural China can produce many benefits and are potentially cost-effective.

I expect that my nuanced analyses of the underlying social processes provide policymakers with further insights into the types, targets, and nature of intervention and prevention programs. While global intervention programs (e.g., community youth centers offering a range of services such as tutoring, health care, and counseling) are urgently needed and will benefit this highly marginalized group, I have identified several other entry-point programs that can be potentially cost-effective. First, my study demonstrates that caregiving arrangements play a critical role in shaping children's behavior, with certain types of caretaking arrangements consistently associated with children's poorer behavioral and emotional outcomes. In particular, this study highlights that children cared for by one-grandparent caretakers are especially vulnerable, consistently faring worse than children in households with other caretaking arrangements. The vulnerability of children and adult caretakers in one-grandparent-caretaking households suggests that programs tailored particularly for this type of caretaking are urgently needed and are likely to improve children's behavioral and emotional outcomes significantly. The empirical finding that this vulnerability is a product of complicated interaction between marginal household economic status, caretakers' poor physical and mental health conditions, and suboptimal caretaking practices suggests that programs adopting a holistic approach may benefit children and caretakers in these households the most. For example, programs providing financial assistance, community-based intervention (e.g., space for sports activities), and school tutoring may collectively improve the well-being of children and adult caretakers.

Prevention and intervention programs for other caretaking arrangements (e.g., maternal migration or two-grandparent caretaking), instead, may focus on providing parenting/caretaking training lessons for at-home caretakers as well as school tutoring for children. The finding that at-home fathers encounter daunting challenges when navigating gender boundaries, for example, suggests that the development of programs targeting traditional social norms regarding gender and masculinity is imminent and potentially effective. My findings also reveal that grandparent caretakers provide much-needed emotional and physical care for children left behind but are often reluctant to serve as disciplinary agents. These findings indicate that programs focusing on parenting/caretaking practices and caretaker–child communication are needed for children cared for by grandparent caretakers.

An important finding—which has yet to attract researchers' attention—is that migrant parents perform "responsible parenting" by bringing children to host cities during summer breaks, offering a good opportunity for children to develop intimacy with their parents and to minimize the feelings of ambiguous loss. Children's experiences of these urban visits, however, are marred by extremely poor living conditions, parents' overloaded working schedules, and a lack of familiarity with urban culture, essentially leaving children hopelessly isolated and trapped in their small apartments. Nonprofit organizations, including national organizations such as "Care for Children" and local college student associations, may develop programs targeting these children, providing needed services such as city tours, space for sports activities, and tutoring. These programs can potentially broaden children's knowledge and understanding of urban culture, reduce their anxiety and depression, and improve child–parent relationships. Moreover, these programs are cost-effective compared with rurality-based programs, which may have difficulties recruiting volunteers and providing services to children living in remote areas.

Final Remarks

This book focuses on children left behind in rural China, identifying critical structural and micro factors associated with the emergence of this subpopulation as well as potential social mechanisms leading to their emotional, psychological, and behavioral outcomes. Severely constrained by multiple institutional barriers, children left behind, at-home caretakers, and migrant parents strive to maintain a functional household and achieve intergenerational mobility. These translocal households, however, face numerous uncertainties, and their efforts can be utterly shattered by rapid and unexpected social changes. Granted, modern China has already witnessed a lion's share of dramatic social changes since the founding of the People's Republic of China in 1949, including the Great Leap Forward Campaign from 1958 to 1961, the Cultural Revolution from 1966 to 1976, and the Reform and Opening Up since 1978. All of these movements, along with the massive rural-to-urban migration discussed in this book, have dramatically altered people's life trajectories (e.g., education, employment, and marriage trajectories). But more seems to be coming.

One imminent social change with potentially far-reaching effects is the so-called "Crop Plantation Landscaping" in rural China, which is promoted by the central government and consists of activities such as leveling uneven soil and removing ridges separating land belonging to different rural households. The explicit purpose of this movement is to minimize the detrimental effect of labor migration on agricultural productivity, transforming the traditional subsistence economy into a large-scale farm economy. Indeed, despite their legal rights to farm their families' land, all families in the two villages where I conducted my field observation had leased their land to one family, from whom each household received a certain amount of compensation for the rent. Although rarely discussed in the public discourse, this government-promoted program has the potential to effectively deprive rural residents of the right to subsistence farming, a social security cushion for migrants, and a symbolic connection between migrants and their home villages. The critical question here is, with the *hukou* system largely intact and the symbolic connection between peasants and land now removed, what are the life choices for left-behind children—most of whom will become the next generation of migrant workers? In particular, if China's economy slows down and jobs disappear, where can these children go? Without any farming skills and little emotional connection to the land, will this new generation of migrant workers settle down permanently in urban areas or have to float like their parents? Will they still be treated as secondary citizens by the state and the urban residents? With a higher level of education and a better understanding of the rural–urban inequality than their migrant parents, how will the second-generation migrants react to and cope with the institutionally induced discrimination and their marginalized socioeconomic status? Importantly, how will the central and local governments respond to these urgent issues and reform the *hukou* and the educational system? With the second generation of rural-to-urban migrants soon becoming the majority and the economy currently slowing down, the clock is ticking.

ACKNOWLEDGMENTS

This book would not have been possible without the Chinese migrant parents, children left behind, and parent/grandparent caretakers involved in the research projects. I am grateful for the confidence and trust of them, who have welcomed me to their homes and shared their life stories with me without any reservation. Their positive attitude toward life even when it is filled with much adversity, self-reliance, and kindness compels me to write their stories.

During the development of this book project and the subsequent data collection, I received much support from friends, colleagues, and family members. I want to thank my two older sisters, Xiaoyi Chen and Xiaohua Chen, and their family members (my two nephews and two nieces), who have provided a lot of ideas for the development of this project. Their life experiences, particularly long years of *dagong* in coastal provinces, inspired me to study and understand the left-behind children population in rural China. I am also grateful for Mr. Zhou—the principal of a middle school I interviewed. Without Mr. Zhou, I would not have had access to the middle schools in Peace County to collect survey or interview data. Finally, I owe a debt to my research assistant Julie Ford, who meticulously proofread all chapters of this book and provided many insightful comments, even when she was busy with her classwork and research.

Earlier versions of the chapters have been published in *The British Journal of Criminology*, *Current Politics and Economics of Northern and Western Asia*, and *Victims & Offenders* and have been presented at American Society of Criminology conferences. I would like to thank the editors and reviewers of these journals and the conference audiences for their critique and advice. I also would like to acknowledge academic funding support from Tulane University for the two projects "Internalizing and Externalizing Behavior of Left-Behind Children in Rural China and "Left-Behind Children and Caregivers in Rural China," and the book subvention grant from the Tulane University School of Liberal Arts. This book could not have been carried out without Tulane University's generous financial support.

Last but foremost, I owe a great deal of debt to my own family. My wife, Ruiyi Jiang, provides excellent care for our son, which enabled me to go to China many times to work on this project. I am also deeply grateful to and for our son Jerry. I have seen him grow up from an innocent child to a strong and resilient teenager during the last few years. He has never ceased to amaze me with his courage, positive attitude, and genuine kindness toward life and the people around him.

REFERENCES

ACWF (All-China Women's Federation). (2013). *The Research report of left-behind children and migrant children in rural China*. Southwest China Normal University Press.

Agnew, R. (1992). Foundation for a general strain theory of crime and delinquency. *Criminology*, 30(1), 47–88.

Alinejad, D. (2019). Careful co-presence: The transnational mediation of emotional intimacy. *Social Media+ Society*, 5(2), 2056305119854222.

Anand, M. (2020). *Gender and mental health: Combining theory and practice*. Springer Singapore.

Antia, K., Boucsein, J., Deckert, A., Dambach, P., Račaitė, J., Šurkienė, G., Jaenisch, T., Horstick, O., & Winkler, V. (2020). Effects of international labour migration on the mental health and well-being of left-behind children: A systematic literature review. *International Journal of Environmental Research and Public Health*, 17(12), Article 12.

Antman, F. M. (2012). Gender, educational attainment, and the impact of parental migration on children left behind. *Journal of Population Economics*, 25(4), 1187–1214.

Asis, M. M. (2006). Living with migration: Experiences of left-behind children in the Philippines. *Asian Population Studies*, 2(1), 45–67.

Ba Nguyen, D., & Van Nguyen, L. (2022). Mental health among left-behind children in Vietnam: Role of resilience. *International Journal of Mental Health*, July 12. https://doi.org/10.1080/00207411.2022.2098562.

Bai, Y., Neubauer, M., Ru, T., Shi, Y., Kenny, K., & Rozelle, S. (2020). Impact of second-parent migration on student academic performance in northwest China and its implications. *Journal of Development Studies*, 56(8), 1523–1540.

Bai, Y., Zhang, L., Liu, C., Shi, Y., Mo, D., & Rozelle, S. (2018). Effect of parental migration on the academic performance of left behind children in north western China. *Journal of Development Studies*, 54(7), 1154–1170.

Baker, L., & Silverstein, M. (2012). The wellbeing of grandparents caring for grandchildren in China and the United States. In S. Arber & V. Timonen (Eds.), *Contemporary grandparenting* (pp. 51–70). Policy Press.

Baron, R. M., & Kenny, D. A. (1986). The moderator–mediator variable distinction in social psychological research: Conceptual, strategic, and statistical considerations. *Journal of Personality and Social Psychology*, 51(6), 1173.

Biao, X. (2007). How far are the left-behind left behind? A preliminary study in rural China. *Population, Space and Place*, 13(3), 179–191.

Boss, P. (2002). Ambiguous loss in families of the missing. *The Lancet*, 360, s39–s40.

Boss, P. (2009). *Ambiguous loss: Learning to live with unresolved grief*. Harvard University Press.

Boss, P. (2016). The context and process of theory development: The story of ambiguous loss. *Journal of Family Theory & Review*, 8(3), 269–286.

Braithwaite, J. (2015). Rethinking criminology through radical diversity in Asian reconciliation. *Asian Journal of Criminology*, 10(3), 183–191.

Branje, S. (2018). Development of parent–adolescent relationships: Conflict interactions as a mechanism of change. *Child Development Perspectives*, *12*(3), 171–176.

Broderick, C. B. (1993). *Understanding family process: Basics of family systems theory*. SAGE.

Bronfenbrenner, U. (1979). *The ecology of human development*. Harvard University Press.

Bronfenbrenner, U. (2005a). Ecological systems theory (1992). In *Making human beings human: Bioecological perspectives on human development* (pp. 106–173). SAGE.

Bronfenbrenner, U. (2005b). *Making human beings human: Bioecological perspectives on human development*. SAGE.

Bronfenbrenner, U., & Morris, P. (2007). The bioecological model of human development. In R. M. Lerner & W. Damon (Eds.), *Handbook of child psychology*, Vol. 1, *Theoretical models of human development* (6th ed., pp. 793–828). Wiley.

Bryan, J., Moore-Thomas, C., Gaenzle, S., Kim, J., Lin, C.-H., & Na, G. (2012). The effects of school bonding on high school seniors' academic achievement. *Journal of Counseling & Development*, *90*(4), 467–480.

Burt, C. H. (2020). Self-control and crime: Beyond Gottfredson & Hirschi's theory. *Annual Review of Criminology*, *3*(1), 43–73.

Carranza, M. (2022). The cost of "a better life": Children left behind—beyond ambiguous loss. *Journal of Family Issues*, *43*(12), 3218–3243.

Chan, K. (2019). China's hukou system at 60: Continuity and reform. In R. Yep & J. Wang (Eds.), *Handbook on urban development in China* (pp. 59–79). Edward Elgar.

Chan, K. W., & Ren, Y. (2018). Children of migrants in China in the twenty-first century: Trends, living arrangements, age-gender structure, and geography. *Eurasian Geography and Economics*, *59*(2), 133–163.

Chang, F., Jiang, Y., Loyalka, P., Chu, J., Shi, Y., Osborn, A., & Rozelle, S. (2019). Parental migration, educational achievement, and mental health of junior high school students in rural China. *China Economic Review*, *54*, 337–349.

Chang, H., Dong, X., & MacPhail, F. (2011). Labor migration and time use patterns of the left-behind children and elderly in rural China. *World Development*, *39*(12), 2199–2210.

Chao, R. K. (1994). Beyond parental control and authoritarian parenting style: Understanding Chinese parenting through the cultural notion of training. *Child Development*, *65*(4), 1111–1119.

Chao, R., & Tseng, V. (2002). Parenting of Asians. In *Handbook of parenting: Social conditions and applied parenting* (2nd ed., Vol. 4, pp. 59–93). Lawrence Erlbaum Associates Publishers.

Chen, F., & Liu, G. (2012). The health implications of grandparents caring for grandchildren in China. *Journals of Gerontology Series B: Psychological Sciences and Social Sciences*, *67*(1), 99–112.

Chen, F., Liu, G., & Mair, C. A. (2011). Intergenerational ties in context: Grandparents caring for grandchildren in China. *Social Forces*, *90*(2), 571–594.

Chen, H., Wang, X., Liu, Y., & Liu, Y. (2020). Migrants' choice of household split or reunion in China's urbanisation process: The effect of objective and subjective socioeconomic status. *Cities*, *102*, 102669.

Chen, L. J., Yang, D. L., & Ren, Q. (2015). *Report on the state of children in China*. Chapin Hall, University of Chicago.

Chen, M., Rizzi, E. L., & Yip, P. S. F. (2021). Divorce trends in China across time and space: An update. *Asian Population Studies*, *17*(2), 121–147.

Chen, R., & Zhou, L. (2021). Parental migration and psychological well-being of children in rural China. *International Journal of Environmental Research and Public Health*, *18*(15), 8085.

Chen, X. (2009). The link between juvenile offending and victimization: The influence of risky lifestyles, social bonding, and individual characteristics. *Youth Violence and Juvenile Justice*, *7*(2), 119–135.

Chen, X. (2017). Parental migration, caretaking arrangement, and children's delinquent behavior in rural China. *Asian Journal of Criminology, 12*(4), 281–302.

Chen, X. (2021). Parental migration and children's problem behaviours in rural China: Testing an integrative theoretical model. *The British Journal of Criminology, 61*(6), 1592–1611.

Chen, X., & Jiang, X. (2019). Are grandparents better caretakers? Parental migration, caretaking arrangements, children's self-control, and delinquency in rural China. *Crime & Delinquency, 65*(8), 1123–1148.

Chen, X., Li, D., Liu, J., Fu, R., & Liu, S. (2019). Father migration and mother migration: Different implications for social, school, and psychological adjustment of left-behind children in rural China. *Journal of Contemporary China, 28*(120), 849–863.

Chen, X., Liang, N., & Ostertag, S. F. (2017). Victimization of children left behind in rural China. *Journal of Research in Crime and Delinquency, 54*(4), 515–543.

Chen, X., Wu, Y., & Qu, J. (2022a). Parental migration and children's exposure to polyvictimization in rural China. *Journal of Interpersonal Violence, 37*(19–20), NP17429–NP17453.

Chen, X., Wu, Y., & Qu, J. (2022b). Parental migration and risk of sexual assault against children in rural China. *Crime & Delinquency, 68*(4), 613–643.

Chen, Y., Huang, R., Lu, Y., & Zhang, K. (2021). Education fever in China: Children's academic performance and parents' life satisfaction. *Journal of Happiness Studies, 22*(2), 927–954.

Cheng, J., & Sun, Y.-H. (2015). Depression and anxiety among left-behind children in China: A systematic review. *Child: Care, Health and Development, 41*(4), 515–523.

China Youth and Children Research Center (2001). *Research report on Chinese children: Survey data*. China Youth Press.

Choi, S. E., & Zhang, Z. (2021). Caring as curing: Grandparenting and depressive symptoms in China. *Social Science & Medicine, 289*, 114452.

Conger, R. D., Ge, X., Elder, G. H., Lorenz, F. O., & Simons, R. L. (1994). Economic stress, coercive family process, and developmental problems of adolescents. *Child Development, 65*(2), 541–561.

Cotton, C., & Beguy, D. (2021). Long-distance mothering in urban Kenya. *Journal of Marriage and Family, 83*(2), 482–497.

Darling, N. (2007). Ecological systems theory: The person in the center of the circles. *Research in Human Development, 4*(3–4), 203–217.

Dittman, C. K. (2018). Long-distance parenting: the impact of parental separation and absence due to work commitments on families. In M. R. Sanders & A. Morawska (Eds.), *Handbook of parenting and child development across the lifespan* (pp. 511–533). Springer International Publishing.

Dong, B., Yu, D., Ren, Q., Zhao, D., Li, J., & Sun, Y. (2019). The resilience status of Chinese left-behind children in rural areas: A meta-analysis. *Psychology, Health & Medicine, 24*(1), 1–13.

Dong, Y., Wang, W., Li, S., & Zhang, L. (2021). The cumulative impact of parental migration on schooling of left-behind children in rural China. *Journal of Rural Studies, 86*, 527-541.

Dreby, J. (2010). *Divided by borders: Mexican migrants and their children*. University of California Press.

Du, Y. (2000). Rural labor immigration in contemporary China: An analysis of its features and the macro context. In L. West & Y. Zhao (Eds.), *Rural labor flows in China* (pp. 67–100). University of California Press.

Elliott, D. S., & Ageton, S. S. (1980). Reconciling race and class differences in self-reported and official estimates of delinquency. *American Sociological Review*, 95–110.

Elliott, D. S., Ageton, S. S., & Canter, R. J. (1979). An Integrated Theoretical Perspective on Delinquent Behavior. *Journal of Research in Crime and Delinquency, 16*(1), 3–27.

Elliott, D. S., Huizinga, D., & Ageton, S. S. (1985). *Explaining Delinquency and Drug Use*. SAGE.

REFERENCES

Ettekal, A. V., & Mahoney, J. L. (2017). Ecological systems theory. In K. Peppler (Ed.), *The SAGE encyclopedia of out-of-school learning* (pp. 230–241). SAGE.

Falicov, C. J. (2012). Ambiguous loss: Risk and resilience in Latino immigrant families. In *The New Immigration* (pp. 211–220). Routledge.

Fan, C. C. (1999). Migration in a socialist transitional economy: Heterogeneity, socioeconomic and spatial characteristics of migrants in China and Guangdong Province. *International Migration Review*, *33*(4), 954–987.

Fan, C. C., & Li, T. (2020). Split households, family migration and urban settlement: Findings from China's 2015 National Floating Population Survey. *Social Inclusion*, *8*(1), Article 1.

Fan, C. C., Sun, M., & Zheng, S. (2011). Migration and split households: A comparison of sole, couple, and family migrants in Beijing, China. *Environment and Planning A: Economy and Space*, *43*(9), 2164–2185.

Fang, Y., & Shi, Z. (2018). Children of migrant parents: Migrating together or left behind. *Habitat International*, *76*, 62–68.

Farrington, D. P. (1986). Age and Crime. *Crime and Justice*, *7*, 189–250.

Fellmeth, G., Rose-Clarke, K., Zhao, C., Busert, L. K., Zheng, Y., Massazza, A., Sonmez, H., Eder, B., Blewitt, A., Lertgrai, W., Orcutt, M., Ricci, K., Mohamed-Ahmed, O., Burns, R., Knipe, D., Hargreaves, S., Hesketh, T., Opondo, C., & Devakumar, D. (2018). Health impacts of parental migration on left-behind children and adolescents: A systematic review and meta-analysis. *The Lancet*, *392*(10164), 2567–2582.

Fu, M., Xue, Y., Zhou, W., & Yuan, T. F. (2017). Parental absence predicts suicide ideation through emotional disorders. *PLoS One*, *12*(12), e0188823.

Fu, Y., & Law, Y. W. (2018). Chinese adolescents' meaning-focused coping with prolonged parent-child separation. *Journal of Adolescent Research*, *33*(6), 752–773.

Fuligni, A. J. (1998). Authority, autonomy, and parent–adolescent conflict and cohesion: A study of adolescents from Mexican, Chinese, Filipino, and European backgrounds. *Developmental Psychology*, *34*(4), 782–792.

Gaetano, A. M., & Jacka, T. (2004). *On the move: Women and rural-to-urban migration in contemporary China*. Columbia University Press.

Gao, Y., Li, L. P., Kim, J. H., Congdon, N., Lau, J., & Griffiths, S. (2010). The impact of parental migration on health status and health behaviours among left behind adolescent school children in China. *BMC Public Health*, *10*(1), 56.

Ge, Y., Song, L., Clancy, R. F., & Qin, Y. (2019). Studies on left-behind children in China: Reviewing paradigm shifts. *New Directions for Child and Adolescent Development*, *2019*(163), 115–135.

Giordano, P. C. (2010). *Legacies of crime: A follow-up of the children of highly delinquent girls and boys*. Cambridge University Press.

Gordon, R. A. (2015). *Regression analysis for the social sciences*. Routledge.

Graham, E., & Jordan, L. P. (2011). Migrant parents and the psychological well-being of left-behind children in Southeast Asia. *Journal of Marriage and Family*, *73*(4), 763–787.

Grasmick, H. G., Tittle, C. R., Bursik, R. J., Jr., and Arneklev, B. K. (1993). Testing the core empirical implications of Gottfredson and Hirschi's general theory of crime. *Journal of Research in Crime & Delinquency*, *30*: 5–29.

Guo, J., Chen, L., Wang, X., Liu, Y., Chui, C. H. K., He, H., Qu, Z., & Tian, D. (2012). The relationship between Internet addiction and depression among migrant children and left-behind children in China. *Cyberpsychology, Behavior, and Social Networking*, *15*(11), 585–590.

Ho, E. S., & Chiang, L. N. (2017). Long-distance filial piety: Chinese families in Australasia caring for elderly parents across borders. *Translocal Chinese: East Asian Perspectives*, *11*(2), 278–311.

Hoang, L. A., Lam, T., Yeoh, B. S. A., & Graham, E. (2015). Transnational migration, changing care arrangements and left-behind children's responses in South-east Asia. *Children's Geographies*, *13*(3), 263–277.

Holdaway, J. (2018). Educating the children of migrants in China and the United States: A common challenge? *China Population and Development Studies*, *2*(1), 108–128.

Hu, B. Y., Wu, H., Winsler, A., Fan, X., & Song, Z. (2020). Parent migration and rural preschool children's early academic and social skill trajectories in China: Are "left-behind" children really left behind? *Early Childhood Research Quarterly*, *51*, 317–328.

Hu, F. (2012). Migration, remittances, and children's high school attendance: The case of rural China. *International Journal of Educational Development*, *32*(3), 401–411.

Hu, F. (2013). Does migration benefit the schooling of children left behind? Evidence from rural northwest China. *Demographic Research*, *29*, 33–70.

Hu, H., Lu, S., & Huang, C.-C. (2014). The psychological and behavioral outcomes of migrant and left-behind children in China. *Children and Youth Services Review*, *46*, 1–10.

Hu, S. (2018). Parents' migration and adolescents' transition to high school in rural China: The role of parental divorce. *Journal of Family Issues*, *39*(12), 3324–3359.

Hu, S. (2019). "It's for our education": Perception of parental migration and resilience among left-behind children in rural China. *Social Indicators Research*, *145*(2), 641–661.

Hu, Y., & Scott, J. (2016). Family and gender values in China: Generational, geographic, and gender differences. *Journal of Family Issues*, *37*(9), 1267–1293.

Huang, W., Chen, X., & Wu, Y. (2023a). Education fever and adolescent deviance in China. *Crime & Delinquency*, 00111287231174421.

Huang, W., Chen, X., & Wu, Y. (2023b). Tough or no love? Parental migration and children's exposure to corporal punishment and neglect in rural China. *Victims & Offenders*, *18*(1), 217–236.

Jaramillo E. (2022). China's hukou reform in 2022: Do they mean it this time? CSIS, April 20. https://www.csis.org/blogs/new-perspectives-asia/chinas-hukou-reform-2022-do-they-mean-it-time-0.

Jiang, H., Hu, H., Zhu, X., & Jiang, H. (2019). Effects of school-based and community-based protection services on victimization incidence among left-behind children in China. *Children and Youth Services Review*, *101*, 239–245.

Jingzhong, Y. (2011). Left-behind children: The social price of China's economic boom. *Journal of Peasant Studies*, *38*(3), 613–650.

Jingzhong, Y., & Lu, P. (2011). Differentiated childhoods: Impacts of rural labor migration on left-behind children in China. *Journal of Peasant Studies*, *38*(2), 355–377.

Klahr, A. M., McGue, M., Iacono, W. G., & Burt, S. A. (2011). The association between parent–child conflict and adolescent conduct problems over time: Results from a longitudinal adoption study. *Journal of Abnormal Psychology*, *120*(1), 46–56.

Kong, S. T., & Meng, X. (2010). The educational and health outcomes of the children of migrants. In X. Meng, C. Manning, L. Shi, & T. Effendi (Eds.), *The great migration* (pp. 93–116). Edward Elgar Publishing.

Krisberg, B. A. (2017). *Juvenile justice and delinquency*. SAGE.

Kruttschnitt, C. (2013). Gender and crime. *Annual Review of Sociology*, *39*(1), 291–308.

Lam, T., & Yeoh, B. S. A. (2018). Migrant mothers, left-behind fathers: The negotiation of gender subjectivities in Indonesia and the Philippines. *Gender, Place & Culture*, *25*(1), 104–117.

Lan, X., & Sun, Q. (2022). Exploring psychosocial adjustment profiles in Chinese adolescents from divorced families: The interplay of parental attachment and adolescent's gender. *Current Psychology*, *41*(9), 5832–5848.

Lee, M.-H. (2011). Migration and children's welfare in China: The schooling and health of children left behind. *The Journal of Developing Areas*, 165–182.

REFERENCES

Lewis, G., Collishaw, S., Thapar, A., & Harold, G. T. (2014). Parent–child hostility and child and adolescent depression symptoms: The direction of effects, role of genetic factors and gender. *European Child & Adolescent Psychiatry*, 23(5), 317–327.

Li, S. D., Liu, T.-H., & Xia, Y. (2023). A comparative study of parenting practices and juvenile delinquency between China and the United States. *Deviant Behavior*, 44(4), 636–651.

Li, W. (2018). Migration and marital instability among migrant workers in China: A gender perspective. *Chinese Journal of Sociology*, 4(2), 218–235.

Li, X., Feigelman, S., & Stanton, B. (2000). Perceived parental monitoring and health risk behaviors among urban low-income African-American children and adolescents. *Journal of Adolescent Health*, 27(1), 43–48.

Liang, W., Hou, L., & Chen, W. (2008). Left-behind children in rural primary schools: The case of Sichuan Province. *Chinese Education & Society*, 41(5), 84–99.

Liang, Y., Wang, L., & Rui, G. (2017). Depression among left-behind children in China. *Journal of Health Psychology*, 22(14), 1897–1905.

Liang, Z., Yue, Z., Li, Y., Li, Q., & Zhou, A. (2020). Choices or constraints: Education of migrant children in urban China. *Population Research and Policy Review*, 39, 671–690.

Liu, J. (2009). Asian criminology—challenges, opportunities, and directions. *Asian Journal of Criminology*, 4(1), 1–9.

Liu, J. (2018). The Asian criminological paradigm and how it links global north and south: Combining an extended conceptual tool box from the north with innovative Asian contexts. *The Palgrave Handbook of Criminology and the Global South*, 61–82.

Liu, P. L., & Leung, L. (2017). Migrant parenting and mobile phone use: Building quality relationships between Chinese migrant workers and their left-behind children. *Applied Research in Quality of Life*, 12(4), 925–946.

Liu, R. X. (2015). The effects of gender and bonds with parents and grandparents on delinquency among Chinese adolescents. *Sociological Focus*, 48(1), 68–87.

Liu, R. X. (2019). Harsh parental discipline and delinquency in mainland China: The conditional influences of gender and bonding to paternal grandparents. *Sociological Focus*, 52(4), 274–291.

Liu, Z., Li, X., & Ge, X. (2009). Left too early: The effects of age at separation from parents on Chinese rural children's symptoms of anxiety and depression. *American Journal of Public Health*, 99(11), 2049–2054.

Logan, J. R., & Bian, F. (1999). Family values and coresidence with married children in urban China. *Social Forces*, 77(4), 1253–1282.

Lu, Y. (2012). Education of children left behind in rural China. *Journal of Marriage and Family*, 74(2), 328–341.

Lu, Y., Yeung, J. W.-J., Liu, J., & Treiman, D. J. (2019a). Health of left-behind children in China: Evidence from mediation analysis. *Chinese Journal of Sociology*, 2057150X19872685.

Lu, Y., Yeung, J. W.-J., Liu, J., & Treiman, D. J. (2019b). Migration and children's psychosocial development in China: When and why migration matters. *Social Science Research*, 77, 130–147.

Lucas, R. E. B. (1997). Internal migration in developing countries. In *Handbook of Population and Family Economics* (Vol. 1, pp. 721–798). Elsevier.

Luo, W., Tong, Y., & Cheung, N. W. T. (2018). Rural-to-urban migration and adolescent delinquent behaviors: Evidence from Hunan and Guangdong in China. *Eurasian Geography and Economics*, 59(2), 246–266.

Ma, A. (2014). China raises a generation of "left behind" children. CNN.com. http://www.cnn.com/2014/02/04/world/asia/chinachildren-left-behind/.

REFERENCES

Ma, L., Chen, M., Che, X., & Fang, F. (2019). Farmers' rural-to-urban migration, influencing factors and development framework: A case study of Sihe Village of Gansu, China. *International Journal of Environmental Research and Public Health*, *16*(5), Article 5.

Ma, X., Wang, F., Chen, J., & Zhang, Y. (2018). The income gap between urban and rural residents in China: Since 1978. *Computational Economics*, *52*(4), 1153–1174.

MacKinnon, D. P., & Dwyer, J. H. (1993). Estimating mediated effects in prevention studies. *Evaluation Review*, *17*(2), 144–158.

Madianou, M., & Miller, D. (2011). Mobile phone parenting: Reconfiguring relationships between Filipina migrant mothers and their left-behind children. *New Media & Society*, *13*(3), 457–470.

Madianou, M., & Miller, D. (2013). *Migration and new media: Transnational families and polymedia*. Routledge.

Mallee, H. (1995). China's household registration system under reform. *Development and Change*, *26*(1), 1–29.

Marc Jackman, W., & Morrain-Webb, J. (2019). Exploring gender differences in achievement through student voice: Critical insights and analyses. *Cogent Education*, *6*(1), 1567895.

Massey, D. S., Arango, J., Hugo, G., Kouaouci, A., Pellegrino, A., & Taylor, J. E. (1994). An evaluation of international migration theory: The North American case. *Population and Development Review*, *20*(4), 699–751.

Masten, A. S., & Barnes, A. J. (2018). Resilience in children: Developmental perspectives. *Children*, *5*(7), 98.

Masten, A. S., Best, K. M., & Garmezy, N. (1990). Resilience and development: Contributions from the study of children who overcome adversity. *Development and Psychopathology*, *2*(4), 425–444.

Matthews, B., & Minton, J. (2018). Rethinking one of criminology's "brute facts": The age–crime curve and the crime drop in Scotland. *European Journal of Criminology*, *15*(3), 296–320.

Mazzucato, V., Cebotari, V., Veale, A., White, A., Grassi, M., & Vivet, J. (2015). International parental migration and the psychological well-being of children in Ghana, Nigeria, and Angola. *Social Science & Medicine*, *132*, 215–224.

McKenzie, D. J. (2005). Measuring inequality with asset indicators. *Journal of Population Economics*, *18*(2), 229–260.

McLuhan, M. (1964). *Understanding media: The extensions of man*. McGraw-Hill.

Menard, S., & Johnson, M. C. (2015). An intergenerational test of integrated theory. *Deviant Behavior*, *36*(2), 87–100.

Meng, X., & Manning, C. (2010). The great migration in China and Indonesia: Trends and institutions. In X. Meng, C. Manning, S. Li, & T. N. Effendi (Eds.), *The great migration: Rural-urban migration in China and Indonesia* (pp. 3–11). Edward Elgar.

Meng, X., & Yamauchi, C. (2017). Children of migrants: The cumulative impact of parental migration on children's education and health outcomes in China. *Demography*, *54*(5), 1677–1714.

Messner, S. F. (2015). When west meets east: Generalizing theory and expanding the conceptual toolkit of criminology. *Asian Journal of Criminology*, *10*(2), 117–129.

Meyerhoefer, C., & Chen, C. (2011). The effect of parental labor migration on children's educational progress in rural China. *Review of Economics of the Household*, *9*(3), 379–396.

Mu, G. M. (2018). *Building resilience of floating children and left-behind children in China: Power, politics, participation, and education*. Routledge.

Murphy, R. (2014). Study and school in the lives of children in migrant families: A view from rural Jiangxi, China. *Development & Change*, *45*(1), 29–51.

Murphy, R. (2020). *The children of China's great migration*. Cambridge University Press.

Murphy, R., Zhou, M., & Tao, R. (2016). Parents' migration and children's subjective well-being and health: Evidence from rural China. *Population, Space and Place*, *22*(8), 766–780.

National Bureau of Statistics of China. (2021). *China statistical yearbook*. China Statistics Press.

National Bureau of Statistics of China. (2022). *China statistical yearbook*. China Statistics Press.

Oliveira, G. (2018). *Motherhood across borders: Immigrants and their children in Mexico and New York*. NYU Press.

Pan, L., Tian, F., Lu, F., Zhang, X. (Luke), Liu, Y., Feng, W., Dai, G., & Wang, H. (2013). An exploration on long-distance communications between left-behind children and their parents in China. *Proceedings of the 2013 Conference on Computer Supported Cooperative Work—CSCW '13*, 1147.

Pan, S., Parish, W. L., & Huang, Y. (2011). Clients of female sex workers: A population-based survey of China. *Journal of Infectious Diseases*, *204*(S5), S1211–S1217.

Parreñas, R. S. (2005a). *Children of global migration: Transnational families and gendered woes*. Stanford University Press.

Parreñas, R. (2005b). Long distance intimacy: Class, gender and intergenerational relations between mothers and children in Filipino transnational families. *Global Networks*, *5*(4), 317–336.

Parreñas, R. S. (2008). Transnational fathering: gendered conflicts, distant disciplining and emotional gaps. *Journal of Ethnic and Migration Studies*, *34*(7), 1057–1072.

Parreñas, R. S. (2009). Transnational mothering: A source of gender conflicts in the family panel 3: Families and global migration. *North Carolina Law Review*, *88*, 1825–1856.

Perez, R. M., & Arnold-Berkovits, I. (2018). A conceptual framework for understanding Latino immigrant's ambiguous loss of homeland. *Hispanic Journal of Behavioral Sciences*, *40*(2), 91–114.

Platte, E. (1988). Divorce trends and patterns in China: Past and present. *Pacific Affairs*, *61*(3), 428–445.

Pottinger, A. M. (2005). Children's experience of loss by parental migration in inner-city Jamaica. *American Journal of Orthopsychiatry*, *75*(4), 485–496.

Ren, Q., & Treiman, D. J. (2016). The consequences of parental labor migration in China for children's emotional wellbeing. *Social Science Research*, *58*, 46–67.

Rosenfield, S., & Mouzon, D. (2013). Gender and mental health. In C. S. Aneshensel, J. C. Phelan, & A. Bierman (Eds.), *Handbook of the sociology of mental health* (pp. 277–296). Springer Netherlands.

Rutter, M. (1987). Psychosocial resilience and protective mechanisms. *American Journal of Orthopsychiatry*, *57*(3), 316–331.

Shani, A. (2021). Who are China's left-behind children? *Haaretz*, April 22. https://www.haaretz.com/world-news/2021-04-22/ty-article-magazine/.premium/who-are-chinas-left-behind-children/0000017f-e508-df2c-a1ff-ff5996760000.

Shen, A. (2018). *Internal migration, crime, and punishment in contemporary China*. Springer.

Shen, J. (2013). Increasing internal migration in China from 1985 to 2005: Institutional versus economic drivers. *Habitat International*, *39*, 1–7.

Shen, W., Hu, L.-C., & Hannum, E. (2021). Effect pathways of informal family separation on children's outcomes: Paternal labor migration and long-term educational attainment of left-behind children in rural China. *Social Science Research*, *97*, 102576.

Shi, L., Chen, W., Xu, J., & Ling, L. (2020). Trends and characteristics of inter-provincial migrants in mainland China and its relation with economic factors: A panel data analysis from 2011 to 2016. *Sustainability*, *12*(2), 610.

Singer, M. (2020). *Educated youth and the Cultural Revolution in China*. University of Michigan Press.

REFERENCES

Slotta, D. (2022). Number of smartphone users in China from 2018 to 2022 with a forecast until 2027. Statista, December 9. https://www.statista.com/statistics/467160/forecast-of-smartphone-users-in-china/.

Solheim, C., Williams-Wengerd, A., Kodman-Jones, C., Burke, K., St. James, C., Lewis, M., & Sherman, M. (2022). Ambiguous loss: A focus on immigrant families, postincarceration family life, addiction and families, and military families. In S. Browning & B. van Eeden-Moorefield (Eds.), *Treating contemporary families: Toward a more inclusive clinical practice* (pp. 187–218). American Psychological Association.

Solheim, C., Zaid, S., & Ballard, J. (2016). Ambiguous loss experienced by transnational Mexican immigrant families. *Family Process, 55*(2), 338–353.

Stark, O., & Bloom, D. E. (1985). The new economics of labor migration. *The American Economic Review, 75*(2), 173–178.

Steffensmeier, D., Lu, Y., & Kumar, S. (2019). Age–crime relation in India: Similarity or divergence vs. Hirschi/gottfredson inverted j-shaped projection? *The British Journal of Criminology, 59*(1), 144–165.

Steffensmeier, D., Zhong, H., & Lu, Y. (2017). Age and its relation to crime in Taiwan and the United States: Invariant, or does cultural context matter? *Criminology, 55*(2), 377–404.

Su, Y., Tesfazion, P., & Zhao, Z. (2018). Where are the migrants from? Inter- vs. intra-provincial rural-urban migration in China. *China Economic Review, 47*, 142–155.

Suárez-Orozco, C., Todorova, I. L. G., & Louie, J. (2002). Making up for lost time: The experience of separation and reunification among immigrant families. *Family Process, 41*(4), 625–643.

Tang, Z. (2017). What makes a difference to children's health in rural China? Parental migration, remittances, and social support. *Chinese Sociological Review, 49*(2), 89–109.

Taylor, J. E., Rozelle, S., & de Brauw, A. (2003). Migration and incomes in source communities: A new economics of migration perspective from China. *Economic Development and Cultural Change, 52*(1), 75–101.

Todaro, M. P. (1969). A model of labor migration and urban unemployment in less developed countries. *The American Economic Review, 59*(1), 138–148.

UNICEF (United Nations Children's Fund). (2019). Country office annual report 2019: China. Accessed November 23, 2020. https://www.unicef.org/about/annualreport/files/China_2019_COAR(1).pdf.

United Nations Department of Economic and Social Affairs, Population Division. (2022). World migration report 2022. https://worldmigrationreport.iom.int/wmr-2022-interactive/.

Wang, L., Zheng, Y., Li, G., Li, Y., Fang, Z., Abbey, C., & Rozelle, S. (2019). Academic achievement and mental health of left-behind children in rural China: A causal study on parental migration. *China Agricultural Economic Review, 11*(4), 569–582.

Wang, M., Victor, B. G., Hong, J. S., Wu, S., Huang, J., Luan, H., & Perron, B. E. (n.d.). *A Scoping Review of Interventions to Promote Health and Well-Being of Left-behind Children in Mainland China*. 21.

Wang, Q., & Zhou, Q. (2010). China's divorce and remarriage rates: Trends and regional disparities. *Journal of Divorce & Remarriage, 51*(4), 257–267.

Wang, S. X. (2014). The effect of parental migration on the educational attainment of their left-behind children in rural China. *BE Journal of Economic Analysis & Policy, 14*(3), 1037–1080.

Wang, W. (2005). Son preference and educational opportunities of children in China—"I wish you were a boy!" *Gender Issues, 22*(2), 3–30.

Wen, M., & Lin, D. (2012). Child development in rural China: Children left behind by their migrant parents and children of nonmigrant families. *Child Development, 83*(1), 120–136.

Whitbeck, L. B., Conger, R. D., & Kao, M. Y. (1993). The influence of parental support, depressed affect, and peers on the sexual behaviors of adolescent girls. *Journal of Family Issues*, *14*(2), 261–278.

Wong-Villacres, M., & Bardzell, S. (2011). Technology-mediated parent-child intimacy: Designing for Ecuadorian families separated by migration. In *CHI'11 Extended Abstracts on Human Factors in Computing Systems* (pp. 2215–2220).

World Bank. (2009). *Reshaping economic geography*. World Development Report. Oxford University Press.

Wu, C., & Chao, R. K. (2017). Parent–adolescent relationships among Chinese immigrant families: An indigenous concept of qin. *Asian American Journal of Psychology*, *8*(4), 323–338.

Wu, W., Qu, G., Wang, L., Tang, X., & Sun, Y.-H. (2019). Meta-analysis of the mental health status of left-behind children in China. *Journal of Paediatrics and Child Health*, *55*(3), 260–270.

Xiong, Y. (2015). The broken ladder: Why education provides no upward mobility for migrant children in China. *The China Quarterly*, *221*, 161–184.

Xu, H. (2017). The time use pattern and labour supply of the left behind spouse and children in rural China. *China Economic Review*, *46*, S77–S101.

Xu, H., & Xie, Y. (2015). The causal effects of rural-to-urban migration on children's well-being in China. *European Sociological Review*, *31*(4), 502–519.

Xu, L., Silverstein, M., & Chi, I. (2014). Emotional closeness between grandparents and grandchildren in rural China: The mediating role of the middle generation. *Journal of Intergenerational Relationships*, *12*(3), 226–240.

Yan, Y. (2003). *Private life under socialism: Love, intimacy, and family change in a Chinese village, 1949–1999*. Stanford University Press.

Ye, J., & Lu, P. (2011). Differentiated childhoods: Impacts of rural labor migration on left-behind children in China. *Journal of Peasant Studies*, *38*(2), 355–377.

Ye, J., & Murray, J. (2005). *Left-behind children in rural China: Impact study of rural labor migration on left-behind children in mid-west China*. Social Sciences Academic Press.

Yu, L., & Suen, H. K. (2005). Historical and contemporary exam-driven education fever in China. *KEDI Journal of Educational Policy*, *2*(1).

Yue, A., Sylvia, S., Bai, Y., Shi, Y., Luo, R., & Rozelle, S. (2016). *The effect of maternal migration on early childhood development in rural China* (SSRN Scholarly Paper ID 2890108). Social Science Research Network.

Zhang, C. (2020). Are children from divorced single-parent families disadvantaged? New evidence from the China family panel studies. *Chinese Sociological Review*, *52*(1), 84–114.

Zhang, L. (2017). Preliminary study on crime prevention of left-behind children in rural China. *Asian Agricultural Research*, *9*(7), 88–89,92.

Zhang, X., Li, M., Guo, L., & Zhu, Y. (2020). Community-based family workshop intervention improved the social adaptation of left-behind children in rural China. *Frontiers in Public Health*, *8*.

Zhao, C., Wang, F., Li, L., Zhou, X., & Hesketh, T. (2017). Long-term impacts of parental migration on Chinese children's psychosocial well-being: Mitigating and exacerbating factors. *Social Psychiatry and Psychiatric Epidemiology*, *52*(6), 669–677.

Zhao, C., Wang, F., Zhou, X., Jiang, M., & Hesketh, T. (2018). Impact of parental migration on psychosocial well-being of children left behind: A qualitative study in rural China. *International Journal for Equity in Health*, *17*(1), 1–10.

Zhao, X., Chen, J., Chen, M.-C., Lv, X.-L., Jiang, Y.-H., & Sun, Y.-H. (2014). Left-behind children in rural China experience higher levels of anxiety and poorer living conditions. *Acta Paediatrica*, *103*(6), 665–670.

REFERENCES

Zhao, Y. H. (2000). Rural-to-urban labor migration in China: The past and the present. In L. A. West & Y. H. Zhao (Eds.), *Rural labor flows in China* (pp. 231–250). University of California Press.

Zhou, C., Sylvia, S., Zhang, L., Luo, R., Yi, H., Liu, C., Shi, Y., Loyalka, P., Chu, J., & Medina, A. (2015). China's left-behind children: Impact of parental migration on health, nutrition, and educational outcomes. *Health Affairs, 34*(11), 1964–1971.

Zhou, M., Murphy, R., & Tao, R. (2014). Effects of parents' migration on the education of children left behind in rural China. *Population and Development Review, 40*(2), 273–292.

Zhou, R., Wen, Z., Tang, M., & DiSalvo, B. (2017). Navigating media use: Chinese parents and their overseas adolescent children on WeChat. *Proceedings of the 2017 Conference on Designing Interactive Systems*, 1025–1037.

Zhou, S., & Cheung, M. (2017). Hukou system effects on migrant children's education in China: Learning from past disparities. *International Social Work, 60*(6), 1327–1342.

Zuo, J., & Bian, Y. (2001). Gendered resources, division of housework, and perceived fairness—A case in urban China. *Journal of Marriage and Family, 63*(4), 1122–1133.

INDEX

The letters *f* or *t* following a page number denote a figure or table, respectively.

Academic performance, 97, 102*t*, 137, 148; effect of caretaking arrangements, 99; effect of family socioeconomic status, 102*t*; effect of grandparenting, 97; effect of parental migration, 98; frequency of, 97; gendered analysis, 102*t*; measure of, 97
Academic-track high school, 4, 13, 174, 175
ACWF, 2, 15, 27, 32, 37, 99
Affiliation with deviant peers, 21, 123; effect of caretaking arrangements, 123, 123*f*; effect of gender, 123–126; frequency of, 123; mediating effect of caretaking practices, 126; scale of, 123
Age-crime curve, 121
Alpha (α), 52, 58, 63, 145, 163
Alternative caretaking arrangements, 19, 31, 49, 54, 68, 131; measures of, 19; types of, 166
Ambient conditions, 73
Ambiguous loss, 21, 142, 144, 155, 156, 160; cross-over, 155; dimensions of, 156, 160; frequency of, 160; indicators of, 160, 161*t*; latent factors of, 161, 162*t*; reliability of, 161; predictive validity of, 163–164; types of, 155
Ambivalent feelings, 21, 144, 147, 156
Anxiety, 5, 21, 144–150, 152, 155, 163, 165
Association with deviant peers, 121–122, 124–126, 134, 138, 141; predictors of, 139, 139*t*
Asymmetrical relationship, 78
At-home caretaking, 85, 97, 116, 140, 148, 151
At-home father caretaking, 18, 56; measure of, 18
At-home mother caretaking, 18, 148; measure of, 148
At-home parents, 13, 18–20, 63, 68, 109
Autonomy for woman, 91

Baron & Kenny, 99, 103
Baseline model, 105
Behavioral development, 166
Bioecological model, 6–9
Bivariate analysis, 123, 125, 127, 146, 149
Boundary ambiguity, 156, 159

Caregiver-child dyad, 156
Caretaker-child bonding, 53–58; effect of caretaking arrangements, 53*t*; reliability, 58; respect toward caretakers, 59–60; scale of, 58

Caretaker-child conflict, 62–64, 69, 167; effect of caretaking arrangements, 64*t*; reliability, 62; scale of, 62
Caretaker hostility, 102, 105–107, 119; reliability, 105; scale of, 105
Caretaker monitoring and supervision, 49, 51–53, 62, 68, 101; effect of caretaking arrangements, 53*t*; reliability, 52; scale of, 51
Caretaking arrangements, 6, 24–27; alternative, 31; decision making, 23; factors associated with, 30–34, 31*t*; measure of, 6; prevalent types, 26, 26*f*; stability and change, 23, 28–30
Caretaking practices, 46, 49–51; dimensions of, 49
CFPS (China Family Panel Studies), 50
Child-school dynamics, 148
China's National Development and Reform Commission (NDRC), 182–183
Community-based intervention, 185
Composite score, 52, 123, 125, 162
Compulsory Education Law, 36, 183
Conduct problems, 5
Confucianism, 175; traditional family values prescribed by Confucianism, 175
Control variable, 52, 58, 63, 103, 124, 149, 164
Copresent caretakers, 70, 71, 85
Corporal punishment, 63, 65, 69
Crop Plantation Landscaping, 187
Cultural factors, 6, 20, 27, 36, 46, 166
Cultural Revolution, 172, 186
Custody arrangements, 91

Dagong, 4, 5, 19; duration, 86*f*
Delinquency, 6, 14, 120–122; effect of caretaking arrangements on, 141; effect of long-distance parenting on, 137; opportunities of, 138; parental concerns, 138; role model of, 138
Demographic factors, 8, 26, 101
Depression, 5, 62, 97, 142–143
Descriptive analysis, 100, 104, 129
Desire to drop out of school, 21
Deviant behaviors, 21, 126, 129, 139–140; effect of caretaker hostility, 128, 127*t*; effect of caretaking arrangements, 126–127; effect of caretaking practices, 128–129, 127*t*; effect of school, 127–128, 127*t*; frequency of,

203

126; measure of, 126; moderating effect of gender, 127t, 128
Deviant peer association, 123, 125, 128, 140
Dibao, 158
Direct effect, 21, 141
Division of labor, 122, 132; family, 122; gender, 132
Divorce rate, 91
Drowning, 62, 138
Dual-parent migration, 33–34, 43, 46, 84, 101, 112, 132
Duration of parental visits, 92, 93t; effect of age, 93t; effect of caretaking arrangements, 93t; effect of inter-province migration, 93t; frequency, 92
Dynamic processes, 9

Eating bitterness, 1, 4, 180
Ecological system theory, 7, 9; context, 8; person, 8; proximal process, 7; time, 9
Educational performance, 4, 14, 95, 98, 114, 118
Education-based intervention, 185
Education fever, 12, 21, 62, 80, 119, 148, 151
Effect pathway, 103
Emotional detachment, 75, 78
Emotional development, 6, 7, 12, 166, 168–169
Emotional intimacy, 71, 74–76, 81, 95, 132, 151
Emotional well-being, 13, 19, 143, 147–152, 164, 169
Emotional work, 50, 57, 155
Empty space, 156
Evidence-based programs, 166
Exosystem, 9, 11, 12
Exploratory factor analysis, 161–162
Extended family, 6, 12, 16, 25, 27–28, 31, 46, 52, 150, 175
External factors, 166; macro, 13, 166; meso, 13, 166; micro, 13, 166

Face validity, 144
Factor loading, 162
Family background, 99, 101, 103, 124
Family division, 177, 178
Family economic status, 17, 30, 31, 52–53, 64
Family microsystem, 12
Family migration, 11, 25
Family process theory, 12, 49, 50, 122; family dysfunction, 122; family imbalance, 49; specific roles and obligations, 49, 122
Family socioeconomic status, 23, 30, 91, 99; frequency of, 30; measures of, 30
Family structure, 4, 5, 6, 15, 56, 178
Family system, 122, 156, 165
Family values, 27, 171, 175
Family workshop intervention, 185
Farm economy, 187
Father-only caretaking, 131
Father's education level, 30, 43
Feelings of strangeness and abandonment, 160, 162t; frequency of, 160; indicators of, 160; reliability of, 163
Feelings of understanding and appreciation, 161, 162t; frequency of, 160; indicators of, 161; reliability of, 163

Field observation, 15, 24, 53, 57, 97, 131, 146, 175, 187
Filial piety, 38–41, 46, 171, 175, 177; intergenerational exchange, 39; modified version, 40
Five certificates, 184
Fluidity of caretaking arrangements, 29; factors associated, 29–30
Full model, 105

Gender boundaries, 55–57, 69, 115, 155, 167, 186
Gendered analysis, 103
Gender identity, 57; productive selves, 57, 69
Gender roles, 32, 33, 57, 137
General strain theory, 122
Geographically separated family, 12, 13
Geographically separated parents, 71, 155, 160
Get ahead, 137
Going outside, 44, 142
Grandparent availability, 33
Grandparenting, 4, 6, 20, 21, 24, 34, 36–40; as a cultural adaptation, 38; as surrogate parents, 4, 6, 24, 37, 66, 68, 167; economic incentive, 37
Great Leap Forward Campaign, 186
Guang, 51, 58, 61, 62

Harsh discipline, 20, 49, 62–64, 68, 69, 136, 141; effect of caretaking arrangements, 64t; measure of, 63
High school entrance examination, 16, 183
Hukou system, 6, 10, 13, 24, 45, 182; incremental changes, 182–183; location-based, 182; reform of, 182–183; types, 10

Immediate family, 12–13, 20, 70
Income effect, 180
Income inequality, 3
In-depth interview, 6, 20, 49, 53, 58, 156, 172
Indigenous concepts and measures, 60
Indirect effect, 104
Information and communication technologies (ICT), 11, 168
Institutional discrimination, 33, 121
Institutional reform, 166
Integrated theory of crime and delinquency, 122
Intensive distance parenting, 74
Interactive processes, 9–10
Intergenerational mobility, 13, 23, 96, 119, 131, 157, 178, 186
Intergenerational transmission, 147
Internal migration, 3, 20, 23–24, 57
Internet bar, 126
Inter-provincial migration, 88, 90
Intimacy with parents, 22, 165
Intrafamilial interaction, 70
Intralocal family, 23
Intra-provincial migration, 90
Involvement in minor delinquency, 128–129, 136, 139–140; descriptive statistics, 129; effect of caretaker hostility, 130, 130t; effect of caretaking arrangements, 129–130; effect of caretaking practices, 129–130, 130t; effect of parental marital

INDEX

status, 129–130; effect of school, 129–130, 130*t*; moderating effect of gender, 130*t*, 129; reliability of, 129; scale of, 129

Left-behind Children (LBC), 1–2; Definition, 1–2; global population size, 2; population size, 2
Left-behind-child syndrome, 5
Left-behind experiences, 22; effect on problematic behaviors, 140
Left-behind father, 44, 58, 90, 101, 115, 118, 125, 155
Left-behind mother, 20, 43, 44, 90, 101
Life stressor, 6
Living in a school dorm, 20; measure of, 20; frequency of, 17*t*
Logistic regression, 63, 129, 130*t*
Loneliness, 142–143
Long-distance communication, 72–78, 81; asymmetrical relationship, 78; factors associated with the frequency, 76–77; frequency, 75–79; intensity, 77; primary media, 72–75; types of, 72; topic, 79–81
Long-distance parenting, 6, 10, 14, 20, 70–71, 85, 95, 151; dimensions of, 70–71; measures of, 70–71
Longitudinal Gansu Survey of Children and Families, 98
Longitudinal study, 112

Macrostructural factors, 10, 24, 182
Macrosystem, 9, 13
Malnutrition, 5
Marital status of biological parents, 17; measure of, 17; sample characteristics, 17*t*
Maternal grandparents, 11, 27, 47, 142, 157, 181
Maternal migration, 26–27, 31–34, 101; measure of, 27; prevalence, 26*f*
Mediating effect, 98, 99, 128, 131, 136; approach by MacKinnon & Dwyer, 128
Mediator, 99, 169
Megacities, 5, 10, 18, 24, 183
Mental health, 6, 14, 143, 147, 155, 185
Mesosystem, 9, 12, 13
Meta-analysis, 143
Microsystem, 9, 12
Migrant schools, 11, 167
Migrant-sending communities, 6, 10, 13, 36, 117, 183, 184
Migration-specific protective factors, 164
Migration-specific risk factors, 164
Mixed methods, 15, 165
Mobile parenting, 20, 70, 72, 94, 154, 165, 168–170
Moderate, 100, 109, 117, 125, 180
Moderating effect, 100, 109
Moderator, 101, 131
Mother-away families, 141
Mothering, 50, 57, 69, 115, 159, 167
Mother-only caretaking, 131
Multilocal family, 37, 41, 70, 108, 116
Multimedia, 73
Multimedia communication, 73
Multinomial logistic regression, 31
Multistage cluster sampling, 16

Multivariate ordinal regression, 83, 88, 89, 93, 127
Multivariate regression model, 52, 64, 101, 139
Mutual responsibility system, 10

National Bureau of Statistics of China, 1, 10, 24, 37, 80, 173
National University Entrance Examination, 183
National Youth Survey, 122
Negative emotions, 13, 133, 136, 145*t*; effect of caretaking arrangements, 145*t*; effect of sex, 145*t*
Night self-study classes, 77
Non-LBC, 26–27, 145–147, 150; measure of, 27; prevalence, 26*f*
Normalization of migration, 146, 164
Normative mental development, 6
Normative physical development, 6
Nuclear family, 44, 133, 148, 165, 177, 178
Number of siblings, 17, 103; measure of, 17; sample characteristics, 17*t*

One-grandparent caretaker, 26, 27, 101, 180
One-grandparent caretaking, 27, 31–33, 52–54; measure of, 27; prevalence, 26*f*
Opening Up and Reform, 172
Other fathers, 38, 50
Other mothers, 38, 50
Overarching theoretical model, The, 9, 14, 14*f*, 19, 118, 122

Panel data, 112
Parental absence, 6, 15, 122, 142, 144, 157, 174, 179
Parental concerns, 81, 138–140, 152
Parental consent, 16
Parental divorce, 8, 45, 91, 142, 170
Parental education, 16–17, 51–53, 103; frequency, 17*t*; measure of, 16–17
Parental migration, 24, 45; macro-institutional factors, 45; micro-individual factors, 45; status, 14*f*
Parent-child communication, 75–79, 97, 116–117, 152, 168, 170
Paternal grandparents, 11, 27–29, 43
Paternal migration, 26, 31–34; measure of, 27; prevalence, 26*f*
Patriarchal order, 175, 177
Patriarchal system, 11, 14, 49, 170; neotraditional version, 50
Pauline Boss, 144
Perceived family economic status, 16–17, 30–31, 103; measure of, 16–17; sample characteristics, 17*t*
Person, 8; person forces, 8; person resources, 8; personal traits, 8
Personal agency, 171
Person-environmental interaction, 171
Physical anxiety, 21, 142, 143, 165
Physiological symptoms, 144–148; effect of ambiguous loss, 164; effect of caretaking arrangements, 145*t*; effect of long-distance communication, 153*t*; effect of parental marital status, 153*t*; effect of sex, 145*t*; measure of, 145; reliability of, 145

INDEX

Pinyin, 110, 112
Planned system, 182
Polymedia, 115
Population registration systems, 6
Positive parenting, 62, 112
Predictive validity, 22
Prevention and intervention programs, 186; recommendations, 184–186
Primary caretakers, 4, 18, 23, 25, 35
Principal component analysis (PCA), 162
Problematic behaviors, 19, 121–122; dimensions of, 121–122; effect of long-distance parenting, 137
Propensity score matching, 146
Proportionate stratified sampling, 16
Protective factor, 22, 71, 125, 128, 129, 164, 171–172
Psychological anxiety, 142
Psychological development, 15, 19, 91, 152
Psychological distance, 94
Psychological outcomes, 6, 14, 19, 21, 142, 143
Psychological problems, 144–146, 148–152
Psychological well-being, 5, 10, 14, 21, 142–144, 146–151; effect of ambiguous loss, 163t, 163; effects of academic performance, 148, 149t; effects of caretaking hostility and rejection, 148, 149t; effects of school bonding, 148, 149t
Punitive caretaking practices, 136

Quality of caretaking practices, 49, 97, 99, 103, 107; positive caretaking, 112

Rachel Murphy, 12, 40, 178
Reciprocal processes, 10
Reconfigured family structure, 6, 19, 166
Reference category, 31, 102t, 106t, 107
Reference group, 31, 31t, 102t, 106t, 107
Reliability, 22, 145, 161, 163
Remittance, 3, 18, 41, 96, 146, 147, 164, 177, 178
Remote parenting, 95, 99, 144
Resilience, 6, 170–175; definition, 171; holistic approach, 171; individualistic perspective, 171
Resilience development, 172, 175, 179; effect of farming, 179–181; effect of household chores, 179–181; influence of education, 172–175; role of family values, 175–179
Response category, 104, 123
Responsible parenting, 94, 158, 168, 186
Risk factors, 55, 121, 150
Rurality-based program, 186
Rural to urban migrants, 1, 11, 25; economic rationality, 26; push-pull factors, 24; size, 1; theory of neoclassical economics, 25
Rural-urban income gap, 10, 14, 45, 51
Rutter, Michael, 171

Sample characteristics, 15, 17t
School bonding, 21, 104–107; effects of caretaking arrangements, 106t; effects of caretaking practices, 106t; gendered analysis, 105f, 106t; measure of, 104; reliability of, 104

School involvement, 97, 116–119, 116t; effect of distant parenting, 116t
School performance, 6, 101–104; parental caring about, 116; parental concerns on, 116
School tutoring, 17, 50, 108; by grandparents, 107–112
Self-control, 8, 124–125; measure of, 124; reliability of, 125
Self-injurious behavior, 144; rate of, 144
Self-injury, 144–149, 150–153, 163–164; effect of ambiguous loss, 164; effect of caretaking arrangements, 145; effect of long-distance communication, 153t; effect of parental marital status, 153t; effect of sex, 145; measure of, 144
Skip-generation households, 4, 17
Smartphone, 71, 168; size of users, 71
Social anxiety, 143–145, 148–150, 152–155; effect of ambiguous loss, 164; effect of caretaking arrangements, 145; effect of long-distance communication, 153t; effect of parental marital status, 153t; effect of sex, 145; measure of, 145; reliability of, 145
Social bonding theory, 122
Social development, 6, 49
Social learning theory, 122
Social stigma, 91
Social withdrawal, 144–145, 148–150, 152–154; effect of ambiguous loss, 164; effect of caretaking arrangements, 145; effect of long-distance communication, 153t; effect of sex, 145; measure of, 145; reliability of, 145
Socioeconomic status, 90
Sole-grandparent caretaker, 42, 58, 60, 114
Sole-grandparent caretaking, 41, 42, 56
Sole-parent caretaking, 34, 43; effect of familial factors, 43; effect of situational factors, 43
Sole-parent migration, 46, 69, 84
Son preference, 85
Spring festival, 41, 84, 90, 160
Standardized regression coefficients, 116, 117, 128, 130
State Council Decision on Basic Education Reform and Development, 183
State feminism, 50
Stem family, 177, 178
Stepwise regression, 99
Striving team, 40, 56, 118, 147, 154, 155, 178–179
Structural factors, 6, 8, 20, 24, 30
Subgroup analysis, 100; based on gender, 102t, 103, 106t, 107
Subsistence economy, 187
Substitution effect, 180
Suicidal ideation, 5, 142; rate of, 144
Surrogate parent, 4, 6, 24, 37, 66, 68, 167
Survey, 15–16

Temporal separation, 73, 81, 94
Test of the linear combination of coefficients, 52
Text-based communication, 72
Three-step procedure, 99

INDEX

Time, 9; micro-time, 9; meso-time, 9; macro-time, 9
Time zone, 94, 168
Traditional labor division, 85
Traffic accident, 62, 138
Translocal family, 11, 13, 29, 117, 154, 172, 178
Transnational migration, 2–3, 142; size, 2–3
Tuition fee, 36, 96; costs of private schools, 96
Tutoring, 108–112; by grandparents, 108–110; by at-home parents, 109–110
Two-grandparent caretaker, 101, 180
Two-grandparent-caretaking, 27, 31–32; measure of, 27; prevalence, 26f

UNICEF (United Nations Children's Fund), 2
Unidirectional communication, 78
Unstandardized regression coefficients, 53, 64, 83, 83, 89, 127t
Urban *hukou*, 10, 173, 182, 184
Urban-rural dual structure, 2
Urie Bronfenbrenner, 6–9

Varimax rotation, 162
Victimization, 5, 61, 135, 138
Virtual presence, 154
Visits of children to migrant parents, 117; effect of caretaking arrangements, 83t; effect of children's sex, 83t; frequency, 82
Visits of migrant parents, 85, 94; duration, 88; effect of caretaking arrangements, 89t; effect of family economic status, 89t; effect of inter-province migration, 89t; effect of parental marital status, 89t; frequency, 86f, 86–88; predictors of, 89t
Voice-based communication, 72

WeChat, 11, 71–73; audio chats, 72, 116; size of users, 71; texting, 72; video chats, 70, 72, 74–79, 116
Well-being, 3, 5, 6; general, 6, 13, 19; physical, 6; emotional, 13, 19, 143, 147–148, 152, 164
Working "outside", 23, 37, 44, 108, 119, 146, 161, 180

ABOUT THE AUTHOR

XIAOJIN CHEN is an associate professor in the Department of Sociology at Tulane University in New Orleans. His research interests include life-course criminology, the well-being of socially and economically disadvantaged children, and the application of advanced statistical techniques. His recent research focuses on the well-being of children of rural-to-urban migrants in rural China.

Available titles in the Rutgers Series in Childhood Studies:

Amanda E. Lewis, *Race in the Schoolyard: Negotiating the Color Line in Classrooms and Communities*

Donna M. Lanclos, *At Play in Belfast: Children's Folklore and Identities in Northern Ireland*

Cindy Dell Clark, *In Sickness and in Play: Children Coping with Chronic Illness*

Peter B. Pufall and Richard P. Unsworth, eds., *Rethinking Childhood*

David M. Rosen, *Armies of the Young: Child Soldiers in War and Terrorism*

Lydia Murdoch, *Imagined Orphans: Poor Families, Child Welfare, and Contested Citizenship in London*

Rachel Burr, *Vietnam's Children in a Changing World*

Laurie Schaffner, *Girls in Trouble with the Law*

Susan A. Miller, *Growing Girls: The Natural Origins of Girls' Organizations in America*

Marta Gutman and Ning de Coninck-Smith, eds., *Designing Modern Childhoods: History, Space, and the Material Culture of Children*

Jessica Fields, *Risky Lessons: Sex Education and Social Inequality*

Sarah E. Chinn, *Inventing Modern Adolescence: The Children of Immigrants in Turn-of-the-Century America*

Debra Curtis, *Pleasures and Perils: Girls' Sexuality in a Caribbean Consumer Culture*

Don S. Browning and Binnie J. Miller-McLemore, eds., *Children and Childhood in American Religions*

Marjorie Faulstich Orellana, *Translating Childhoods: Immigrant Youth, Language, and Culture*

Don S. Browning and Marcia J. Bunge, eds., *Children and Childhood in World Religions*

Hava Rachel Gordon, *We Fight to Win: Inequality and the Politics of Youth Activism*

Nikki Jones, *Between Good and Ghetto: African American Girls and Inner-City Violence*

Kate Douglas, *Contesting Childhood: Autobiography, Trauma, and Memory*

Jennifer Helgren and Colleen A. Vasconcellos, eds., *Girlhood: A Global History*

Karen Lury, *The Child in Film: Tears, Fears, and Fairy Tales*

Michelle Ann Abate, *Raising Your Kids Right: Children's Literature and American Political Conservatism*

Michael Bourdillon, Deborah Levison, William Myers, and Ben White, *Rights and Wrongs of Children's Work*

Jane A. Siegel, *Disrupted Childhoods: Children of Women in Prison*

Valerie Leiter, *Their Time Has Come: Youth with Disabilities on the Cusp of Adulthood*

Edward W. Morris, *Learning the Hard Way: Masculinity, Place, and the Gender Gap in Education*

Erin N. Winkler, *Learning Race, Learning Place: Shaping Racial Identities and Ideas in African American Childhoods*

Jenny Huberman, *Ambivalent Encounters: Childhood, Tourism, and Social Change in Banaras, India*

Walter Hamilton, *Children of the Occupation: Japan's Untold Story*

Jon M. Wolseth, *Life on the Malecón: Children and Youth on the Streets of Santo Domingo*

Lisa M. Nunn, *Defining Student Success: The Role of School and Culture*

Vikki S. Katz, *Kids in the Middle: How Children of Immigrants Negotiate Community Interactions for Their Families*

Bambi L. Chapin, *Childhood in a Sri Lankan Village: Shaping Hierarchy and Desire*

David M. Rosen, *Child Soldiers in the Western Imagination: From Patriots to Victims*

Marianne Modica, *Race among Friends: Exploring Race at a Suburban School*

Elzbieta M. Gozdziak, *Trafficked Children and Youth in the United States: Reimagining Survivors*

Pamela Robertson Wojcik, *Fantasies of Neglect: Imagining the Urban Child in American Film and Fiction*

Maria Kromidas, *City Kids: Transforming Racial Baggage*

Ingred A. Nelson, *Why Afterschool Matters*

Jean Marie Hunleth, *Children as Caregivers: The Global Fight against Tuberculosis and HIV in Zambia*

Abby Hardgrove, *Life after Guns: Reciprocity and Respect among Young Men in Liberia*

Michelle J. Bellino, *Youth in Postwar Guatemala: Education and Civic Identity in Transition*

Vera Lopez, *Complicated Lives: Girls, Parents, Drugs, and Juvenile Justice*

Rachel E. Dunifon, *You've Always Been There for Me: Understanding the Lives of Grandchildren Raised by Grandparents*

Cindy Dell Clark, *All Together Now: American Holiday Symbolism among Children and Adults*

Laura Moran, *Belonging and Becoming in a Multicultural World: Refugee Youth and the Pursuit of Identity*

Hannah Dyer, *The Queer Aesthetics of Childhood: Asymmetries of Innocence and the Cultural Politics of Child Development*

Julie Spray, *The Children in Child Health: Negotiating Young Lives and Health in New Zealand*

Franziska Fay, *Disputing Discipline: Child Protection, Punishment, and Piety in Zanzibar Schools*

Kathie Carpenter, *Life in a Cambodian Orphanage: A Childhood Journey for New Opportunities*

Norbert Ross, *A World of Many: Ontology and Child Development among the Maya of Southern Mexico*

Camilla Morelli, *Children of the Rainforest: Shaping the Future in Amazonia*

Junehui Ahn, *Between Self and Community: Children's Personhood in a Globalized South Korea*

Francesca Meloni, *Ways of Belonging: Undocumented Youth in the Shadow of Illegality*

Xiaojin Chen, *China's Left-Behind Children: Caretaking, Parenting, and Struggles*